# THE ARCHITECTURE OF
# ARTHUR ERICKSON

# THE ARCHITECTURE OF ARTHUR ERICKSON

## ARTHUR ERICKSON

Douglas & McIntyre
Vancouver/Toronto

Douglas & McIntyre Ltd.
1615 Venables Street
Vancouver, British Columbia V5L 2H1

Published simultaneously in the United States of America by
Harper and Row, Publishers, Inc.

Canadian Cataloguing in Publication Data
Erickson, Arthur, 1924–
   The architecture of Arthur Erickson
   ISBN 0-88894-610-4
   1. Erickson, Arthur, 1924–   2. Architecture, Modern
— 20th century.   I. Title.
NA749.E75A36   1988   720'.92'4   C88-091193-X

All care has been taken to trace ownership of images in this
book. Omissions will be corrected in subsequent editions,
provided notification is sent to the publisher.

Design by Barbara Hodgson
Typeset by PolaGraphics Ltd.
Colour separations by Cleland-Kent Western Ltd.
Printed in Canada by Hemlock Printers Ltd.
Bound in Canada by North-West Book Company Limited

*Title page: Napp Laboratories in Cambridge, England;
designed in 1979.* TIMOTHY HURSLEY/THE ARKANSAS
OFFICE

# CONTENTS

# FOREWORD

Arthur Erickson is a member of the third or fourth generation of modern architects. This means among other things that, unlike the fathers of the modern movement, he has never felt compelled to adhere to the orthodoxies established by the early pioneers. And it also means that Erickson has had available to him an extraordinarily rich and varied vocabulary developed by those same pioneers from, roughly, the beginning of the century to the 1960s.

To understand the significance of this, one should remember that the pioneers — unlike innovators in other fields — spent much of their time breaking old molds and establishing their own vocabulary. The rules governing their new language of architecture were clear and immutable: roofs were flat, plans were open, materials were "modern" (glass, steel, concrete and, of course, plastics), and everything was "expressed" (articulated, modular, and otherwise high-tech). Anyone who bent those rules was suspected of being romantic, sentimental, and probably bourgeois to boot.

In retrospect, all of this sounds more than a little grotesque; and it is, of course, slightly exaggerated. But it should be remembered that, rightly or wrongly, the pioneers of the modern movement believed themselves to be surrounded by enemies: initially, their enemies were supporters of the École des Beaux-Arts, an institution clearly representative of various defenders of privilege, and determined to impose the styles of earlier autocracies upon a new, democratic society; and, later, their enemies were supporters of fascist and other authoritarian regimes, whose architecture was designed to convey a sense of military and political oppression.

Erickson's generation of modern architects faced very little ideological opposition: by the late 1950s, when he began to practise in Vancouver, modern architecture was a fact, accepted by governments, business and the general public alike. World's Fairs — a good measuring stick of public taste — were uniformly "modern." Movie sets — an even better indicator — were modern or futuristic. The faces of leading modern architects were beginning to appear, routinely, on the covers of popular magazines and on the front pages of newspapers. The modern movement was fully accepted, and the battle was won.

Or so it seemed. In retrospect, what had won was a kind of modern "style." The style that emerged all over the world after World War II, and that had won acceptance, *faute de mieux*, was little more than a logical, reasonably economical, and not very interesting set of diagrams that made a fair amount of commercial and technological sense. Cities around the globe were being "sanitized" as the Germans put it — i.e., torn down and rebuilt — in the same pragmatic, uninspired image; so that it soon became impossible to tell if one was visiting Houston, Bombay, Rio, Toronto, Nairobi, or certain parts of Paris. Commercial architects, organized in mega-offices run like insurance companies, were grinding out blueprints by the acre for miles upon miles of curtain-walled boxes to house offices, apartments, schools, factories, museums, churches, and even high-rise cemeteries — all roughly identical in everything but height, and all

*Pages 6/7: The Pacific Northwest house in Seattle, Washington; designed in 1979.*

*Facing page: The night skyline forms the backdrop for the Roy Thomson Hall in Toronto, Ontario, designed in 1976 and opened in 1982. The hall's glass skin provides a view from the street of the excitement within.*
TIMOTHY HURSLEY/THE ARKANSAS OFFICE

equally destructive of the human spirit and of art.

There were, however, a very few architects — often working alone, often ignored at first by their contemporaries — who held a very different view of architecture. In the United States this small band included the likes of Louis Kahn and Paul Rudolph; in Japan it included people like Fumihiko Maki and Tadao Ando; and in Canada it included — most visibly — Arthur Erickson.

Half a century ago, the French/Swiss architect Le Corbusier defined architecture as "le jeu savant, correct, et magnifique des volumes assemblés sous la lumière." He did not say that architecture was the reasonable packaging of cubage for profit — he put it just a little more poetically.

Arthur Erickson's work is perhaps best defined in those poetic terms chosen by Le Corbusier. What strikes one most forcibly about Erickson's buildings, especially if one is an architect too, is how difficult they are to describe in conventional terms. A certain house may be best described by the way sunlight enters it and moves across a wall or a floor; by the way an interior space meets the hillside; by the way one moves from one space into the next, and is seduced by views of the landscape and the smell of flowers. An urban superblock in Vancouver may be best described by the way in which people are almost tempted to skip and dance through it, to enjoy its many indoor and outdoor spaces; and by the way they respond to the surprises found around every other corner. A university campus may be best described not so much in terms of available facilities and amenities but in terms of majestic views from a mountain top. And a museum may be best described by the way its structure frames the landscape and by the way its hilltop site seems to meet the ocean visible several miles in the distance.

How do you draw an elevation, or a section, or even a plan of sunlight travelling across a wall, or of a view from a mountain, or of the intersection of dissimilar but related spaces? These very special qualities, this ability to conjure up a "magnificent play of volumes under light," these are the talents that set Erickson and a few others apart from most of their contemporaries.

Like everyone else of his generation, Erickson owes a debt of gratitude and of inspiration to architects like Frank Lloyd Wright, who was one of the first to bring the sun and the earth into contemporary architecture; and to Mies van der Rohe, whose 1928 Barcelona Pavilion remains *the* virtuoso exercise in space-in-motion — without which Erickson and others could not have accomplished similar sleights of hand with such assurance.

And Erickson undoubtedly owes a debt of gratitude to the likes of Alvar Aalto for the attention Aalto always paid to the people within his buildings; to the likes of Luis Barragan, who knows more about how to make space with colour and light than any latter-day minimalist; and, of course, to Le Corbusier, who not only knew more about the architecture of his and our time than most of his contemporaries but learned equally from the architecture and the art of past centuries and past civilizations — and reinterpreted them for us in his own, inimitable forms.

For Erickson, like all first-rate architects, is also a considerable scholar, with an avid interest in all aspects of the natural and the man-made environments, regardless of their place and time. There are aspects of his work that remind you of Fatehpur Sikri and of Isfahan and of certain gardens in China and Japan (all of which he visited and studied enthusiastically). And there are other aspects of his work that demonstrate his intimate knowledge of the terraced gardens left by Greek and Roman builders around the edges of the Mediterranean and beyond.

In a sense, Arthur Erickson is really a masterful landscape architect by inclination — a landscape architect who conceives of each building as an interval on a natural or man-made site, an interval differentiated from a nearby stream or pool or cliff by being roofed-over and sometimes walled-in. To him, one feels, a building is really a point of interest on a panorama that may extend all the way to the horizon. His work, in that respect, goes beyond Le Corbusier's definition, in that it is a play of spaces as well as forms — with the spaces sometimes extending as far as the eye can see.

Erickson's buildings, to repeat, are almost impossible to describe by conventional means, using an architect's conventional T-square and triangle. They really have no conventional façades, no false fronts that address the general public and the public press. His buildings address, instead, the sensibilities of those who live in them and use them, who look out, more often, than in. As you walk through his houses or his urban complexes, you feel that the architect has revealed to you a new way of experiencing your world, and that he had *you* in mind when he created this space or that view.

To photograph such buildings and to convey such intentions in still photographs is very difficult. That so much of the quality of Erickson's work emerges from the photographs in this book is remarkable. David Hockney, the artist with whom Erickson has occasionally collaborated, has tried in his giant photographic collages to transport the observer into the very midst of the scenes depicted. Perhaps the reader of this book should try to do the same — to transport himself or herself into the very centre of the images reproduced on these pages, and to imagine what it might be like to experience such views, such space, such light, and such art. It could be quite rewarding.

*Peter Blake*
*Washington, D.C.*

# PREFACE

The course of any successful career is an adventure of directions explored and ideas pursued. However, unlike an artist or businessman, an architect cannot easily refer to a gallery of work or some badge of wealth as evidence of his progress. It is the lot of the architect to envision much and realize little. Yet the numerous stillborn projects and lost competitions are key to explaining an architect's path; how he developed from one project to another, why he designed one thing one way, and something else another. I have been fortunate regarding the built evidence of my efforts. Nevertheless, it seems only a book, which can gather together the built and unbuilt schemes, accords a full picture of a working life.

Now, in mid-career, I may be less modest than in 1975, when I published in Canada a photographic essay on only twelve built projects titled *The Architecture of Arthur Erickson.* It received limited circulation outside our borders, as did *New Yorker* writer Edith Iglauer's slender 1981 profile, *Seven Stones: A Portrait of Arthur Erickson, Architect.* However, I must have been well served by the architectural press, for in the years since I have been surprised and gratified by the international recognition of my peers. When I finally decided to undertake a sequel compilation of my work, addressed to this broader audience, my publishers firmly responded: put everything in, and from the beginning. And so, for the first time, I have gathered it all, from the houses in 1950s Vancouver to design ideas for projects from California to the Middle East and China that may not be built until well into the 1990s.

An architect's enthusiasm is transparent in his architecture, whether it is his joy in the craft of building, the composition of eloquent spaces, the making of provocative forms, or his concern for whom he is designing, and where. The source of ugliness in architecture is equally obvious: indifference; in our time, to the challenge of a mechanized building industry that belies both art and craft by reducing the building process to the on-site assembly of premade parts. But how can mundane materials be made into something more evocative and powerful than the sum of their parts? For two decades, I preferred in situ concrete because its qualities testify both to the skill of the maker and the sensitivity of the designer. Athenians had their Pentelic marble; we have our concrete.

Today, the reaction to an overly mechanical century that previously informed my career seems to be dissipating to reveal a sparkling field of new opportunities. In part, this is because the powers of science and technology — the foundation of the Modernists' common optimism — are moving into a wondrous new mode. I am entranced by the possibilities, as by the arrival of a caravan with marvels from a distant land. But the promiscuous delights of youth have been replaced by the thoughtful discriminations of maturity; methods and means, however novel, remain only tools for creating. What the future brings must always be tested for how it can serve my basic drive for clarification.

Beyond the provision of shelter, architecture invests mute forms with meaning. A building, like any other work of art, if it would speak cogently across time, has first to be true to its own circumstance and place.

In realizing this book, I am indebted to Allen Steele for compiling the text from scribbled fragments and filling out faithfully the sense of my words. To a valued associate, Alan S. Bell, I owe thanks for undertaking the difficult task of gathering the images, uncovering them in forgotten boxes and wresting them from photographers. Over recent years, Barbara E. Shapiro has performed a similar task with my sketches, such as they are. I thank the eminent architect, writer and teacher Peter Blake for graciously contributing an introduction. And I thank publisher Scott McIntyre for his zeal, as well as his editor, Saeko Usukawa, and his designer, Barbara Hodgson, for their skill in giving an artful form to this sprawling collection.

Even before I set up my own firm, I was perhaps too independent, too jealous of my design prerogatives. Those who are sceptical that one man could produce this body of work can take satisfaction in the back of the book, along with those who want to know how an architect really works — there you will find a list of project credits. Without the determination, sound instincts and solid talents of these colleagues, my ideas would have all remained feeble sketches.

This is their book, too.

PART I

# EXPLORATIONS

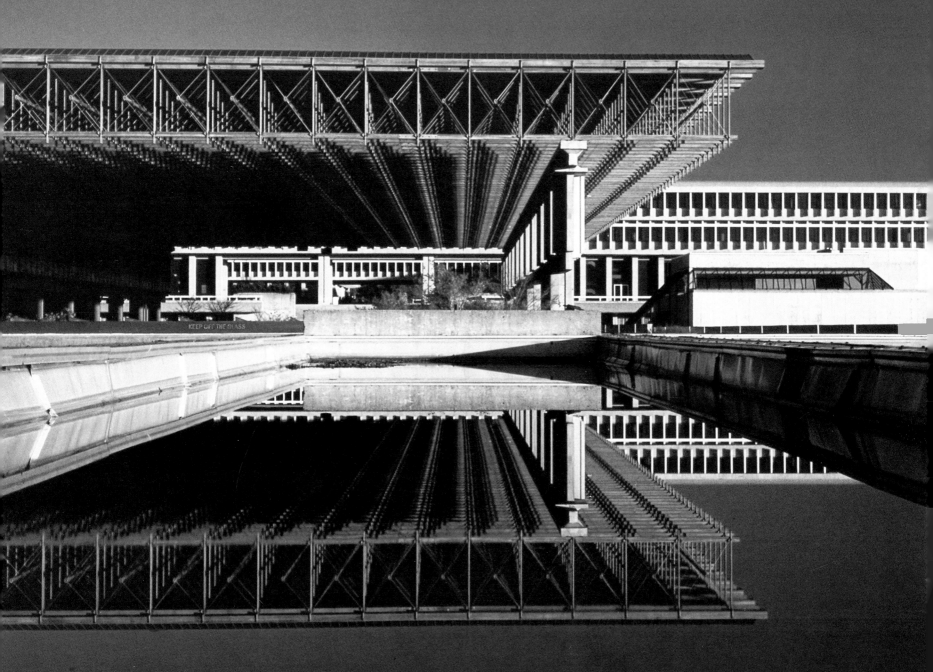

# EXPLORATIONS

When I was growing up in Vancouver, British Columbia, the city was closer in spirit to California than to the twin centres of Canada, Toronto and Montreal. Like the American West, the Canadian West was a land of economic promise. However, the people who headed for the Pacific coast were often less interested in making their fortune than in gaining a fresh start in life. Such people took tolerance for granted, were optimistic about the future and were not terribly bound by the past.

My parents moved to Vancouver from Toronto after the First World War, and only after my mother had convinced my father that they would marry despite the loss of both his legs at the Battle of Amiens. Had they stayed in the East, they might have seemed an eccentric couple, she with her restless mind and strong opinions, he genial and outgoing while never conceding his handicap. But Vancouver was new without being unsure, small without being tight, and its people democratically held that good character and good minds were the equal of a large bank account. The Ericksons soon knew everyone in the community, and the conversation of the varied guests around our dining room table was the beginning of my education.

The comfortable, indulgent home life supported the interests and adventures of my brother and myself. The consuming hobbies of my boyhood were botany, ichthyology and especially painting — after covering the walls of my bedroom with Lucius Beebe–inspired underwater scenes, I moved on to my brother's room with a South American jungle. Painting brought me a small but sig-

nificant recognition by the leader of Canada's famous Group of Seven painters, Lawren Harris, who arrived to make his home in Vancouver in 1939, another seeker of a new life. He invited me to submit a painting to a show of nonobjective American art he had organized; and though I was still in high school, he and his wife Bess included me in their Saturday night salons. His gift to me was a foundation of assurance in my work that I carried into my next creative venture, architecture.

I fell into architecture quite by chance in one of those numinous moments that bless the most important turnings of our lives. Like thousands of other young men during the Second World War, I went into military service. Mine took me to India and Southeast Asia as a Japanese-language interpreter attached to British Intelligence Force 136, and I returned with a taste for foreign cultures that prompted me to consider a career in the diplomatic service. However, a preparatory summer course in economics and politics discouraged me; my feeling was for the expression of history, for a people's whole culture, not in its manifest direction by a few self-important leaders. Then in the summer of 1947 I found in an issue of *Fortune* magazine an article on Frank Lloyd Wright's Taliesin West with colour photographs. Suddenly it was all clear to me. If such a magical realm was the province of an architect, I would become one. McGill University was the first to respond to my frantic last-minute applications to professional school, and I was off that fall. I never looked back.

A few years before, McGill had thrown off the trammels of a beaux arts program and

*Page 14: The Robert Filberg house in Comox, British Columbia; designed in 1958.* ARTHUR ERICKSON

*Page 15: The Point Grey Townhouses in Vancouver, British Columbia; designed in 1963.* JOHN FULKER

*Facing page: Simon Fraser University, designed in 1963, in Burnaby, British Columbia. The view looks through the main mall roof to the academic quadrangle.* SIMON SCOTT

had become fanatically Bauhaus. The basic design course was taught by Gordon Webber, a man of compelling presence and disciple of Moholy-Nagy and György Kepes of the re-established Bauhaus in the Chicago School of Design. His exercises were intended to purge the mind of preconceived formal sets and then to let it explore the essence of materials, light, line, plane and volume through drawings and constructs in creative play. Webber himself exemplified — in his dress, manner, observations and thoughts — a new prophet challenging all cherished precepts and forcing students into their own creative resources.

Mies van der Rohe, Walter Gropius and Marcel Breuer were the masters to be emulated; and John Bland, the director of the McGill School of Architecture, led us on pilgrimages to their ateliers in the United States. Another professor primed us in the tenets of Le Corbusier. Nothing in his studio would be accepted unless it followed the master's dictums: pilotis, roof gardens, and interior and exterior walls freed from structure. Nevertheless, Le Corbusier's admiration for classical Greek architecture came as a revelation, for others taught that architectural history started with the spatial compositions of the High Renaissance and the Baroque periods. Frank Lloyd Wright's work was given only a grudging tolerance, so by the end of my third year I had been cleansed of any romantic or muddy tendencies that Mr. Wright might have planted. I had become a paragon of the new rationalism. Then, on my way back from Vancouver to McGill for my final year, I stopped by Taliesin East on its Wisconsin hilltop.

Walking up from the bottom of the hill, I could not find the entrance and came instead through the garage with its more than a dozen cars all painted in Wright's special red. Beyond was a small court girdling the crown of the hill where a single jet of water played with a branch of overhanging pine. The roof eaves swept below the hilltop. Here in brash,

brassy America was a place that shared the peace and timelessness of an Italian monastery. From some cool inner precinct floated the delicate sound of a harpsichord. I wandered into a comfortably low space that unfolded into a broad golden room. It was empty but felt charged with a quiet presence. When later that afternoon I finally met Mr. Wright, he was not the fearsome autocrat I had been told about. Rather, he was full of mischief and humour. I enthusiastically accepted his invitation to join his atelier-commune. Here was the rare chance to live one's art. Wright's seductive offer was shortly topped by John Bland when I reached Montreal. If I would stay on and complete my studies at McGill, there was a good chance that I could win a scholarship for a year's travel abroad.

And so after graduation I embarked on a two-and-a-half-year odyssey, following the development of Western architecture from its beginning in sequence through the Middle East, Greece, Italy, France and Spain, then finally to England and Scandinavia. In these formative years I confirmed how misleading was all the history I had been taught. History is not about war and politics, continually rewritten to justify some current point of view, but about the great adventure of the human spirit. The astonishing beauty of the Greek temples lies in a geometry not calculated by any architect but born in the eye of the sculptor: the buildings had been carved out, not built up. The Gothic arch was not an engineering breakthrough but an exotic fashion borrowed by the European barbarians from the civilized Moors. I learned how courageous early builders had been — how bold in their ideas — and how timid we are in comparison despite our vastly superior array of techniques. The best buildings defied the inertia of their times and carried their culture forward in great strides. Stirring works, they exuded an inner life — a contained vitality like the stillness of the athlete or the dancer poised. This commanding inner presence became for me the criterion of great art.

I learned, too, how inseparable a building's appearance is from climate and place. Only by seeing a building in its context can one comprehend its essence. Nothing about a woodcut or a sketch, a transparency or a photograph can convey the physical presence and power of some early Christian chapel or Michelangelo's Campidoglio. As trees, while true to the form of their species, create a twist of the trunk, a reach of the branch and a root structure in response to their particular bit of rock and soil, each archetypical building — a house, a hospital, a museum or a university — will vary in its response to its particular context of place and time. With my functionalist training, I confirmed that architecture finds its language at the point where the inner requirements of a building meet the conditions external to it. This "dialogue" between a building and its setting — rural or urban — became for me the source of meaning in architecture. From then on, site provided the context and motivation of my buildings.

Context comprises not only the obvious matters of topography, orientation, climate and surrounding structures, but also the more elusive ones: the general character of the site and the quality of light. Over and above its peculiarities of shape, ground cover, climate and position, any natural site fits into a "genre" of meadow, vale, forest, hillside, cliff face, lakeshore and so on. These general categories of site have to be recognized, understood and accepted before they can be enhanced by an architectural addition.

The act of recognition is not always easy. In my own garden, for example, only after burying what had been an English border garden beneath a high mound of earth did I recognize that the character of the site was that of a forest clearing. Then, having deduced this, I could strengthen it by adding forest plants, wild grasses and a shallow pond. Only when the character of the site is understood is it possible to think about building, for every building should have a sense of place. If architecture is, as I believe it to be, not a statement but a response, the response is not only to those human needs for shelter but to strong locational needs as well. Too often we think that the site exists merely to grace a building, but we can learn from the ancient Greeks or the villagers of the dramatically folded Mediterranean coastline that a site can be made still more beautiful by the buildings placed on it.

The urban site is a more problematic design exercise. Of course there are obvious factors that tie a building physically into a city, like access, services, existing uses and traffic flow — all of which must be analyzed before even starting to design — as well as the visible surroundings. The modernists very often seemed to ignore neighbouring buildings, giving their own a sense of isolation or even defiance of the context.

The success of an urban building is dependent upon its relationships to its neighbours and the spaces around it. One reads architecture in comparison. A well-detailed building stands out until a better detailed one comes along beside it. The setting is critical for any beautiful object — a jewel, a ceramic vase or a sculpture. Since urban surroundings are usually given, the trick is to make them appear as if they were made for the building. Even though the building is a new intruder, it can appear as though it has orchestrated its own skyline, its own approaches and their unfolding spaces. You compose against the negative and positive factors of street space and building mass. You use scale as the most effective device to proportion massing and detail. Surface material, colour, pattern and their expression through detail are just smudges on your palette. The final reading of the building can only be made against the buildings around it.

The temperate marine climate of my native Pacific Northwest Coast, in which the

19

*In the Erickson garden in Vancouver, laid out in 1960, a travertine marble slab projects into an artificial pond planted with water lilies, rushes and wild irises. Above the transplanted wild grasses, several species of bamboo and rhododendron provide an evergreen privacy barrier under taller native dogwoods and pine trees. The visual layers of foreground, water, berm and tall trees give this small city garden the illusion of depth.* Simon Scott

*Rear view of the 1,376-square-foot first house for painter Gordon Smith in 1953, sited on an acre of dense woods in West Vancouver, British Columbia. The bedroom is on the left; the kitchen, dining and living room are in the centre; the two-storey studio is on the right. The exterior finish is stucco and vertical cedar siding. A glazed overhang on the second level lets light in, protects against rain and blurs the indoor-outdoor distinction: this device recurs over the years.*

majority of days are overcast, probably made me particularly sensitive and instinctively responsive to light. Light gives life to architecture by its changing volumetric effects and subtle intimations of mood. Of all the reasons for the changes that take place in a building's form from one region to another, the aesthetic reasons — how well something looks in the particular light of the region — are paramount. Simple geometric solids, like the Egyptian pyramids or the domes of the Middle East and Persia that look strong and majestic in those desert regions, would appear monotonous and unrelieved in the flat light of northern Europe. On the other hand, the spires and lacelike silhouettes of northern architecture, highly evocative against the white skies of the north, would look ineffectual against the dark sky and brilliant light of the desert. The international styles that swept Europe — the Romanesque, Gothic or Baroque — were almost instinctively modified following the local dic-

tates of light and culture. What was, in England, a charming domesticity, would in France have passion and intellectual clarity, in Italy be generous and full of grace, and in Spain have a feverish intensity. Light can be hard and glaring, or ineffably soft and luminous. While the light in Spain danced on the surfaces, the flat northern light and white skies of England and Germany demanded rather a two-dimensional silhouette. Surfaces that pulsed in high relief and deep volume in Italy were reduced to a shallow sparkling surface pattern in the desert.

Not only how light affects our perception of form but how it penetrates our building interiors deeply influences architectural style. In the north the problem has always been how to get enough light in, and in the south how to keep it out. Equivalent phenomena have quite opposite significance in contrasting climatic zones. Therefore, how to get the light in or keep it out, how to deal with it once it is in, how to have it illuminate form and activate surfaces: these are the central problems giving rise to the array of solutions that distinguish regional styles. Place the Friday Mosque of Isfahan in the middle of London, and it will look like a Turkish bath; move the Sainte-Chapelle from Paris to Fez, Morocco, and it will look like some mad northerner's trollish fancy. Light is one determinant of form that has always limited the appeal of an international style of architecture.

I became convinced that how we see things as a consequence of light is fundamental to the formation of human perception and imagination. In southern countries the earth is directly illuminated by sun and the sky is dark, whereas in northern countries the sky is predominantly white with light diffusing through cloud cover and the earth is dark. Such different lights must affect the psyche. People of different climates have different perceptions, different sensibilities, different ideas about reality. It is no accident that algebra and monotheism came out of the desert where sand, sky and stars are irreducible absolutes moving in constant relation to each other. Nor is it surprising that ghosts and poetry have thrived in countries of mist like Japan and England where subtle, illusive light brings out the uncertainties of existence. In Japan especially, where mist and diffused light are in almost constant combination, an architecture unlike any other in the world developed, an architecture of mood exemplified by the teahouse, revealing elusive ambiguities in the soft light of the forest floor. Light accounts for the exquisite moods of Japanese teahouses, the exuberance of the Baroque transparents, the mystery of Gothic naves and the golden splendour of Byzantine chapels.

The Northwest Coast of North America is a particularly difficult area with its watery lights, which are capable of sombre and melancholy moods. The coast demands that buildings be transparent to light, by means of walls of glass or devices like skylights that permit a gentle introspective light to bathe the walls, or water to reflect the sky's brightness from the earth's dark surfaces.

When I returned from Europe to Vancouver in 1953 and entered my trade, I proceeded to get fired from the large offices for my unrealistic proposals — glass *brise-soleil* for an intrinsically boring post office building — and my bohemian ways — a lunch of an unwrapped loaf of bread and a slab of cheese sticking out of my drawer was too eccentric. Fortunately I met Geoffrey Massey, a Harvard graduate who had moved west pursuing the rumour that exciting modern work was being done here. We joined forces for a few years, Geoff keeping regular employment while I worked out of the waterfront house we shared in West Vancouver. The artist Gordon Smith was our first brave client in 1953. Our design was a blend of Bauhaus formal concepts with West Coast sensibility to wood construction, the first

such modern example to win a Canadian national award for architecture. Along with our first house and first award came our first lesson about modifying design in the face of a client's needs. It is one thing to win over a client in your own office-lair and another to dictate on site to one who is serving as his own carpenter.

A house the following year was for Ruth Killam, an old and cherished friend whom Geoff later married. Within its post-and-beam structure we explored the use of skylights to bring in sun to the north side of the house. The site was inspiring: a peninsula of blue-grey rocks jutting into the salt water.

*The 1955 Killam-Massey house in West Vancouver looks east up Howe Sound from its exposed point. The pyramidal skylight, a geometrized version of the rock outcrop, covers the kitchen/dining/living room area. Although it was customary to use a quiet stained wood in the Pacific Northwest, this house is an unabashed lighthouse white with silver wood infill in honour of its marine location.* ARTHUR ERICKSON

We reflected the character of the site in the pyramid of the living room roof, the room itself open to a basin in the rocks and the sea view. We made it white — unusual for the region — and won another award.

For one who is at the beginning of a career, trying, teaching can be a needed salary; it is not necessarily for those who do not "do." My first application for such a subsidy was turned down by the University of British Columbia. Then in 1956 a McGill classmate, Douglas Shadbolt, helped me get on at the University of Oregon. At the time it had a remarkable School of Architecture, given form in the 1920s by an idealistic teacher and disciple of Louis Sullivan, W. R. B. Willcox. In contrast to the practised aloofness of the beaux arts teaching, Oregon educated in the truest sense of the word, "leading out" through dialogue. As the teacher, you could ask a student only questions designed to draw him out and make him think for himself. You offered no opinion or advice. This put the student in the position of being forced back on his own resources, of having to discover his own way; and as so often happens in the creative process, it is in a state of desperation when you are grasping at anything to save yourself that you get that sudden, almost cathartic, revelation. Sadly, the sterling Oregon method and its pass-fail system of grading could not survive the explosion of student and faculty numbers that hit after I left.

The University of British Columbia took me on in 1957, and I proceeded to "unteach" there for many years. Sharpened by the Oregon technique, I shocked students into experiencing things freshly by approaching their cherished precepts in an unexpected way. Once I invited a dance teacher to instruct the students in how to move their bodies for balance, rhythm and sense of space. Then I asked them to draw themselves in some position that they had been in and to support that position thoroughly with a structure. In only one week they came up with a marvellous range of devices. If I had simply asked them to design a piece of furniture for sitting or reclining, they would have been completely bound by their preconceived notions of a chair or lounge. Now they understood on a deeper level what furniture was all about.

In 1958 I organized a small architectural services team out of my office at the University of British Columbia. Early commissions were modest. There were porches to be closed in, living rooms to be extended, and kitchens to be remodelled in some of the great old houses of Vancouver; and even a Japanese garden with mounds and rocks simulating a creek bed.

Then there were the more ambitious projects, such as a pool house for Dal Grauer, my first client of the Medici mold. He had been a Rhodes scholar, and as head of the province of British Columbia's giant hydroelectric corporation, he was practically the equal of the premier. With his family, he was immersed in literature and the arts, and they lived in a handsome white neoclassical house.

An inventor friend of mine, Blythe Rogers, was experimenting with fibreglas-reinforced structural shapes, and I persuaded him to undertake casting eight tulip-shaped shells for the cabana roof. It was the beginning of an adventure. The complex plaster mould for the fibreglas forms collapsed. Another mould was built and another unsuccessful form produced. Finally, six acceptable forms were produced, but then the company went bankrupt. I had to hire a truck and steal my client's confiscated shells at night. The Grauers never knew the extent of the calamity when they enjoyed their pristine, exotic pool house. I sent off photographs to the professional magazines only to learn that a similar vaulted form had been produced for the American pavilion at a Moscow exposition. This was my first experience with the synchronicity of ideas that bedevils all innovators.

I continued to use fibreglas "sandwiches" — sheets with a variety of core materials —

*Facing page: The fibreglas roof of the cabana stands in front of the changing and pool equipment rooms of the Grauer house in Vancouver. Hollow steel pillars drain off the rainwater. The tulip shells are lit from inside at night, making a Moorish delight fitting for the New Romanticism of the late 1950s.* SELWYN PULLAN

*Top left: The translucent fibreglas patio roof, added in 1960 to the Boultbee house in Vancouver, provides shelter from the strong sun and enhances weaker light. The lacquered steel pillars contain lights.* Arthur Erickson

*Bottom left: The roofline of the 1961 Danto house steps rhythmically down its Vancouver site, perhaps the first Erickson house to move so. The interior and exterior walls are split-faced concrete block.* Arthur Erickson

*Right: A sketch for the Danto house shows the stepped roofline-terrace theme. Side patios and covered terraces extend the 3,300-square-foot house.*

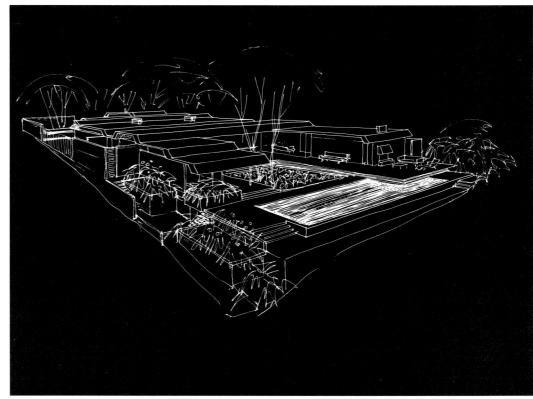

in my projects. A grand statement in their use was made in the golden gable of the living room wing added to the E. Leonard Boultbee home in 1960. Inevitably the addition swallowed the original house, and its exotic glowing roof made quite a picture in the old *Architectural Digest,* with its policy at that time of featuring the decorator and ignoring the architect.

An eclectic group of houses followed in the early 1960s. Out of antipathy for the hipped roof, I often avoided shakes or shingles and made roofs of stone or sod. I always challenged myself to come up with an original solution. As I had learned from Mr. Wright, materials themselves could determine the form of a building. A Vancouver city house for Julius Danto was built entirely in concrete block, using different widths of coursing to produce striated walls that, uncut by windows, stepped down a terraced property, the roofline following in counterpoint. A series of gateways opened through the successive

walls across the upper and lower terraces, like stages in a theatre set. Another block house, for H. A. Dyde, by contrast nestled between berms of natural grasses on the prairies near Edmonton, Alberta.

For Henri Fuldauer's house in West Vancouver, the roof was composed of deep inward sloping beams sheathed in board and batten inside and out. This and the supporting rough wood columns provided a gallery with a high ceiling across the south side of the house, off which the other rooms opened. The gallery in turn opened onto a long terrace from which the property dropped off to a view of the distant city. The same formal idiom was translated more smoothly into an unbuilt concrete house for Lionel A. J. Thomas, a university colleague.

The John N. Laxton house, precariously set on a West Vancouver vertical slope, had its wood frame and bracing exposed like the Kiyomizu Temple; the framing above was filled in with plaster like a half-timbered

Top left: The Dyde house was built in 1960 on the exposed treeless plains outside of Edmonton, Alberta. The sketch shows an early use of paired beams, as well as mounded earth in protective berms as an anchoring device.

Bottom left: A 1960 conceptual sketch of the Thomas house proposes the first in situ concrete house. The building would express the plasticity of the material in a composition of piers and trays hovering over the rocky knoll of its Vancouver site.

Right: The 1963 Fuldauer house in West Vancouver has steeply pitched roof planes that provide a skylight to the interior, as well as extra height for important spaces and an upstairs study; they also break the flat roofline. The house opens south towards the view.
JOHN FULKER

*Left: In a move beyond the usual exposed rough-cut lumber for supports, the 1963 Bayles house in West Vancouver uses posts of peeled tree trunks. The rustic look is carried through to roofs that are covered with moss.* ARTHUR ERICKSON

*Top right: View of the Laxton house living room terrace and glass roof eyebrow; the 1964 house was placed on long cedar poles to fit on its cliff-face site in West Vancouver overlooking a salt-water view. These are carried into a half-timbered look in the exposed frame and plaster infill for the house.* JOHN FULKER

*Bottom right: The 1963 Baldwin house near Vancouver is a lake pavilion in rough-sawn cedar and glass. The living room is upstairs, entered from grade, and the family room is downstairs, fronting on the shallow pond installed to bring the lake visually closer to the house. The chain strung from a beam is after an Asian rainwater lead, used through the years in preference to a drainpipe.* SELWYN PULLAN

*Facing page: The Lloyd house is set back 65 feet from the front property line of a small, narrow city lot in an ordinary Vancouver neighbourhood, exploiting the southern exposure. The excavation for the basement studio and a pond for light supplied earth to make a berm for privacy. River rock covers the roof. The interior is lit by a skylight that runs over the ridge beam. At 1,120 square feet and a cost of $15,000 in 1962, this was a modest house.* SIMON SCOTT

Elizabethan cottage. It was a rocky, forested site, and the straight trunks of the trees are echoed in the stilts, as are their lowering boughs in the roofline.

Another wood-frame house, for William F. Baldwin, was sited on Deer Lake a few miles east of Vancouver. The building appeared to illegally extend into the water on wooden piers, but the opposite was true — we brought the lake to the house by excavating the shoreline. Placid and without tides, lakes allow an intimate relationship with buildings most famously exploited in the lake palaces of Moghul India.

In Ted Bayles's West Vancouver house, the rustic quality dominated through the use of brick walls and posts of peeled tree trunks set upside-down as at Knossos. To complement the moss- and lichen-covered rocks of the site, the roofs were covered with moss and lichen instead of the usual shingle treatment of the Northwest. The rustic hand-crafted nature of the house was carried to wood-framed glass doors and windows.

The Denys C. Lloyd house had a modest $15,000 budget and a small Vancouver city lot with handsome old dogwood trees. Instead of backfilling the basement excavation, I extended the depression out so that the basement could have full-height windows and look into a sunken pond. The fill made a mound at the front of the lot, which, planted with bamboo and native grasses, gave the house more privacy. The neighbours confounded us by complaining to city hall about the garden; they preferred lawns and picket fences — we were going against context.

In 1963, towards the end of this evolutionary period in my career, I did a multiple-housing project called Point Grey Road Townhouses. Lois Milsom (then Spence), the developer for the five-townhouse project on a rundown but excellently sited set of waterfront lots, had been my pupil, and the project was essentially her senior thesis. Our challenge was to oblige five clients with different requirements to merge in a single unified

*Left: Floor plan of the five-unit Point Grey Townhouses built in Vancouver in 1963. The north side is all glass to take advantage of the view; the south side has skylit wells and courtyards.*

*Top right: The Point Grey Townhouses consist of a double unit with five bedrooms and a swimming pool, and four units with two or three bedrooms. A five-foot six-inch module of used brick and flying beams acts as the unifying device and accommodates even the unit designed by another architect.* SIMON SCOTT

*Bottom right: The largest Point Grey unit faces its pool. The used-brick columns are topped by fir spans stained green-grey by a treatment Erickson introduced to the region.* JOHN FULKER

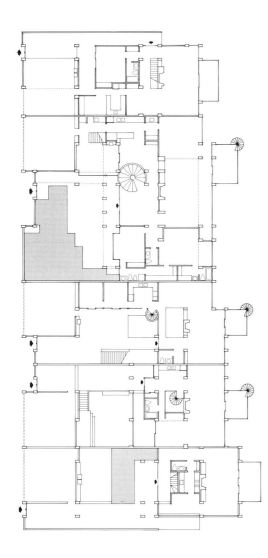

block. The only common denominators were the materials and the way of building. We chose used brick masonry, with wood for beams and details. An effective link was the repetition of a simple dominant beam form. The development was the first of such attached dwellings in Vancouver and resulted in new building laws to accommodate them. Lois's clients were lucky; spearheaded by her vision, property values in the area tripled.

Another multiple-housing project in Vancouver was Shannon Mews. Shannon was a splendid Italianate villa, the family manse of Austin Taylor, whose daughter Pat had married the writer William F. Buckley. In 1966, developers were planning a set of apartments for the property. For sentimental and architectural reasons, I assisted Pat, an old friend, in convincing them to keep the mansion and stables as well as the rose and Italian gardens. The ultimate 1971 scheme hid the new economical construction behind the large trees of the estate.

Like any young man beginning his profession, I was still testing for a direction. I struggled with the light and the beauty of Northwest Coast sites, but the lingering images of the great architecture on the shores of the Mediterranean had a subtle, subduing effect on my modernist enthusiasm. At the same time it was natural for me as a beginner to be preoccupied with the peripherals of detail, materials and structural innovation. These design concerns continued until my first large building commission with Geoffrey Massey, Simon Fraser University, when out of necessity I shifted attention from surface to the underlying sinew and bone of simple structure. And yet I never sacrificed the overall layout of a building to the demands of structure; structure came after the design, not as its basis, reversing the assumed order of Modernism. Later when my career took off, Modernism itself, led by I. M. Pei and Louis Kahn, was entering a classical period with which I was quite comfortable in identifying myself.

*Top: Shannon Mews in Vancouver has 160 units with one, two and three bedrooms arranged over a 10-acre former estate in L-shaped two-storey components, mostly hidden in the trees.* SIMON SCOTT

*Bottom: The open formal gardens of Shannon are preserved, as is the Georgian-style main house, which was converted to common rooms and a few apartments. The built project was initiated in 1971; its simple design does not attempt to engage the Classicism of the old building but rather hides discreetly — and inexpensively — in the trees. Construction is brick with exposed wood beams.* SIMON SCOTT

# FILBERG HOUSE

In 1958 Robert M. Filberg became my first patron, a wealthy man who was willing to back a full-scale architectural expression of my artistic nature. We were also contemporaries and friends, and the project was a nice match of our youthful ideals. Rob wanted to build a retreat-conference centre for world thinkers and leaders, with a main gathering place and smaller cabins scattered about the property. In a region of spectacular sites, his Vancouver Island acreage, near the town of Comox, was perhaps the most unusual and dramatic that I have ever built on. The property, part fields and part forested, covered the crown of a bluff two hundred feet above the inland sea between the island and the mainland. With that vantage there was nothing cramped or limited or lowering. On one side the vista looked back at a glacial peak on the island, and on the other it swept miles down the Strait of Georgia towards more mountains, rugged foothills and islands. Only a century before, Indian war canoes had passed this way, but to me the light was the thing — and it was pure Mediterranean.

To enhance the natural features of the site, we brought in a bulldozer and reshaped the ground, trying to act for the centuries to form a rise under the tall maples and a natural fall of land towards the cliff edge. We even cut a formal allée through the forest to get a view of the beach below. Thus, well before the house design was started, the powerful axes were established, joining the most compelling points of the distant landscape. The views just had to be brought through. The site radiated light, and I gave the house perforated screens, skylights and contoured ceilings so that even in the dullest

coastal weather it was suffused with luminosity. Many of its elements reflect New Romanticism, the 1950s equivalent of the 1980s postmodern fashion.

Rob Filberg died before he could realize the rest of his dream, and the house survives alone on its promontory, like a knight's pavilion with its large audience room and single bedroom quarters.

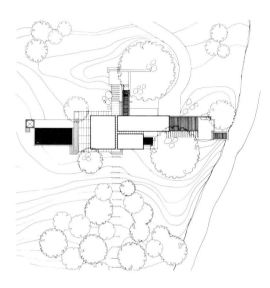

*Top: The plan shows the 1958 Filberg house, sited for light and view, on a high Vancouver Island bluff.*

*Middle: The living room of the Filberg house is its major space. The lattices and other details reflect the site's Mediterranean feel.* SIMON SCOTT

*Bottom: A section through the 2,500-square-foot Filberg house. The living room is on the left. The den and bedroom are up a short flight of stairs; the bedroom deck is over the garage at right.*

*Facing page: A view of the side reflecting pool of the Filberg house with the bedroom balcony to the right.* ARTHUR ERICKSON

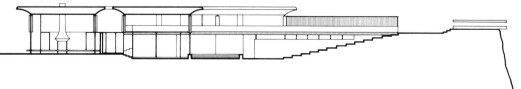

# SIMON FRASER UNIVERSITY

*Left: A view of Simon Fraser University from the top of the berm inside the academic quadrangle shows the pond and the main steps down to the mall. The quadrangle is a tranquil, contemplative space that encourages meditation by such touches as the simple, strong focal form of the berm, the regularity of the architecture, and the water and planting. Designed in 1963 for a mountaintop site in Burnaby, British Columbia.* SIMON SCOTT

*Right: Steps lead from the university's covered mall to the academic quadrangle; faculty offices and seminar rooms are in the elevated quadrangle structure, lecture theatres are underground. Vertical accents provide a rhythm in combination with horizontal masses and ensure that concrete rather than glass reads as the dominant material. The idea of elevating offices above a circulation area recurs in other projects.* SIMON SCOTT

*Facing page: View through the covered mall of the university: the glass canopy measures 133 feet by 297 feet. The hybrid space-frame roof, designed by structural conceptualist Jeffrey Lindsay, uses horizontal wood members, vertical tubular steel members and cable tension members.* SIMON SCOTT

In 1963, the age of the instant university and the eve of the multiversity, Geoffrey Massey and I joined forces again to enter a competition for the design of the British Columbia government's new Simon Fraser University. The rules called for a typical North American campus of scattered individual buildings for each faculty. Although we did not enter on a lark — we assembled a team and spent weeks of long hours developing our scheme — we hardly expected to win, as our design contravened the conditions. With that and our lack of experience, our chances seemed doubly diminished. Geoffrey and I went to the announcement ceremonies only because we were curious to see the other entries. We were truly surprised when we won.

After visiting some of the earliest extant universities, Al Azhar of the eighth century in Cairo, Bologna of the tenth century, and the colleges of Cambridge and Oxford begun in the thirteenth century, I had concluded that North American universities were nineteenth-century aberrations. Even when organized around Oxbridge quadrangles, fragmentation was the dominant theme. The American campus, with forestry and business, chemistry or law each separately housed, created physical boundaries that

fostered false intellectual divisions. I believed that above all a university should express universality of knowledge; that fragmentation into faculties and departments, each isolated in its own world, contradicted its purpose. Knowledge is connecting; higher education had to be more than the sum of its parts. The intellect develops from the process of interchange. I wanted to express at Simon Fraser University a new ideal based on the ancient models; the new university should be a community of learning.

The design began with a rethinking of the North American university campus in our time. We found that the separate buildings housing the various departments all contained the same fundamental entities: classrooms, laboratories, offices and lounges. Most academic facilities could be broken down into a few basic types that could then be reassembled not in individual enclaves but in continuous large clusters, allowing for the cross-fertilization of knowledge through proximity and sharing of spaces. This also made possible a more efficient utilization of facilities. The question remained of how to regroup these spaces. And here my own frustrations at college, in trying to find places in which to meet friends or talk informally with professors, came to the surface. After all, only a part of learning takes place in the classroom; the memorable experiences most often happen outside, in hallways, the library, the cafeteria, the dorms — all the meeting places of the campus.

If the learning process is a community process — a matter of dialogue, response, stimulation and redefinition — culminating in achieved knowledge that is a subject of contemplation, then the university has a twofold character that should be reflected in two major spaces: the social space for the interchange of ideas, and the intellectual space for contemplation. As a complement, two other types of space were needed: recreation and housing.

We applied these conceptual entities to the new university's site, the thousand-acre summit of a small mountain east of Vancouver. The mountain's spine swings between two small peaks. In 1963 the tremendous suburban flood was only predicted, and the mountain seemed remote and unfriendly, with a greater rainfall even than other parts of the Vancouver area. Today, its forested slopes are lapped by housing.

We began with an academic quadrangle in the tradition of Oxford and Cambridge. Within it, a "philosopher's walk" bordered a quiet green central space. To one side were the science laboratories, on the other the humanities, connected by an underground concourse with the lecture theatres off it. Standing in a ring above were smaller seminar rooms and more intimate teaching areas. Because professors should be among their students, their offices were distributed throughout. In keeping with the sense of contemplative quiet, the quadrangle must be a perfect square with no variation in its façade, like the *plaza mayor* of Salamanca, sufficiently monotonous that only the sky above, the outlook underneath and the garden within would command attention.

The second major space, the social crossroads of the university, was inevitably outside the library, with all the common facilities grouped around it: theatres, art galleries, communication centre, bookshop, pubs and cafeterias, lounges and student government offices. In this central mall, students and teachers would at one time or another run into everyone at the university. Such a space needed an umbrella, a huge glass one to let the light in but to keep off the interminable Northwest Coast rain.

Next came the more informal recreational space, located around the gymnasium and student union. Finally, there were the residences, with smaller scale, domestic spaces between them. Each of these four major spaces had its own character, yet was connected by the covered walkway that spanned the mountain ridge.

*Facing page: Two or three inches of water on the gravel roofs of the university's northern classroom section enhance the view, serve as insulation and carry through the Javanese terrace image. Walkways lead to meeting platforms. The water was a useful conceit that maintenance engineers did not tolerate for long.* SIMON SCOTT

Top: Perspective of the competition-winning scheme
for Simon Fraser University. The main access road
intersects the campus between the gymnasium and the
covered mall. Student residences are at the far left,
faculty housing at the upper right. The terraced playing
fields sculpt the mountain as done by ancient peoples
in Peru, Mexico and Java. Ken Burroughs

Bottom: The 1972 updated master plan of Simon Fraser
University shows the east-west axis of the campus
spine on the mountaintop's slightly saddle form. From
the left are the student residences with courtyard,
gymnasium, transportation centre, central mall and
library, academic quadrangle, administration building
and parking areas.

The walkway structure eventually became the spine of the university. Linking all buildings, it logically carried all the services of the university, acted as a delivery and communications route and held as much parking as possible. The walkway was raised above ground because on a mountain one of the problems is to get people to their destinations with a minimum of climbing. The central mall became a high-level pedestrian bridge, a hanging garden between the academic quadrangle at the top of one rise and the residential section at the top of the other rise, a distance of some thousand feet.

From the time of our original hike up to the rude clearing on the mountaintop, it had been obvious that tall buildings would aggravate the problems of ascent and descent. They would also look strangely diminutive and inadequate on the huge mountain, for the scale was not that of Europe where a castle might spike naturally from some crag. We decided on an axis that followed the ridge of the mountain. By spreading the buildings out and cutting them into the hillside in terraces so that the university hugged the summit, building and mountain would appear to be part of each other. The edges of the complex would dissolve into the land form, a sculpted fit suggested by Fatehpur-Sikri in India, Monte Alban in Mexico and the water-terraced hills of Java. Implicit in the quadrangle-mall unit was a one-building concept that meant expansion would always occur at the periphery; growth by accretion. The university would spread down the mountain in the same low, land-hugging terraced form dictated by the central core.

Simon Fraser University was to open and admit its first two thousand students two years after the project was begun. To achieve this impossible schedule, the four runners-up in the competition were commissioned for the final design and working drawings of five of the buildings — the library, quadrangle, science block, gymnasium and theatre — and asked to follow our schematic drawings and work under our supervision. In addition to our fellow architects, there were five contractors stumbling over one another on the site. So Geoff and I, the two house designers, plunged ahead through a couple of chaotic years. We chose to develop in full detail the building that tied them all together, the central mall. Our focal point was a huge glass roof a block long over the central mall. The roof was engineered by Jeffrey Lindsay, a disciple of Buckminster Fuller, and it met much skepticism. But Lindsay was not only a brilliant visionary, he was a meticulous engineer. In 1968, as a result of a freakishly heavy snowfall that brought down structures all over the city, several hundred panels of glass broke, and in the ensuing publicity he received much of the blame. Insurance companies and lawyers sorted it out, so Lindsay was never vindicated in court. In fact, Lindsay had nothing to do with the substitution of cheaper, inferior glass for the type he had specified. The repaired span sheltering the hub of university life stands as his finest achievement.

One of the major drawbacks of the university was its distance from the city. To overcome this, though not requested in the master plan, we advocated providing for a large built-in residential population and proposed to locate a new town centre on the very edge of the campus. When this plan was rejected, our later master plan opened the possibility of five thousand to ten thousand students living in as a necessary step to lessen the university's rarified isolation. Unlike mediaeval Arabic and many European universities tucked in the fertilizing currents of city life, the ordinary university allows escapism to flourish within its almost industrial precincts. Simon Fraser is purposely an urban complex. At Simon Fraser, students and teachers daily encounter the whole community. This intensity of involvement is the basis of culture. Simon Fraser proved it by attaining a high academic standard within a few years of its inauguration.

In the late 1960s the architecture of Simon Fraser was blamed for student unrest because the design turned the student body inward and made them socially conscious. What the critics did not see was that the architecture also helped solve the political friction and for the same reason: no one could escape the social responsibility of coming to terms with adversaries in so compact an environment. During the years of student unrest, no damage was ever done at Simon Fraser. In fact, the students showed an uncharacteristic sensitivity and became guardians of the university architecture. They campaigned against an unsightly gas station and against temporary buildings where trees should have been. In the spirit of the time, we all joined together in a poppy planting rite one golden spring dusk, as part of an effort to save the grass meadows surrounding the campus from being chopped to stubble.

*Top: A view of the steps from Simon Fraser's transportation centre, a dropoff point to the mall for buses and visitors' cars. The domed skylight over a steady progression of stairs draws people upward.* JOHN FULKER

*Bottom: Two sections of the university, the first a transverse section through the academic quadrangle, laboratories and classrooms — natural and physical sciences are on the right, humanities and social sciences teaching areas are on the left. The second is a longitudinal section through the central spine, from the transportation centre on the left to the academic quadrangle on the right.*

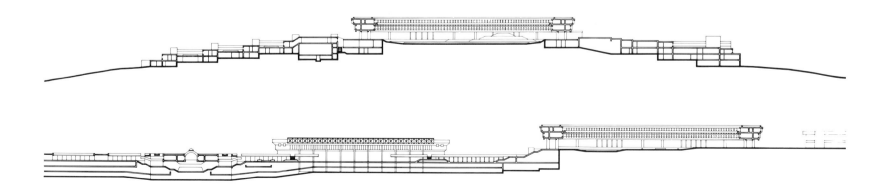

PART II

# PROGRESSIONS

# PROGRESSIONS

In architecture as in any of the arts, experience teaches economy of expression. But if I had not seen the arts and sacred buildings of Japan, expressions of a millennium of experience, I would have come very late to value that certain artlessness which yields the freshness of the simple statement. A proliferation of novel techniques or materials, in themselves empty, too often bury the craft of building; and as a young man, feeling as strictures anything I had not come to on my own, I was eager to test new architectural avenues and building products. Then in 1961 a travelling fellowship enabled me to spend several months in Japan, and I discovered in the Orient the ultimate rebellion — living in Japan was to live in opposition to European aesthetics.

I was a student again in Kyoto, but I immediately found that I could learn only if I suspended entirely my innate, occidental references for judgement. This act of mental discipline capped my creative rebelliousness with objectivity. To realize that Western architecture was just one narrow field expressing one culture-bound view of the world enabled me to look at first Japan and then other cultures as equally valid avenues of expression. I began to see myself as an architectural anthropologist, never tempted to go native with my sympathies, but always curious, always respectful of other ways of doing things, and applying that same detached attitude to my own life and work at home. My energy thus captured by objectivity, I subsequently looked for solutions that would avoid fashion or doctrine and would address the realities of context and purpose.

After Japan, I could say with conviction that it is better to be simple and still remain independent of Mies's structuralist minimalism. As a West Coast architect, I already knew the Japanese idiom, and my work was often superficially influenced by it. The trip made me aware of the aesthetic principles behind their refinement of detail, though in practice the sensitivity to mood and illusion and the craftsmanship the Japanese apply to form, jointing, surface and pattern could not be duplicated in the West, much less the profounder attributes of their architecture. The sum of it remained part of the Japanese civilization.

The first noteworthy buildings I saw were the ancient temples of Nara, and I could not understand them. To me they were rather feeble wooden structures, alone and unprepossessing, the antithesis of what my reading had led me to expect. The refreshing, Mondrianesque compositions that graced the publications of Bauhaus writers were nowhere to be seen. Even though I was lucky enough to be the only foreign resident of Jikoin, a small Zen temple near Nara, and could study it from sympathetic proximity, the architecture seemed to lack any exuberance or joy. Instead, it expressed only a sombre, mediaeval resignation.

The temple has a famous courtyard garden for meditation that "borrows" the distant view of real hills and pagodas. The garden's clipped hedges in the foreground represent waves that silently crash on the toy sand beach. In the morning the temple's paper walls were slid aside, and its many rooms became a single platform surrounded by gardens. Sunlight streamed through the

*Page 38: The second Smith house, designed in 1964 for a site in West Vancouver, is a study of post-and-beam architecture.* JOHN FULKER

*Page 39: The Canadian Pavilion at Expo '70 in Osaka, Japan, has a kinetic canopy composed of five rotating 60-foot-diameter umbrellas.* ERNEST SATO/ JOHN TAKEHAMA

*Facing page: The design of the Museum of Anthropology at the University of British Columbia in Vancouver began in 1972.* EBERHARD OTTO

trees, and freshly rinsed stone paths exuded a damp, caressing smell. But even these carefully tended beauties could not dispel completely the darkness of ancient associations.

After a few weeks I moved to a sister temple in Kyoto and finally began to penetrate the mystery of Japanese art. One evening at the shop of Robin Curtis, an antique dealer who lived in Kyoto, I saw a collection of Chinese Sung porcelains, and I started to explain to him how easy their beauty was to see with their clear celadon surfaces and noble symmetry. On the other hand, an adjacent group of Japanese pottery seemed awkward and rural with earth-toned glazes and deliberately misshapen asymmetry. ''You show your ignorance,'' Robin said, ''for one is just as fine as the other.'' I took this as a challenge, and the next morning I went to the Kokedera Temple to view a particularly renowned teahouse that I had previously disdained, vowing not to leave until I too could feel the fineness of this highly contrived Japanese style. It was a rustic structure, but too precious.

Each of the teahouse's four columns rested in studied conceit on different elements: a stone, a log, a slab of rock and the earth. Professorial patience gave way to stubborn determination as I sat in a viewing shelter across a small garden lake from the teahouse, waiting for some hint of true art from this tiny, acclaimed shack. Noon came and hunger started to erode my sense of mission. Then I heard a rustling, which sounded like a flock of busily feeding birds or monkeys moving through the trees. Instead, half a dozen women emerged from the foliage, a flock themselves, dressed alike in simple blue cotton kimonos pulled up between their legs and tucked into obis, their heads covered with blue bandanas and half-moon-shaped straw bonnets. They were pruning the trees, but not with shears and saws as we use in Canada. They wielded tiny nail scissors and expertly attacked the leaves, not the branches. They trimmed the pine needles as if clipping hair. I could not believe their efforts would have any effect on the jumbled forest of a garden in front of me. Yet where they had passed, it opened up with an airiness and spaciousness that gave every plant the room to fulfill itself with grace. Relieved of the need to compete and extend, each tree became a more perfect expression of its species, something an untended tree could never be. By this careful, unnatural intervention, the garden became more expressive of nature's beauty.

So I understood that in all traditional Japanese art the subject was nature, not man; the opposite of the Western tradition. I remembered the texts that describe the Western fascination with the human form and how it acts as the basis of our humanistic architecture, giving it its proportions, symmetry and strength — its attributes of physique and character. Humanism has shaped our aesthetics. But the Japanese base the canons of their aesthetics on the tree form. The tree is rooted, not detached as is man, and its roots fan out in heavy cords to tiny, disappearing hairs, mirroring the fanning of its trunk to branches and twigs and fine-veined leaves scattering into the sky. A building, therefore, should not stand on the ground but be rooted in place. Its structure grows upward like a trunk and ends in the sweep of the eave, like a branch gesturing towards heaven. The movement has neither beginning nor end. Like a temple drum beat, it fades to infinity. The static proportions and muscular tensions of Western architecture are replaced with a reaching, spiralling gesture, which to the uninitiated seems weak but actually reflects powers more profound than man himself.

Japan has its own rhythmic patterns. Rhythm pervades all things and is at the root of all architecture. Rhythm gives measure and provides the right tempo to a building, be it stately or graceful, quick or ponderous, gentle or slow. As in music, spatial rhythm arises out of the tempo of a culture. To support a structure is easy, but to support it so that the structure is in consonance, improving the intention of the design, is much more difficult.

Western culture with its evangelistic focus on destination uses rhythm to mark our progress to our objective. In Japan, space is nondirectional. The passage, not the destination, is what matters, and one proceeds as if to an Oriental rhythmic beat, which is not a persistent sound but changes logarithmically, coming slowly into the audible range and fading lightly out of hearing into infinity. Such a spatial rhythm does not pace out the human path but underlies a more subtle sense of growth and change. In our culture, we seem to need an accompanying rhythm to draw us on through difficult or uninteresting spaces, such as a flight of stairs or a corridor. Rhythm gives us more pleasure in movement if it provides a sense of purpose and achievement.

Structure should emerge out of the rhythmic need inevitably, as an intrinsic part of the architectural scheme, not predetermined, for then it can inhibit the architectural purpose. Structure must be a means, not an end. How well a building expresses its intent depends on the fusion of its spatial and structural rhythm, the syntax of its spaces and, for eloquence, its details. Japan showed me a very different sense of rhythm and encouraged me to build almost without detail, in a seemingly elemental and effortless way — which of course requires mastery of detail. It also taught me about surface and the appreciation of the nature of materials, upon which I developed my method of counterpointing the elegance of materials with the ruggedness of forms. Wood and concrete, for example, are rough and elemental materials, which, placed without the intervening details of frames and stops in juxtaposition with the sheen of glass, heighten the specific attributes of each.

Intrinsic to rhythm is the modulation of space. Space is the supreme aesthetic adventure. If meeting the purposes of a building is the major task, making the spaces to celebrate those events is an architect's peculiar delight. And why not, when the spaces we shape conform to the Western conviction that man is the centre and measure of all things? The Orient has a different view of space. The pattern of space does not follow the human path because there it is symbolic. In the Japanese house, space wells out on all sides like a series of concentric circles until it merges with the space of nature, symbolized by the garden. Around the core of the house is wrapped the divisible living space, and around this an inner veranda and then an outer veranda, with the border of the garden carefully laid out; and then the garden itself, expanding beyond its boundaries into untamed nature. In this nondirectional order, the path and the different uses of space for sleeping, eating or visiting can be anywhere; spaces are arranged like a series of folding screens to be put up or down at will.

In the Western house a very specific arrangement of spaces, each tailored to a special use, unfolds along the human path. Furthermore, with its scale relative to its setting, its flexibility of disposition, its intricacy relative to its size, and its peculiarities of personal needs and tastes, the house is a special category of architecture that defies generalization. More than any other building form it can respond to the subtlest changes of grade, outlook and climate of a site, and meet intimate personal demands. Although the house is the most comprehensible building form and the most familiar, it is the most complex.

Despite their complicated compositions, the houses I designed after the Japanese experience benefited from my having been reassured about the value of simplicity of expression. Because a house is small, the ideas that are in the forefront of my mind leap out to be tested here first — more easily than in a more conventional, less complex and larger building. After Japan, my houses ceased to be composed of a variety of materials and instead became as much as possible expressions of one material — reminiscent almost, of sculpture.

The firm of Erickson/Massey, formed for the Simon Fraser University project, quickly attracted more business, but my restless vision encouraged me to make proposals to individuals or corporate bodies that I believed needed prompting to make some kind of architectural gesture. Such was the Centennial Museum; I approached Vancouver city council with the museum project to take advantage of federal grants for Canada's celebration in 1967. My proposal was an extendable series of pavilions along a waterfront site. I gave them striking high sweeping roofs, like sea barriers. The council liked the notion of a museum but gave the project to another architect. This initial disappointment did not, however, check my propensity for such actions.

As far back as 1956 I had begun to express myself on the subject of Vancouver's overall development in terms of how the city should look. In that year I had drawn the massing outline of a large-scale housing project for its then uncrowded West End. Today it is a zone of dense apartment towers like Rio de Janeiro or Hong Kong. Anticipating this, I proposed to make the skyline the value and to organize the housing as the texture of a dramatic sweeping structure. Thus the cityscape would complete the theatrical setting that the looming, rugged mountains provided. Through the years, I worked on a number of studies, papers and development proposals on this kind of scale. Although I would hesitate today to impose my will on my native city in such wide swaths, in the 1950s and 1960s the schemes reflected less an egotistical vision for development than a mere professional's better idea of what the customary Canadian combination of large private landownership and invest-

ment and public planning could achieve for a whole city.

The idea of an aesthetic envelope — "individual buildings a thing of the past" — persisted in a 1968 proposal for a residential development in Montreal. The client was Canadian Pacific Railway's real estate company, Marathon, and the site was a former railway yard. I gave the large single structure a shape that picked up the convolutions of the surrounding freeways. Called Cité des Terrasses, for its sweeping profile of balconies that gave its residents both light and views, desirable and scarce features in the sprawling city, it also had a green refuge in a central park. The structure would have been a stupendous urban feature, but its high density and height were against it. I held that these qualities could in fact work in favour of community values, as proved through history, but you had to design for them. The familiar condominium fortress-tower exhibits little thought for the common welfare. I offered a scaled-down version called Fisherman's Quay to Vancouver in 1969, to be placed on a salt-water arm opposite the downtown. The base of the ten- to twenty-storey housing towers attacked the problem of how tall buildings should be grounded; the flared legs of the inverted Y-form brought the ground several stories up the face of the building and thus gave it a rooted and welcoming aspect particularly suitable for housing. The area opened between the legs would admit air and light to the ground or could be used for common facilities such as a swimming pool and meeting rooms.

In contrast to the sculptured high-rise projects, the angled form of the stacked roof of the Expo '67 pavilion became a valid solution for lower urban buildings. I used it in 1968 for a Sikh temple in Vancouver. The temple had to be simple, symmetrical and contained behind a walled space. I discovered later to my delight that the plan of a series of diminishing rectangular prisms, each shifting 45 degrees on axis, was typical of roof construc-

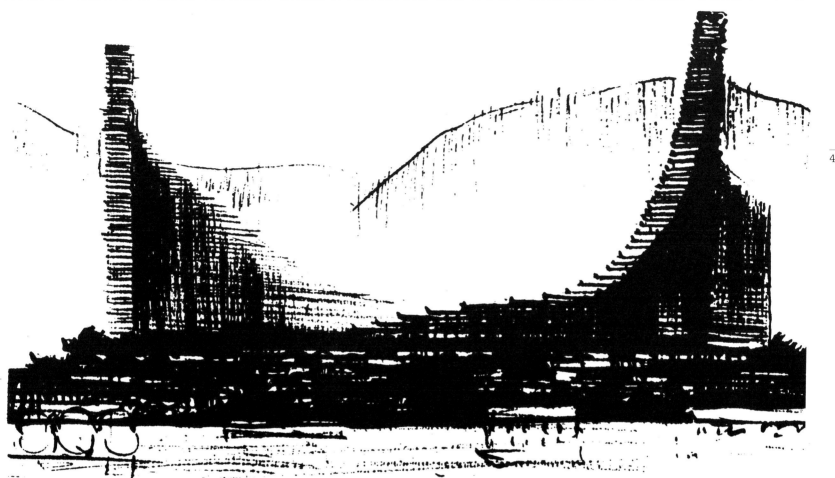

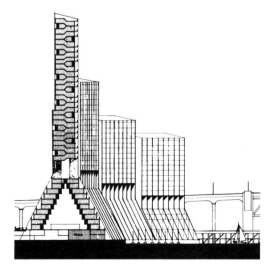

tion in northern India, where shorter available timber could span only across corners. Sheathed in travertine tile, the stepped structure supported the stainless steel outline of a dome.

Angled forms also distinguished a low-rise, very dense village proposed in 1969 for Banff National Park in the Canadian Rockies. As one of North America's natural wonders, Banff has a heavy visitor load. Over the years the haphazard placement of new service areas and the expansion of established private facilities gave a shabby edge to the superb alpine views and the proud old matronly hotels at Banff and Lake Louise. When the government permitted a new development at the base of the Lake Louise ski area, we knew that careful planning was required to fit it in without spoiling what the visitors were there to see. Basically, Village Lake Louise sat on the parking lot of the ski area — no new disruption of the environment there. The second point in its favour was that it

contained structures within a unified design environment, low set and of wood. Nestling in as inconspicuously as possible, it represented our time's response to the scenery that the turn-of-the-century chateau hotels had attempted to romanticize with their grandiose style. The angled, stepped forms get as much of the required square footage onto as small an acreage as possible. The project was defeated by parties even more conservation-minded than I.

Then, two years later, we were the runner-up in the prestigious, international competition for the French government's modern art museum project, the Centre du Plateau Beaubourg. The winners, Piano and Rogers, gave Paris a huge exoskeleton with the fascination of a tinkertoy construction, as popular now as it was then controversial, and a completely anomalous intruder in its neighbourhood. There was no question that all entries would be absolutely contemporary, but ours attempted as carefully as possible to fit snugly in the surrounding historic Marais district with its famous Les Halles market and fine old *hôtels.*

Paris is the most geometric city in the world; solid built-up blocks make the streets and squares read very strongly because the buildings form uninterrupted walls of consistent height, articulating that geometry. Our design conformed to the existing squares, traffic and block patterns as well as the heights of surrounding buildings. We clad the outside walls in mirror, an echo of Versailles, to reflect and blend with the context. From the outside, our building would dissolve in these reflections; only on the inside, upon entering the craterlike centre court, would visitors suddenly find themselves in a twentieth-century museum of art. The stepped court uses on a smaller scale the same 45- and 90-degree angles that appeared in Village Lake Louise.

Although the wall was not a prime concern with me until years later, I did use it in the Sikh temple and, in 1968, the Erickson/Massey building. Both were simple volumes enclosing naturally skylit spaces. The outside walls are quiet, solid enclosures. The professional staff has no distracting view; that is left for the secretarial floor. Even my office is just a skylit cubicle. The structure of the office building is present in the solid timber tree forms that rise from the main floor to support the roof. Ferns and bamboo complete the forest effect.

The opening of a second office for the buildup and duration of Expo '67 in Montreal was the beginning of a cross-continent commute that has characterized my life since. After the fair ended, we moved our tiny shop to Toronto to begin work on the Bank of Canada commission in Ottawa. I was pleased to have a proper business reason for travel and started to spend more time in eastern Canada, dropping down frequently to New York. At first it was difficult to wrench away from the comfort of home and garden and my small treasures. I lugged suitcases of

clothing changes from coast to coast. But shortly I developed a healthy detachment, and I realized how unimportant possessions were. All I needed was health and ability, the prospect of work and some kind of simple refuge — cached with an extra suit — at the end of the journey.

*Top: The Vancouver office of Arthur Erickson Architects is a simple warehouse structure with exterior walls of split-faced concrete block, designed in 1968. A window in the rear opens into the employee lounge area; otherwise, there are no views. A skylight detaches the roof from the walls. The roof is supported by rough-sawn branching fir columns; the interior walls are bare concrete and white-painted gypsum.*
DICK BUSHER

*Bottom: The Centre du Plateau Beaubourg, a 1971 competition submission for a contemporary art museum in Paris, is given a sheath of mirrors to reflect the surrounding historic buildings, thus acknowledging rather than dominating the fragile Marais district. The structure encourages casual pedestrian traffic by entrances to the courtyard through angled corner openings. The landscaped amphitheatre terraces are planned for public activity. The angled forms introduced in the Expo '67 pavilion are still being explored.*
SIMON SCOTT

# GRAHAM HOUSE

The popular image of Vancouver shows a city skyline set directly against the base of a spectacular wall of mountains rising straight up out of its harbour. You might think that the closeness of the mountains is a photographic trick, but there is only a mile of steep foothill between the sea and the escarpment. This strip is West Vancouver, where a geography of wide desirable views and short nasty drops has converted home builders into architects' clients. Some promontories, however, are harder than others to build on. The David Graham house in 1963 launched my reputation as the architect you went to when you had an impossible site.

The Grahams had a rock scree in West Vancouver dropping sixty feet from an overhanging cliff to a ledge over the salt water. First of all, my clients wanted to know, how would you get down to it? The only solution I could see was a multistorey house set against the cliff like a ladder. Its pleasure would be in the discoveries of the descent itself. And as an architect spends as much effort on the roof and sides as the interior of the house, why not make all accessible? In the Graham house, all parts of the structure are exposed as you make your way gradually, bit by bit, down the site. Instead of being thrown up first, the choicest aspects of the site are left to the last, and the best view is arrived at through artful seduction.

As I hiked about the site and looked at the bay below, I thought of the Villa d'Este near Rome, where the whole garden, laid against a hillside, is a play on water. As with the villa, you are granted an overview as you arrive at the Graham house. Then you duck under an overhanging ledge and the view disappears,

until a door opens and you peer down a series of steps and landings that finally reach the sea. Each descending level expands on either side to heighten anticipation. The first, the dining room, has a reflecting pool on one side and a swimming pool on the other. The next is the living room, hanging over rocks with pines on either side and a long view of the sound and high peaks. Finally, another short descent brings you to the master bedroom hanging over the sea, with a bathroom which enhances that water experience by means of submarine windows looking into the swimming pool.

The descending arrangement demanded overlapping volumes, which I translated into overlapping railing-height walls with glass in between. Where solid, wall panels have the heavy texture of vertical board and batten. For their composition, my mind shifted from the eighteenth-century sophistication of a villa to the more regional rusticity of a log cabin.

*Facing page: In the 1963 Graham house, rough board and batten siding contrasts with the smooth beams.* EZRA STOLLER/ESTO

*Top: The Graham house was the first use of roofs to extend living areas.* EZRA STOLLER/ESTO

*Bottom: A sketch of the Graham house shows the horizontal beams balanced on a rocky ledge.*

# SMITH HOUSE 2

Three years after the Japan trip, I was ready to draw on my heightened awareness of surfaces and materials. In the Japanese craft tradition, the juxtaposition of textures acts to give each a sensuous quality that encourages the eye to act as a fingertip: polished wood next to rough wood, silk versus stone. Gordon and Marion Smith were both artists and visually acute people, the perfect clients for such an exercise. They were very trusting as well, in spite of their limited budget and fund of experience with Geoff and me years ago in 1953, and refused to give any directions. I decided to put the house together with rough fir beams direct from the mill, in a rudimentary, structural way like a log cabin. Sheets of glass unbroken by mullions would provide the sensual contrast of a glassy sheen.

My commitment to using one basic material required me to order both posts and beams cut from the same size of wood. Surprisingly, the effect countered the usual tension of support so fundamental to architecture. Instead, the house gained a sense of extraordinary repose. This discovery took my growing devotion to the strong horizontal to a logical conclusion. Several years later, with the Museum of Anthropology, the device could be seen as a direct descendant of the Northwest Coast Native longhouse, which was built of huge log beams laid across posts also rendered from five-hundred-year-old cedars.

I wanted the Smith house to reveal the site in the same way that I had found it revealed to me when I first walked onto it. Through the forest clearing I discovered the fern-covered rift between the rocks; then, at the end, the

distant sea view through the vertical stems of young firs. I customarily made it a practice to place a house on the worst part of the site, so that the virtues of the site could be left undisturbed for enjoyment from the house.

After you approach through the forest and step up to the entrance, you see across the courtyard and under the living room bridge the light from the sea far away through the fir trees. The inner courtyard is an architectural reiteration of the forest clearing — a moment of containment before the release of space into the surroundings. Progressive discovery of the house and site is made possible by overlapping and stepping up each wing of the house in a kind of spiral. The passage starts at the *porte-cochère*, climbs up to the kitchen-dining wing, up to the living room, then to the bedrooms and continues outside to the roof of the porte-cochère, up to the roof of the kitchen and so on, inferring an endless spiral.

At each corner is an anchor point — the

*The southwestern corner of the second Smith house in West Vancouver, designed in 1964, opens to an extensive terrace off the kitchen. EZRA STOLLER/ESTO*

*Facing page: The living room of the second Smith house spans a slight declivity between two rock outcroppings on a prominence over the sea view. It was a first experiment in making posts and beams of equal dimensions, regardless of structural requirements, and continued the drive to reduce the number of materials and forms. The wood was treated with copper arsenate to achieve gold, green and olive tones similar to a patina. EZRA STOLLER/ESTO*

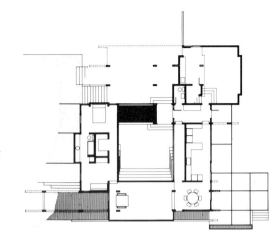

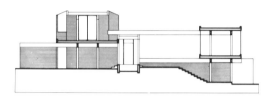

*Left: Floor plan and section of the second Smith house, which spirals around a central court, with a carport and fish tank closing the fourth side. On the right is the studio; the kitchen and dining areas look out on a large patio. The living room spans the court and leads to the bedroom wing. The section through the court shows the two-storey studio on the left, the entry and the living/dining room over the descending steps. The house has one bedroom and a den.*

*Top right: The living room fireplace of the Smith house is bush-hammered concrete. The interior finishes and colour are the same greenish hues as the exterior.*
GORDON SMITH

*Bottom right: The central courtyard of the Smith house restates the forest clearing genre of the site.*
JOHN FULKER

studio at the entrance corner, the dining terrace at the viewpoint, the living room terrace into the forest, and the bedroom terrace edging the forest. Whereas the living room is a suspended box of rough wood and glass, the studio is a skylit solid enclosure with narrow slits of windows giving an even illumination to all the walls. It is the only white room in a house where all other finishes, structure, floors, panelling and even linen wall fabric are treated with a preservative, achieving a green-gold hue. The Smiths, to my great frustration, would not give me any instructions about their new house. They like to tell the story that the one choice they made for themselves was the colour for the studio floor. He chose olive, he said, for practical purposes. He got white.

Within a short distance of the Smith house on a rocky but forested hillside, I did a sort of reprise of its strong wood horizontals in a multiple-dwelling develop-

*Left: The 1979 Montiverdi Estates consists of 20 detached units on a seven-acre forested site in West Vancouver near the Smith and Graham houses. Montiverdi draws on both: strong horizontals that counterpoint the trees and rocks, the use of box beams, the play of smooth glass and rough wood, and the incorporation of roofs as deck space. KIYOSHI MATSUZAKI*

*Right: An entry to a Montiverdi residence: the houses are 2,000 to 3,000 square feet and have custom configurations. The walls are generally transparent on the east and west sides, opaque on the north, screened or transparent on the south. The uppermost houses are most vertical and have roof decks; the houses below are low, with planting on the roofs to extend the forest floor. JOHN FULKER*

ment in 1979. Subdivided and sold as individual lots, the acreage would have lost the serenity that made the property attractive in the first place. So the sensitive developer of Montiverdi Estates asked us to design a prototype unit, which with variations in size and internal arrangements could be placed about the site while keeping the woods as intact as possible. As the houses were sold, we worked with their owners to incorporate desired modifications.

The unifying theme of bands of beams and wood siding counterpoints the site's mossy granite ledges and pristine grove of perfectly straight-trunked firs and hemlocks. The house floors are stepped and stand on slender vertical posts. The application of my characteristic deference to nature to the problem of multiple housing seems not to have been thrown off by the numbers. In its way, Montiverdi is the inverse of the Royal Crescent at Bath, which is all architecture and no nature. Whichever way the houses are arranged, they automatically compose themselves with the trees and rock face.

The living room of the 1967 Catton house in West Vancouver, overlooking Howe Sound. The sculptured form of the brick fireplace is a focal element that follows the roof angle and reveals the view behind it. The exterior wood theme carries into the interior. JOHN FULKER

Facing page, top: The south side of the Catton house has a deck off the living room and kitchen on the lower level. The children's bedrooms, with their own decks, are above on the garage level. The house is a theme on a single material, one-inch by three-inch siding. By wrapping the exterior in stained cedar boards, the house appears to be carved from a single block of wood. The structure is placed on its rocky slope in West Vancouver, not built out of it, and is attached by iron links to the stone. JOHN FULKER

Facing page, bottom left: Section of the Catton house: the roof peaks over the garage and descends over the children's bedroom level.

Facing page, bottom right: Roof/site plan of the Catton house: a skylit stairwell bisects the house, starting on the highest, bedroom level beside the garage. All the balcony spaces are carved out of the block outline, itself inspired by the Swiss farmhouse.

# CATTON HOUSE

The David Cattons were old friends who gave me full freedom to design their house in 1967. In contrast to earlier houses that melded their forms to sites, the Catton house sits on its rocky, West Vancouver lot as a separate entity. It is like a solid volume eroded at the sides, top and bottom. The overall form — suggested by Swiss farmhouses I had recently seen — came from the need to open to the distant views while blocking out the prospect of the railway below and the immediate neighbours. Even though not every client wants the privacy that the personal structure of a house should give, I provide it in any case.

The Catton house forms a rhomboid shaped to the slope of the rock. The direct view below of the railway is constrained by the porch railing, which acts both as an acoustic and visual barrier. Since the bedrooms are concealed in recessed roof terraces and the descent though the house from the entrance allows only brief glimpses out, it is at the living room level that the full impact of the sea and mountains is felt. Here three kinds of view are selected, with each framed differently: south to the sea, often bright from the afternoon sun, in a lofty triangle above the floor that drops away seawards; west to the quiet hillside, in a long horizontal slot through the roof; north to the mountains in a low triangle above the fireplace.

It is an economical house for a family of five, each member needing a private domain, so the plan is tight and spaces compact. Because it is a frame house of exposed surfaces rather than exposed structure, walls, floors, ceilings, and even roof are

sheathed in the same material — three-inch-wide cedar boards — so the house reads like a piece of sculpture carved from a single block of wood. This use of a single material throughout resulted in perhaps the greatest coherence of any of my houses — almost total plastic unity.

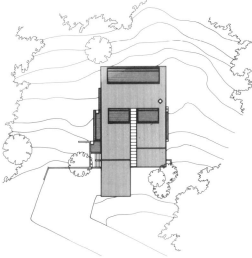

*Top: The Hilborn house, designed in 1970, is located in eastern Canada and is different from the wood post-and-beam West Coast house. Here, vertical brick wall panels establish the rhythm and support the horizontal planes. The walls define the terraced slope while the glass-enclosed rooms flow out onto lateral terraces.* Simon Scott

*Bottom: An axonometric sketch of the Hilborn house conveys the way the walls define the slope of the site. As piers, they extend above and beyond the limits of the house. Light and space run between them east to west. Trellises connect some piers and cover the terraces and roof decks. Although the verticals appear stark in the sketch, the brick terraces and sod roof root them to the site.*

*Facing page, top: A side view of the Hilborn house: the lowest block contains the living room and the covered swimming pool; above are the master bedroom and, on an upper level, two more bedrooms. The wall planes extend into the landscape, articulating the natural slope of the land.* Simon Scott

*Facing page, bottom: Section of the Hilborn house: a bridge on the right leads from a tennis court to the roof terraces. The living area and swimming pool are on the lowest level, separated by a gallery from the kitchen and family room.*

# HILBORN HOUSE

My first house in eastern Canada was for Dick and Laurette Hilborn in Cambridge, Ontario, west of Toronto. The outlook on nearly all sides of their property is to tamed and gentle countryside. The site drops down a slope of pines and maples to a narrow benchland and from there falls another sharp sixty feet to a river. The 1970 concept emerged quickly, almost casually, on the back of an envelope. Brick being the traditional building material of the area, I proposed a series of terraces between vertical walls of brick that marched rhythmically across the site. These held the horizontal roof planes, terraces and trellises that stepped down the hill. All else was glass.

From the approach you can descend over the roof that holds the upper gardens, or into the house stepping through the long lateral shelves of space that terrace down the hillside. These shelves have walls and floors of brick, and ceilings of wooden slats the same width as the brick. At midpoint they lead into a perspex-roofed garden court and swimming pool defined by walls that continue on until the last brick terrace releases itself into the forest. The piers extend beyond the limits of the enclosure, reinforcing the layered fall of the land. The trellises also extend the space, releasing it gradually, as does the structure in dissolving into the landscape somewhat like a ruin.

When new, the house already seemed long established; it plays curiously with time; it may have been just erected or recently excavated, or gradually be sinking back into the earth. But this is also a quality granted by Ontario, a far older and mellower part of Canada than the West Coast.

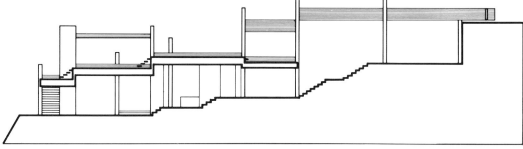

# MacMILLAN BLOEDEL BUILDING

Erickson/Massey was asked in 1965 by J. V. Clyne, the chairman of MacMillan Bloedel, British Columbia's giant forest products company, to look at a headquarters proposal for downtown Vancouver that the company liked financially but not in appearance. Seizing the opening, we declined the ''face lift'' but asked for a month to come back with a counterproposal. This was our first office building and remains my favourite for a good reason; it completely counters the impermanent, jerrybuilt aspect of the modern office building epitomized by hung ceilings and flexible partitioning on the inside and the curtain wall on the outside. With the MacMillan Bloedel building we turned our backs on new technology and went to the oldest and most traditional of techniques, the solid load-bearing wall with minimum openings cut into it.

Our engineer, taking into account earthquake stresses, turned it from a bearing wall into a more logical and contemporary vertical cantilever structure. The wall tapers from a ten-foot thickness at the base to one foot at the top, with the floor structure bridging to the opposite wall. Such a wall demanded poured-in-place concrete, which anyway is preferable to the skin-deep cosmetic of precast concrete. The most difficult thing was to persuade the contractors that this was to be the final finish and to dispense with the construction joints and corner chamfers of finished concrete. Their argument was that the sharp edges would chip and that the pour lines would be untidy, but I wanted precisely such irregularities as surface patina. The structure was bold enough to be complemented by the irregularities that might dis-

tract from a weaker-looking structure. When finished, the concrete turned out magnificently — rough, almost crude at times, but with its own expressive strength. Against it, the mullionless seven-foot square panes of glass were placed in the depth of the structure, effectively contrasting the rugged mass

*Facing page: Night illumination gives a patina to the rough character of the poured-in-place concrete walls of the MacMillan Bloedel building. The seven-foot-square windows and three-foot-wide concrete columns sum up the ten-foot building module.*
EZRA STOLLER/ESTO

*Left: MacMillan Bloedel's elevator lobby is an imposing yet simple space. In it hangs a tapestry by Mariette Rousseau-Vermette, who later contributed work to Roy Thomson Hall.* EZRA STOLLER/ESTO

*Right: The 27-storey, 463,000-square-foot MacMillan Bloedel building, designed in 1965, in Vancouver. The structure tapers upward, on the principle of the vertical cantilever, from a wall thickness of ten feet at the bottom to one foot at the top.* EZRA STOLLER/ESTO

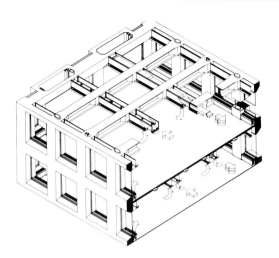

Left: A cutaway isometric view of the MacMillan Bloedel building shows the integrated structural, mechanical and lighting systems. The ceiling coffers are defined by the concrete crossbeams, and the air-conditioning ducts have grooved sides for indirect lighting fixtures. Supply air is introduced at the base of the windows and exhausted through ceiling ducts.

Right: The ceiling of the MacMillan Bloedel lobby; instead of lowering the ceiling to cover a network of mechanical and lighting systems, seven-foot square coffers, matched to the module of window and column and fitted with indirect lighting, allow eleven-foot floor-to-ceiling heights. EZRA STOLLER/ESTO

of concrete with the sheer liquidity of glass.

The interior was now free of the kind of interference that characterizes the deceitfully clean curtain-walled building. No support columns broke up the floors or complicated furniture arrangements. The ceiling pattern inside followed closely the same pattern as the outside wall, a spacing that allowed all the needed variations in office size, with the partitions always ending against solid wall and beam. Instead of the usual fluorescent fixtures, which disrupt the appearance of any building and ensure by their glare the greatest eye discomfort, we substituted where we could an indirect lighting system in the coffers between the beams. The effect in the office space is one of quiet luminosity. And since the building is really a sandwich of two towers, it is narrow enough that no one is far from natural daylight.

I had always deplored the inevitable clutter caused by too many pieces of furniture, equipment, files and papers. I wanted to reduce these to a minimum, which led to the development of the innovative storage wall. Coat cupboards, books, files, additional work surfaces — everything possible was put into the storage wall, leaving only the desks and chairs as movable, freestanding furniture. By reducing the elements and thus reducing confusion to a minimum, more room could be given over to the expression of individual tastes in the work spaces.

The fact that the building is rather rugged in appearance and that it tapers upward like the trunk of a great tree is quite incidental, but nevertheless conforms to the image that MacMillan Bloedel wanted to project. I think of it as my Doric building, uncompromising in its simplicity. Today, even at twenty-seven storeys, it is somewhat tucked away in downtown Vancouver among ever-higher office towers of a more florid, Corinthian taste.

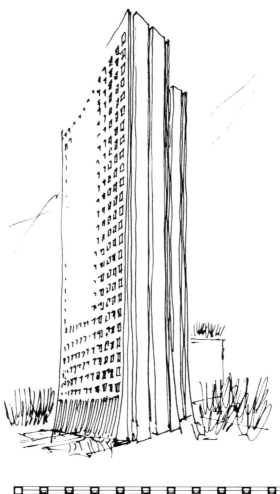

*Top: A conceptual sketch captures the essence of the MacMillan Bloedel building: a tapered, slender, treelike form for the giant forest products company.*

*Bottom: Floor plan of the MacMillan Bloedel building: the slender double towers with column-free interiors meet the need for a large number of executive offices with outside views. A custom oak furniture system of filing cabinets and closets keeps spaces efficient and clear.*

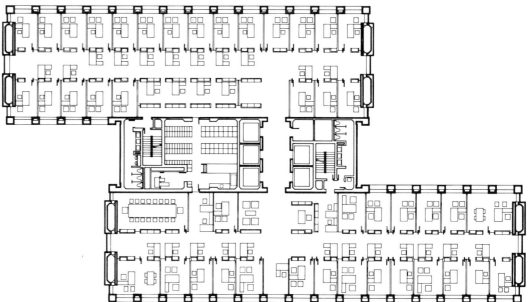

# UNIVERSITY OF LETHBRIDGE

The great North American prairie has a noble quality in its vast spaces and sensuous spareness. A single tree becomes a monument in such a landscape; a house, a fortress; fences and roads and the plough-lines of the fields form an overlying, pervasive geometry. Unlike the desert, which is frankly harsh and defiantly still, the prairie possesses a restless nature of quick mood changes of weather and seasonal switches of its expansive blankets of colour. Human habitation on a land of such a scale and simplicity and busy disregard of human needs seems paltry and absurd. Only the looming clusters of blind-faced grain elevators possess a nobility to match the landscape.

The University of Lethbridge is located on coulee-broken prairie in south-central Alberta. When I first wandered over the site in 1967, I was overwhelmed by the beauty of the folds of land that dipped into long ravines stretching down to a river. The scale was deceptive; the coulee I thought would take five minutes to walk across took three-quarters of an hour. Traditionally, no one built on the coulees — only on the top of the prairie or on the plain of the river. But architecturally the coulees offered extraordinary opportunities: dramatic heights and depths unusual in the prairies, proximity to the river and a microclimate milder than the wind-swept flatlands. The danger of flooding could be controlled.

Standing on the far edge of the coulee, etched against the sky, was the light tracery of an old iron railway bridge, spanning the river. I came to the conclusion that though any buildings upon the exposed flatland should be interred in earth berms so that they would become part of the land, the academic building could span the coulees and, like the old bridge in its rigid flatness, reveal the rich contours of even the most level prairie. The top storey of the university should lie below the tableland in an uncompromising straight line spanning the haunches of the prairie.

*The University of Lethbridge, designed in 1968, sits on the prairie in southern Alberta. In an early master plan, it was to have two long sections. This sketch of the two sections studies a boxier, more articulated alternative than the simple, streamlined form eventually worked out.*

*Facing page: Concrete wall columns lift up the university's residential areas from the coulee floor; their vertical lines break the overwhelming scale.* SIMON SCOTT

*Overleaf: The 912-foot-long nine-storey main block of Project One of the University of Lethbridge floats on the prairie. The building depth responds to the contours of the coulee while the roofline spans it like a nearby railway trestle.* SIMON SCOTT

*Top: The University of Lethbridge is approached from the east and is below the level of the prairie; the western view looks over the Oldman River valley and has wide terraces that incorporate the mechanical plant, whose rooftop is a plaza with stepped seating for student gatherings. The corten (oxidized steel) chimneys of the plant compose a gateway to the river in the background.* SIMON SCOTT

*Bottom: Beneath the residential floor of the university, the vertical supports stand on a concrete terrace that is accessible to the students. The vertical wall columns frame the visual axis leading to an entrance door. The afternoon sun brings out the direct, honest surface texture of the poured-in-place concrete.* SIMON SCOTT

*Facing page, top: The concourse is the main street of the university community. Seminar areas, defined by upholstered couches made of leftover forms from the concrete casting process, double as lounges. The university opened to 1,800 students in 1971.* SIMON SCOTT

*Facing page, middle: Section of the University of Lethbridge: at the top are the laboratories, at mid-level is the concourse, and at the lowest level are the residences.*

*Facing page, bottom: Floor plan of the sixth level, the main student concourse. The steps lead out to the plaza on top of the physical plant.*

Lethbridge carried even further the principle of the intrinsic unity of all knowledge that Simon Fraser University expressed. There would be no differentiation between the sciences and humanities, or between study and relaxation, but only between the differently defined spaces of laboratories, large classrooms, seminar rooms, offices and residences. All space could then be assignable across faculties. Any cross-section of the building would contain all types of spaces from large to small, heavily serviced to unserviced, enclosed or open. Furthermore, since living is very much a part of the process of learning, the residential units also would be an integral part of the cross-section. In the original concept such a free use of space was possible because the students' rooms were the same size as and interchangeable with the professors' offices. Including the students as residents in the academic building would naturally give them a feeling of proprietorship for the whole building, with learning taking place in their own domestic territory; the university was theirs.

The faculty at Lethbridge also went further than that of Simon Fraser in stipulating that much of the instruction would take place at the intimate seminar level and only key lectures would use lecture theatres. The broad, nondirectional space of Cairo's Al Azhar University mosque, where students, merchants and beggars sat or lay on the carpeted floors, listening, praying, reading or just sleeping, again served as a model. Consistent with this concept of an educational marketplace, the main concourse at the midsection of the University of Lethbridge is a vast undifferentiated space separated by groups of trees and stepped benches for the seminars and small classes. Thus the concourse doubles as the main teaching space and as a lounge, an important space for which there is scant accommodation in most university programs.

The largest spaces are at the top of the building to fit the laboratories, which require

the longest spans, heaviest services, good ventilation and exhaust. The smallest spaces, offices and residences, are located towards the base of the building where the greatest loads must be taken. The residences enjoy the more intimate parts of the site — in the bottom of the coulees — where the students can get outside and enjoy the milder climate and its plant life.

Where Simon Fraser turned outward, Lethbridge turned inward because of the severe prairie climate. The building is as compact as possible, and openings are minimal. The brilliant light casts strong shadows, so an undifferentiated form is possible, unlike the Northwest Coast where the light is too flat for such a monolith. Strength on the prairie is monotony on the coast. The top of the boiler house acts as an outdoor assembly area, a theatre over the coulees, and the oxidized steel chimneys form a gateway into the wild folds of the land.

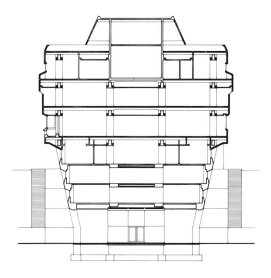

# BANK OF CANADA

The Bank of Canada headquarters in Ottawa was our second office building, and a very different assignment from the MacMillan Bloedel project. It had to incorporate the existing early 1930s office building already on site. An adjacent block held by the public works department was also to be included to provide a major atrium across the main pedestrian walk of the city, giving Ottawa's government and diplomatic personnel a needed meeting place. Ultimately, this projected winter garden of shops and restaurants and clubs was reduced to a small court surrounding the old bank building. The governor of the bank had wanted to offer more than sterile offices to the streets, but we all had to be content with a covered garden giving into a numismatic museum.

As a key facility of the federal government complex on Ottawa's Parliament Hill, the new building had to relate to its context in height, configuration and look. We emphasized the matters of scale and fineness of detail. The surrounding buildings are of rusticated stonework, and the old bank building is finished limestone. A glass wall contrasted nicely with both types of stone. The glass that ties into the earlier building is clear solex. Mirrored solex encloses the new space and reflects the older buildings.

*Facing page: The north side of the Bank of Canada headquarters building in Ottawa, Ontario. The 12-storey towers enfold the original bank with a composition of copper spandrels, mullions and roof and greenish mirrored glass that is consciously more respectful of the surrounding Gothic than the neoclassical style of its parent. SIMON SCOTT*

*A longitudinal section through the Bank of Canada reveals the extensive vaults below. Their careful construction and the phasing process that allowed the bank to remain in its quarters caused the project to take almost nine years to complete, design having begun in 1969. The two office blocks look into the atrium surrounding the original building.*

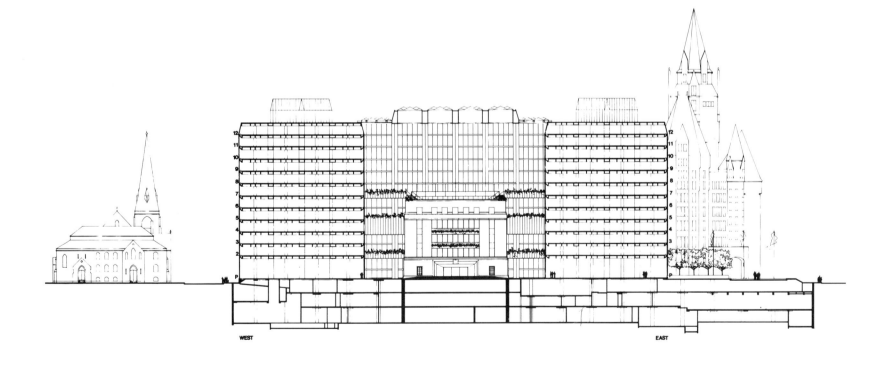

WEST           EAST

*Top: The north face of the Bank of Canada building is oriented to Ottawa's Parliament Hill.* CHRISTOPHER ERICKSON

*Bottom: The ground floor plan of the Bank of Canada building shows the 30-foot by 30-foot grid. The modules next to the garden are vestibules and lobbies for the towers.*

The working arm of the bank was contained in an undistinguished brick building, which we were replacing. In order for the bank to continue to function on site, we devised a scheme whereby twin towers would go up in sequence on either side of the central, finer building. The bank work force never had to leave the site but did have to put up with a seven-year construction span, for the job was complicated by the building of huge vaults below ground. We started the job in 1971; it was completed in 1980.

The tower buildings are based on a tree-shaped structural system: square pods cantilevered from a central column at each floor and divided into eight segments, each containing indirect lighting. Around the pod itself and separating it from its neighbouring pods are air ducts, sprinklers and wiring. The ceiling patterns are the basis of the office partitions, desk and wall storage system we designed. The exterior curtain wall follows the facetted edge of the tree pattern.

The staggered form, the modest height of twelve storeys and the use of copper are all in keeping with Ottawa's predominant style. In order to obtain the right colour for the copper spandrels, mullions and roof, we contacted bronze-casting companies in Italy and Japan. Ultimately, a Japanese team spent six months in Ottawa dipping copper into vats of appropriate acids. The result is what I wished for — an irregular natural patina to contrast with the mechanical slickness of the glazing. If nothing else, the Bank of Canada has one of the most elegant curtain walls in the country.

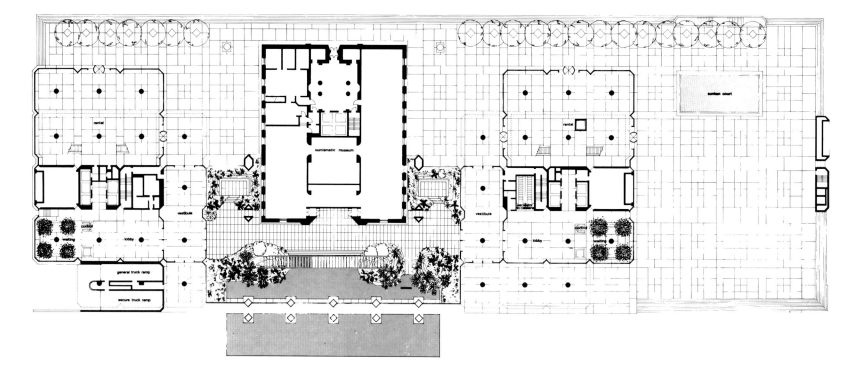

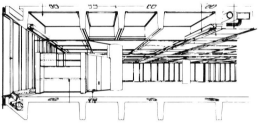

Left: The rear part of the original Bank of Canada building becomes a lunch terrace overlooking the atrium. On the seventh floor, the new towers are linked with bridges. Massive verdigris copper-clad columns support the atrium's roof independent of the three buildings around it. FIONA SPALDING-SMITH

Top right: A view from the floor of the bank's atrium to its glass roof. FIONA SPALDING-SMITH

Bottom right: A section of a storey of the bank building includes a work station and shows the in-floor duct system that provides power to two floors rather than only one. A telephone and power raceway in each ceiling coffer supports floor-mounted outlets as well as the electrified acoustic ceiling panel. The curtain wall, supported on copper spandrels, is at left.

# EXPOSITIONS

Whenever an international exposition is proposed, the cry goes up that it will be a waste of effort and money. But expositions are important not only as international exchanges but because they fulfill a deep instinctive need in people for festivals. The most memorable ones, of course, have a strong architectural component.

A pavilion's purpose is formalistic, with very simple requirements for shelter. But what form? The pavilion is without historical or contextual references. It is not a church or a house with an archetype to play off. Set up abroad, it has to suggest nationality without being scenographic. Set up at home, it has to compete with the surrounding hurly-burly without being cheapened.

The architect works within heavy constraints. The budget is miniscule and materials have to be easy to put up and pull down. There are committees and lots of politics. For me, the lack of definition is more difficult to work through than all the constraints.

An exhibition pavilion is one of those rare projects that the architect pulls out of the air. In this moment the architect passes over to become truly an artist — a sculptor of an abstract monumental form.

My idea for a Tokyo Trade Fair building in 1965 was an obvious one, to represent Canada with a log cabin, but I tried to carry it further by playing off the native Japanese perfectionism that I had just come to know. I thought that a structure of massive, rough-cut lumber would have a good shock value; the few groves in Japan that could have supplied such beams were sacred (and should soon become so in British Columbia). How-

ever, the point was to be felt in the raw power of the very unfinished look of the wood. The building would just be piled up and crudely put together but vigorous, like Canada.

Montreal's Expo '67 was a world's fair with a theme — and architecture. With Jeffrey Lindsay as a special consultant, I developed a concept for the Canadian pavilion. It was an upside-down pyramid, open to the sky and functioning as a reception area. On its base, individual exhibit areas were capped with smaller pyramids. The proposal went ahead, but with such modifications in detail that I withdrew. I made my statement with another pavilion.

Under the general title of Man and His World, subthemes like Man and the Arctic, Man and the Sea, and Man and Space were contained in different theme pavilions to which every country contributed. Canadian architects were asked to demonstrate different construction techniques in different materials on each of these theme pavilions. Our firm was asked to build for Man in the Community and the related Man and His Health. Being from the West Coast, we were given wood as a construction material.

There were so many aspects to the theme of Man in the Community that it was difficult to make a selection for exhibition purposes. The list was so depressing — famine, disease, overpopulation, war, crime, delinquency and so on — that I feared no one would enter such a pavilion. However, working with the exhibit designer, Robin Bush, we decided to accept and express the hard truth of the problems. We would portray them in exhibit capsules ranging in size from one foot to

*The Canadian Pavilion for the 1965 Tokyo International Trade Fair is made of one of Canada's prime exports to Japan, lumber. The structure is built entirely of stacked six-inch by sixteen-inch rough timber like a log cabin. The open interior has a pool for log-rolling exhibitions.* FRANK MAYRS

*Facing page: The Canadian Pavilion at Expo '70 in Osaka, Japan, glows in the evening.* ERNEST SATO/ JOHN TAKEHAMA

thirty feet and group them around a beautiful quiet garden with flowers and birdsong and fish in pools. It would be a kind of miniature Eden that would provide relief from what was contained inside the capsules. In a double switch, reality would be the artificial synthesized world on view in the capsules, while the ideal would be tangible in the charms of the garden.

Over this capsule community I proposed to put up a huge tent of wood, extending the space vertically to infinity in the centre, and stretching it horizontally to infinity on all sides. Jeffrey Lindsay and structural engineer Janos Baracs assisted on the design of the roof structure. It turned out as I had originally visualized, like a basketry of an enormous lath house set over a tropical garden. Jeffrey's solution was ingenious: a series of reducing octagons that rotated 45 degrees, the corner of the one above resting on the sides of the one below. Like all good solutions, it led to an irreducibly simple structure, following the profile of a logarithmic curve. Sound mathematically, it parallelled the earth plane to express horizontal infinity and towered perpendicularly to express vertical infinity.

The largest span at the bottom edge involved glulam box beams over a hundred

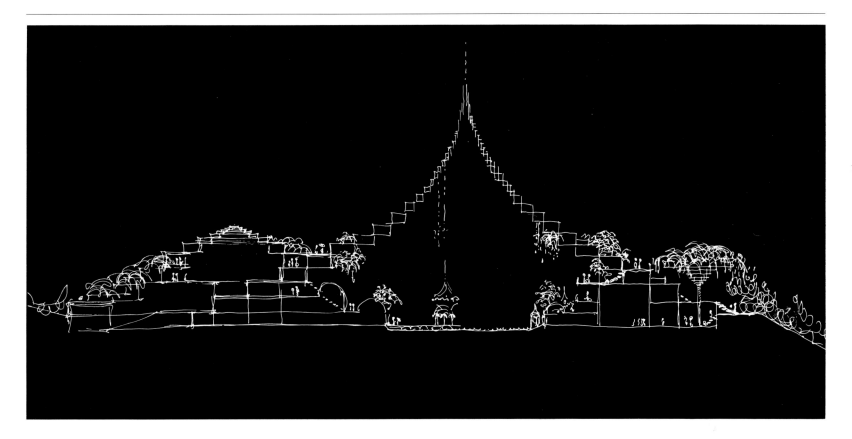

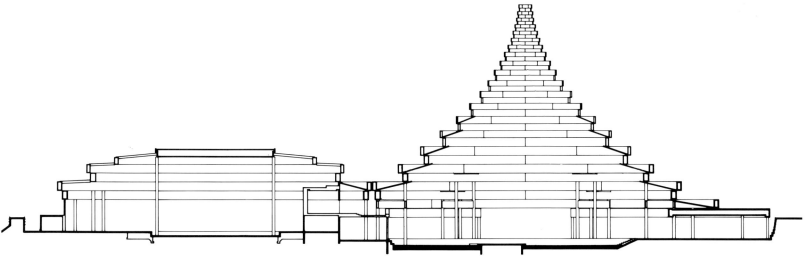

Facing page, top: The original concept for the Canadian Pavilion at Expo '67 in Montreal was developed with Jeffrey Lindsay as special consultant. A large inverted pyramid, open to the sky, is the reception area; the low individual pyramids cover the exhibit areas. HERBERT L. McDONALD

Facing page, bottom: At Expo '67, the Man and His Health pavilion stands to the left of Man in the Community. The tower uses 222 plywood beams in 37 rows, ranging in length from 44 inches to almost 100 feet. MAX SAUER STUDIO

Top: A sketch section through the Man in the Community/Man and His Health pavilions. An elegant spire would distinguish the low pavilion from the powerful masses of its neighbours.

Bottom: A section of the Man in the Community/Man and His Health pavilions: the spire shelters a quiet water garden.

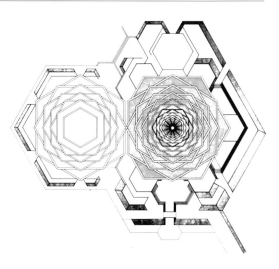

*Left: In the centre of the Expo '67 Man in the Community pavilion, a garden and pool provide a quiet area for hopeful thoughts. The bridge links exhibit areas that open off of the garden.* MALAK

*Centre: Translucent fibre-reinforced polyester roofing was stretched over a plywood lattice framing system. The effect of the interior geometry is to decrease the scale of the huge glulam beams, so effective as an exterior, and enhance the feeling of spaciousness in the pavilion interior.* MALAK

*Right: Roof plan of the Man in the Community/Man and His Health pavilions; Man in the Community (right) is surrounded by subsidiary exhibit areas.*

feet long. Although the six-foot-deep beams, decreasing in size to two-inch by six-inch studs at the apex, were perfect in appearance on the outside, they were too massive for the scale of the space on the inside. The roofing, composed of great shingles of PVC plastic attached to a wood lattice, should logically be placed on the outside; but in order for the outside structure and proportions and the inside space to be effective visually, they were hung — with great difficulty and to the despair of my advisors — from the inside. The effect on the interior space was to give it a sense of peace and limitless space.

The exhibit concept changed several times during the construction of the building, ending as a series of six main exhibits presented by various countries. The garden made a poor start during a typical Montreal winter that extended into May, but to my delight, visitors remarked that the tranquillity of the space provided a special haven for them during the crowded days of Expo — in spite of the subject matter.

We played a second engagement in Japan for Expo '70 in Osaka. Again I faced the problem of representing Canada and at the same time capturing the attention of the mainly Japanese audience. Consider-

ing the complex and miniature scale of the Japanese landscape, I decided that one thing that could be interestingly presented was the emptiness and immensity of the Canadian landscape. I expressed this quality in very large simple forms, four sections of a pyramid pulled apart to open a central court, abstractions of our landscape in size, emptiness and simplicity. Almost immediately the starkness of such monolithic forms worried me. Having just visited Iran, I remembered a Persian garden that used inset mirrors in its plastered *diwan* shell to intensify the beauty of the garden experience. I would invoke that diwan again and again in Middle East designs, but in this instance it inspired me to sheath the whole pavilion in mirrors. Its forms, now mountains of ice, would still work, and the mirror surface would bring down the sky. The sheathing gave a completely new meaning to the structure as something responsive to everything around it, so receptive that the building itself might vanish. To accomplish this, there could be no edge to the building, which meant the mirror had to be detailed so that it merged with the sky. That one detail was the key to the whole thing. Otherwise it would never have disappeared as it often did under a white sky or at night.

Several things about the sky and reflecting

images made the decision to use a mirrored surface successful in the context of Expo '70. For one thing, the sky has great significance in occidental architecture and almost none in Japan, where the earth is what matters. Also un-Japanese was the use of mirrors, which are sacred there. So it was a twofold breaking of convention to display the sky in vast mirrored surfaces. But I knew that the Japanese anticipated with interest the turnaround that foreigners give to their values. The walls were sloped at 45 degrees so that as you approached the building you also directly approached the sky. The Japanese called it the Sky Pavilion.

On the other hand, two factors relating to the mirrors were very positively Japanese. One is the idea of infinity that pervades Japanese art. The Japanese could understand the way the seemingly solid mountain forms would disappear into the infinity of the reflected sky, and how the building would itself disappear in its own endless reflections. The aspect of ambiguity — the uncertainty of what is substance and what is space — is also very much part of their art and philosophy. Substance is inferred, not stated.

Another aspect of the pavilion that appealed to the Japanese was its constant changeability, for they have a deep sense of the impermanence and mutability of life. Some of the changes were caused by the drama of the daily shifts of sunlight. But we picked up the theme in the roof of the central stage, which consisted of five giant umbrellas, engineered by Jeffrey Lindsay, that ceaselessly rotated. The hard-edged patterns of brilliant colour by painter Gordon Smith endlessly rearranged themselves in a kaleidoscope of colour. The movement animated the building as though it had its own vital inner force. Because there was always something happening, like musicians, dancers or an ice review on the stage in the pool, it was also called the Young Pavilion. It drew record crowds and was premiated by the Architectural Institute of Japan.

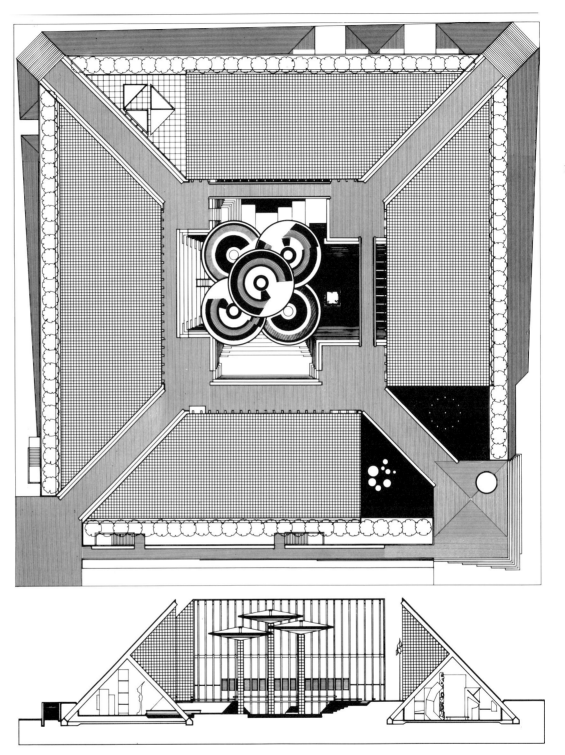

*Top: The Expo '70 Canadian Pavilion in Osaka, Japan, covers 3940 square metres. It consists of four trapezoidal structures; the space between, with a performance stage set in a pool, is protected by five rotating umbrellas on triangular pylons.*

*Bottom: A section through the Expo '70 pavilion indicates slight variations of elevation in the central court to accommodate performance seating and exhibit areas. The mirrored walls could be glacial mountains or expansive skies, both Canadian features.*

When the city of Vancouver hosted the United Nations Conference on Human Settlements (styled Habitat) in 1976, I felt that here was an extraordinary educational opportunity that deserved the attention of every citizen. To get that attention, we would involve the children. With the conference principally discussing housing in the Third World, an elementary shelter would make an appropriate reception centre; why not a structure that children could build? I thought of papier-mâché, using the waste paper that stacks up around everyone's house. Some two thousand ninth-graders were bussed out to a warehouse where they would actually make the parts of the pavilion. We gave them construction helmets to wear, and they laid out their newspapers on premade moulds with paste. When the paper had dried and was removed as separate sections, the children came back and decorated them with the themes of Habitat.

The modular structure was entirely of paper, with paper tubing for struts and edge. Only the connecting bolts were steel. The outer surface was finished with plastic coating. The basic modules were formed of six hyperbolic paraboloid sections. A total of 112 modules formed two pods standing on wooden piers. The shelter was white outside and brightly decorated by the students on the inside, a kind of ''naif Byzantine'' effect. In a small way we were imitating the early cathedral builders: Habitat expressed the efforts of many artists, none of whom knew what the actual outcome of their individual contributions would be.

We were hired by a Spanish developer in 1985 to design a complex of a vastly different size for a site near Madrid. It would be a permanent exhibition facility; like tall buildings, such huge structures take on an antihuman scale of their own and have to be somehow tamed. We worked the four enormous exhibit halls into the sloping site and used water and broad easy steps to make an

*Facing page: The Expo '70 pavilion, like the Expo '67 pavilion, has a visually cool and serene interior using water, plants and unfinished wood. But it also plays with illusion and reality, as the rotating spinners on mirrored pylons continue the game begun by the mirrored exterior.* ERNEST SATO/JOHN TAKEHAMA

*Top: An aerial view of the Habitat reception pavilion in front of Vancouver's old courthouse in 1976. Except for the wooden posts and metal joints, the roof was made entirely of paper and paste, with protective neoprene sprayed on. The geometric module, a hexaphypar, was made up of six equal hyperbolic paraboloid sections. A total of 112 modules were paired and stacked together to form the two pods of the pavilion.* SIMON SCOTT

*Bottom: An interior view of the Habitat reception pavilion: after the children made the hyperbolic paraboloids on molds, using old newspapers brought from home, they pasted on designs they had created on the theme of human habitations.* SIMON SCOTT

interesting environment. By extending the long rooflines with glass, we gave the low mass a delicate and lighter perspective.

We made another pass at temporary glory with a gathering place plan for Expo 86 in Vancouver. Being one of the nonarchitectural expositions, it needed a signature landmark to rise above the formula, prefabricated exhibit buildings. We proposed a crescent-shaped ornamental canal lined with trees and terminating in a lagoon. At the arc's apex we would place a permanent pavilion that would become a museum after the fair. Its grassed roof would be terraced as a theatre down to the water, in which would sit a stage on a rocky, landscaped island. Recalling the visionary theatres of Norman Bel Geddes, the sets could be floated into place in front of the island.

To announce the outdoor theatre season, a great purple tent would unfurl over stage and seating. The gigantic right angle of its support would be in effect a sculpture of steel and glass when the tent was withdrawn into it. With the audience in place on the sloping lawns, the island transformed into a stage and lights hung and banked for performance, the park would have been a gathering place for Expo 86.

The Expo 86 proposal got lost in a shift of political winds, while the company that had invited us to Madrid collapsed under government pressure. After a brief consulting stint on the master plan of Expo 92 in Seville, I could say with some authority that the larger the role you are invited to play in any international fair, the stronger the buffeting winds.

*Top: A 1983 proposal for a focal gathering place at Vancouver's Expo 86: a tall, asymmetrical glass-clad steel structure holds a suspended fabric roof that runs out on a circumferential rail over an amphitheatre. Sets can be floated around from under the seating to be anchored against a permanent island stage. The surrounding canal and tree planting is lined with restaurants and smaller exhibits.* ROBERT MCILHARGEY

*Bottom: A 1985 competition for a permanent 100 000-square-metre trade fair facility on a large site near Madrid utilizes standard inexpensive building components but extends the roof structures to provide lofty sheltered colonnades around an artificial lake, and to reduce the heat and glare of the vast space. Dining and refreshment pavilions set on tree-filled islands would provide a welcome relief to the arduous walking distances.* MICHAEL MCCANN

*Facing page: The mirrored 45-degree slopes of the Canadian pavilion at Expo '70 in Osaka, Japan.* ERNEST SATO/JOHN TAKEHAMA

# MUSEUM OF ANTHROPOLOGY

A complex problem gives up its answer slowly. It takes longer to find its voice and to establish its criteria. To get to the point of design I have to manoeuvre through a field of constructs, or questions, gradually narrowing the range of possibilities. The Museum of Anthropology at the University of British Columbia in Vancouver is an example of how design can flow from particular fixes, in this case striking features of the building's program and its site.

Many years ago, as the Northwest Coast Native culture declined in health and numbers, anthropologists Audrey and Harry Hawthorn, with the aid of philanthropist Walter Koerner, took upon themselves the task of collecting its artifacts for preservation. This was a careful, tenderly accomplished labour of love, and could have been no other for them to have won the confidence of the beleaguered Native peoples. Since the tools and accoutrements of religion and daily life were made of wood and shell, the damp, lush climate and continued use meant their certain loss, while the skills that produced these exquisite and unique objects were also fading. The Native people did not always relinquish ownership of ceremonial objects, but gave them to the Hawthorns for safekeeping when they were not being used. Audrey had put everything except the tall totem poles in a small basement room of the university library, stacked ceiling high when she came to me for help in 1971. Could my "connections" in Ottawa be used to get funding for a museum for the ethnological collection?

The government was forthcoming, and the university donated a magnificent cam-

pus site on the edge of high sandstone cliffs looking out at distant glaciated peaks and the wide straits outside Vancouver harbour. The site had three features that determined the creation of the museum structure. There was the spectacular view from the cliffs — although they are subject to a slow, inexorable erosion, so we could not risk placing the museum on their brink. Farther back on the priceless land, man had left a more permanent mark than nature in tons of concrete, poured as gun emplacements during the last war. Finally, to keep the view from a scenic drive behind unobstructed, the museum had to be a low structure.

*A photographer's trick realizes an architect's vision: the Museum of Anthropology in Vancouver, British Columbia, evokes a Pacific Northwest Native village on a tidal shore.* JOHN FULKER

*Facing page: The precast concrete columns and channelled beams of the Great Hall of the Museum of Anthropology establish a rhythm and appropriate frame for the massive artifacts of Pacific Northwest Native cultures. Design began in 1972 with site models that included models of the large carvings in place. The glass walls, towering up to 45 feet, provide an unobstructed view of the natural setting and enable the carvings to be seen in daylight. The total building area is 70,000 square feet.* SIMON SCOTT

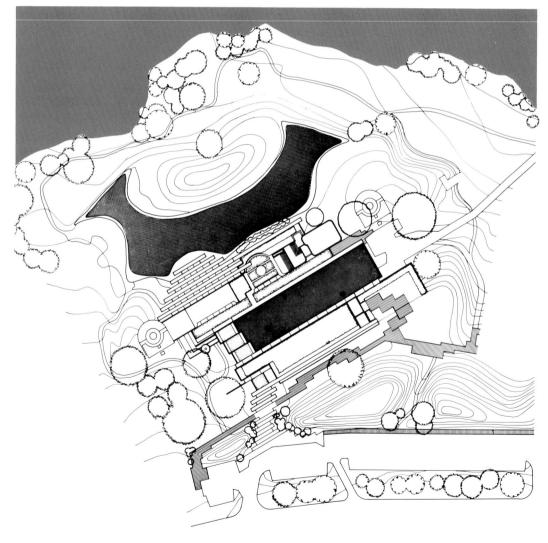

I always go to my first encounter with a site emptied of expectations and prepared for surprises. The cliff prospect, taking off over the sea, immediately suggested the possibility of creating the illusion of a narrow inlet by placing a shallow pond before it with weirs at the outer edge to meld its water visually with the water beyond. Once in place in my mind's eye, the vision recalled a photograph of a Haida village I had seen years before at an exhibition organized by Audrey and the Haida artist Bill Reid. The photograph had shown in an instant the meaning of the massive carvings popularly called totem poles, as well as the motivation of Northwest Coast Native art. The proud houses and massive carvings stood along the curve of a beach, poised between the temperamental ocean and a forbidding forest curtain. Here were a people who respected the powerful spirits of land and sea and lived on the narrow open margin between. Yet they depended on the bounty of both. How natural in their animism to humanize the trees, to carve them with the images of their totems, to express in them their critical relationships with all creatures. The artificial inlet could be the setting for the replica houses and poles that the university intended to bring onto the site, creating the village context that gave birth to the culture. The museum as well would face the inlet, since it was in this relationship merely a protective container for those articles that could not sit outside. We could supplement the thick natural foliage with more ethnobotanically important plants. I expressed this symbolic village in a model of the site. Thus, before we started planning the museum, we had a vision of its landscaping.

Initially, everyone expected to somehow avoid the immovable gun emplacements and to position the museum either above or below them on the site. But working from an initial one-to-five hundred scale site-contour model — which included major trees and neighbouring buildings for a bird's-eye view of the site in relationship to all its surround-ings — and taking into consideration other requirements such as parking, we found that the building would have to straddle the gun emplacements. We turned this obstacle into an opportunity, having worked out the size and relationship of the museum's various spaces. The concrete belt of bunkers, round mounts and ammunition vaults, planted fif-teen feet deep, became the dividing line be-tween the display galleries along the "inlet" and the storage, workrooms, laboratories and administrative rooms of the rest of the facility. Eventually, the bunkers became a handsome, rugged base for the curved walls they supported. The one concrete gun em-placement incorporated into the interior found a fitting destiny as the mount for a dramatic carving by Bill Reid of the Haida genesis legend.

The requirement for a low profile meant that much of the building would have to be buried. The roofs, overlooked by the scenic drive behind, could be planted to enhance the meaning of the site or flooded with water to reflect the view. At least the slope permit-ted a basement storey to emerge at grade at the lower edge.

Next we began working from a larger site model with a scale of three-sixteenths of an inch to one foot and could cut in the emerg-ing footprint of the building. The final fix for the design was the major treasure of the collection: massive carvings and poles rang-ing from twelve to forty feet in height. We made models of each of these pieces since the housing would be just an expression of their placement. As I immersed myself in the project, I learned the extraordinary stylistic differences between the art of the Nuu-chah-nulth of the southern coastal regions, the Kwakiutl of the middle, and the Haida, the Nass and the Tsimshian of the north. They paralleled the differences between the art of Italy and Scandinavia and similarly stemmed from environmental distinctions absorbed into the cultural language. The southern

*Facing page, top: In the original landscaping concept for the Museum of Anthropology, the whole site was left as a natural ethnobotanical teaching resource; a flooded roof for the visible storage area would diminish its intrusion.* CHRISTOPHER ERICKSON

*Facing page, bottom: Precipitous cliffs overlooking the ocean skirt the 11-acre museum site. Three round concrete gun mounts, leftover World War II defences, were impossible to remove. The pond creates the illusion of an inlet.*

*Top:* The Raven and the First Men, *Bill Reid's wood sculpture of a Haida legend, sits under a skylight on one of the gun mounts incorporated into the museum. Interior surfaces are a warm grey concrete with grey carpeting to give the artifacts a neutral, unobtrusive background.* CHRISTOPHER ERICKSON

*Bottom: The three entrance ramp galleries are a low-ceiling approach to the sudden dramatic opening up of the museum's Great Hall. Skylights between the galleries and along their walls give a soft natural light in the area.* CHRISTOPHER ERICKSON

zone shows a naturalistic modelling, the middle zone a dramatic deep painted relief and the northern a shallow, exquisitely carved modulation. I suggested to the Hawthorns that the visitor could be introduced to the three cultural zones by entering through three spaces, each devoted to a zone. The sequence could end in a hall by the pond for the giant poles and house frames. These in turn divided into Haida and Kwakiutl collections on either side. Each side could then be viewed linked with its recreated village on the "shore" of the "inlet."

We placed the miniature reproductions marching down a sloping ramp in three cultural sets, to be softly skylit from above. The visitor would enter through this closed forest way, which would then burst to the encompassing view opened by the tall pieces. From this high space the visitor would pass into a room with a low ceiling for the collections of intimate objects like spoons, rattles, combs and jewellery. These would be suspended in glass cases against a background of young hemlocks screening the glass wall.

At this stage all the volumes had been enclosed except the Great Hall, and now even its shape was foretold. All of our decisions had been made by facing a progress of inevitabilities hardly involving design at all. A model had evolved with everything but the roof of the Great Hall in place. I knew the hall should be cast in a natural light. The first idea was a virtual greenhouse of glass and steel space frames, but the busyness of the structural members would distract from the silent majesty of the large carvings. Even if it was noisy with visitors, the room needed to have a feeling of silence. The superb, seasilvered carvings, sometimes still bearing traces of paint, also needed a simple background for contrast. Unfinished, in situ light grey concrete was the appropriate and obvious choice for construction.

Knowing the Native use of enormous split cedar logs and their exaggerated, luxurious

*The apparent strength of the museum's channelled beams, identical in width to the supporting concrete piers, is structurally misleading: their roof-supporting function is performed by smaller crossbeams. It is for visual unity and simplicity that the concrete channels are made as deep as the posts are wide, and the dimensions of all are the same regardless of spans — which range from 40 to 100 feet.* TIMOTHY HURSLEY/ THE ARKANSAS OFFICE

*Facing page: The post-and-beam structure of the Museum of Anthropology meets the sandy beach opposite a reconstructed Haida village of longhouses and carved poles. To the left is the long deep brow of the masterpiece gallery with its planted hemlock screen.* CHRISTOPHER ERICKSON

*The museum's low masterpiece gallery houses the Koerner Collection of small precious artifacts, many in argillite or silver. After the beach vista of the Great Hall, the gallery is a retreat back into the dappled light of the underbrush. The windows are screened by hemlock trees.* TIMOTHY HURSLEY/THE ARKANSAS OFFICE

*An axonometric of the museum reveals the role of the site's old concrete gun mounts: the two outlying turrets could be left half-buried, and the central one became a display mount. But the adjoining ammunition bunkers were areas that had to be used. Visitors can see the joints of old and new concrete on particular walls. Behind axes established by the gun mounts are the visible storage rectangle, the offices and teaching laboratories.*

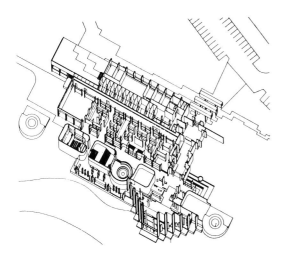

effect, I felt that a similar ponderous weight and disregard for structural reality could pertain here. We could show the same generosity and flamboyant disdain for economy as the Native people in their potlatches and still suggest their reverence for nature; so began the process of establishing supports for a deep-beamed structure.

The flat columns would step in from a gap in the gun emplacements and step up in seven intervals from sixteen feet to forty-five feet to support a ceiling over the highest carvings. Although the columns differed greatly in height, they all had to be of the same width and thickness. The channelled beams ranged from forty feet up to a span of one hundred and eighty feet, and likewise they also had to have the same depth. My strictures were confounding to the engineer, Bogue Babicki, who knew such beams were a practical impossibility. But I had discovered with the second Smith house that defying structural reality in columns and beams — keeping them the same size — brought a mixture of calm and tension that recalled early Doric temples at Athens and Paestum. The scale of the Great Hall gave that tension a monumental serenity, a combination of power and grace that enhanced the majesty of the carvings.

At this point we built a larger scale model in wood. Its reflection in the model lake was enchanting. We began to adjust proportions and continued a give-and-take with the engineer. Finally, in exasperation, he spanned the hall the opposite way with beams crossing the U-channels. This brought in a subtle cross-rhythm to the strong ascending beat of the beams and columns. It also allowed for the precasting and post stressing of most members — a master stroke for both economy and engineering. Thus the structural system is visible after all, but still ambiguous enough to sustain the wonderful mystery of the hall.

In order to avoid the distracting effect of mullions protruding and framing the glass,

we chose a suspension system for the glazing. The hardware was a standard product, but we discarded its aluminum caps to show the beautiful bronze plates and bolts underneath. We gave the skylights between the channels a curved rather than flat profile after looking at them in model form and drawings. The curves relieved the hard edges of the channels and from the back added a kind of organic rhythm.

As a museum, the most important and original feature is its "visible storage." Museums today are like icebergs, with only one-tenth of their collections visible. I have always resented the practice that some other person should determine what I was supposed to see. A closed collection is a censored one. Curators, like teachers, may often shield us from the truth. We need our own broad sources for comparison to understand reality or make value judgements. I believe that every viewer sees in his own way and so makes his own connections.

I expressed my rebellious frame of mind to the curators in the early stages of the program study when the physical needs of the building are described down to the smallest detail. They agreed and developed the idea to its full potential, which became known as visible storage. So as the building proceeded, the interior also developed according to a particular construct. The whole storage area is open to the public and consists of chests with plexiglass-covered drawers and glass-fronted cases with pegboards. Everything is out, the complete collection: the good, the bad, the whole and the fragment are all there. Reference catalogues in book form are next to the chests and cases. All visitors, to the youngest students, can carry out their own investigations.

The exhibitry was in the hands of a display expert, and days before the opening I returned from a trip to find the three entrance galleries hung with so many masks they looked like a bargain basement. The same consultant had also made a ring of the massive carvings in the Great Hall so that they all looked inward at the entrance. Altogether, the effect was to cheapen both the building and the precious objects. I remember the incident for my rare fit of temper. Harry Hawthorn helped to rescue the situation. Speedily, cranes came back to reset the tall poles on two sides, and the galleries returned to a clean order. I recalled how compelling are the caryatids on the Acropolis as they stare out to the distant unknown. These great carvings with their expressionless, primal eyes, their beaks and snouts, should also gaze at nothing as they had once gazed out to sea. The change transformed the Great Hall into a sanctuary.

Philistines had their revenge with the landscaping. Normally landscaping is the final flourish. In this case, it had inspired the initial design with its village setting. Cornelia Oberlander began planting for an ethnobotanical exhibit of plants the Native people used for clothing, food, medicine, crafts and dyes. But at the hands of the university's own experts, the tall sheltering broadleaf maples were trimmed, and the sensitive, lush ecosystem beneath exposed and destroyed. Nursery specimens replaced it. The inlet became a political issue within the university's board, for its location defied conventional thought on preserving the cliffs. We filed a long shelf of reports, essentially arguing that if erosion is caused by water seeping into the sandstone, even rainwater would be checked by the sealed pond bottom. The installation was delayed until there were no longer funds for it. However, a needed building expansion is on the boards. Instead of adding a second wing of low galleries, three compact high halls will be tucked in beside the entrance galleries. They will act as a background for the Great Hall, just as the forest wall stood behind the beach settlements.

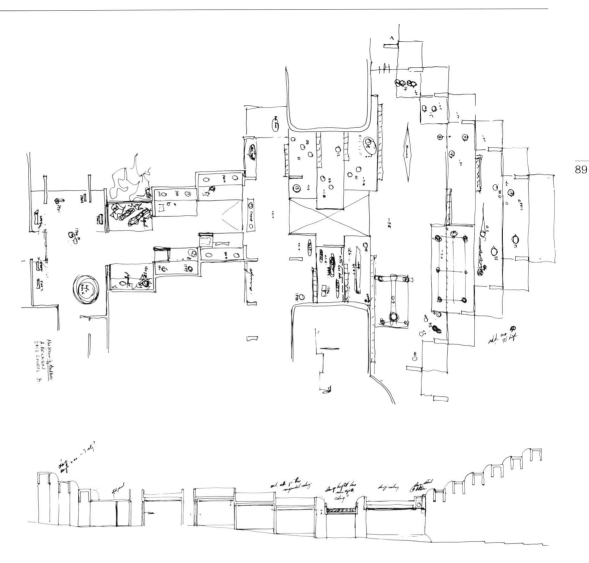

*Top: The Museum of Anthropology was designed around the massive carvings in its collection, as a sketch plan shows. Three smaller galleries are staggered down a gentle slope to the Great Hall, whose space is partially defined by the vise of the immovable concrete bunkers that are on the site.* COLLECTION CENTRE CANADIEN D'ARCHITECTURE/CANADIAN CENTRE FOR ARCHITECTURE

*Bottom: Part of the power of the museum is in the flow of space from the entrance to the Great Hall. A sketch section traces its rhythm, beginning with the three low brows over the entrance that impose a reverential mood.* COLLECTION CENTRE CANADIEN D'ARCHITECTURE/ CANADIAN CENTRE FOR ARCHITECTURE

# PART III

# ACHIEVEMENTS

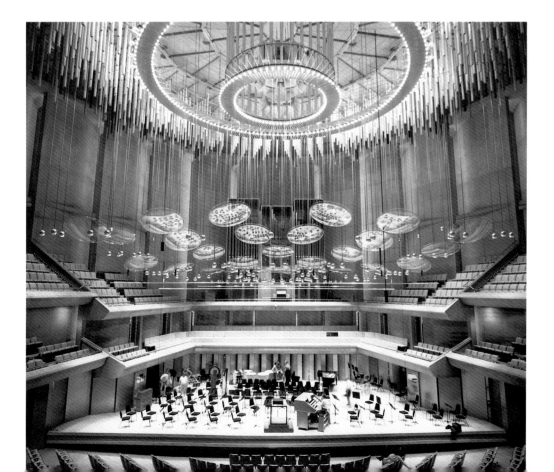

# ACHIEVEMENTS

As I moved into my middle years, I began to bring an easy confidence and versatility to my work. With my strong natural curiosity, I never had been afraid to experiment, but the years of observing architecture around the world had strengthened that drive by assuring me that in truth there were not many new types of buildings, just different ways of expressing what were, essentially, a few archetypes. After Japan, I had come to feel that I was standing outside my own culture and looking in; I had become objective. Now I would question the accepted premises of our projects — not the programs themselves, but those assumptions that cradled them like the dead hand of history, prescribing limits to programs and functional expressions alike. The superb architectural writer, Ada Louise Huxtable, then with the *New York Times*, had remarked about Simon Fraser University that it was the fruit of a "rethink" of the university's mission. I took the term to heart.

At the same time, designing continued to be an arduous process, even if the results I was getting now seemed clearer, stronger and therefore easier to realize than before. But such simplicity by itself had never been a goal for me. Instead, I came to understand that the paring-away process, with its aim of uncovering the heart and force of an idea, is the increasing concern of the maturing artist. The tricks and shortcuts learned in the course of lengthening experience are just added temptations in the unfolding path of our devotion. The fuller awareness of our powers and goals that age brings just makes work all the harder.

In 1972 events set another stage for my career. By affirming my position within Canada, they enabled me to eventually pursue commissions outside. Auspiciously enough, in February of that year, the Canadian edition of *Time* magazine put me on its cover; a cumulative recognition, I suppose, for the recent completion of the photogenic Lethbridge University, the winning of the lucrative Royal Bank of Canada award and controversy over my proposal to replace an aging Vancouver cathedral with a dramatic new monument. Publicity for a design architect feeds the business, since as many clients seek you out as you are hunting in predictable channels. But with the historic exception of Mr. Wright, architects are as a rule a quiet breed, and I found that the experience of fame, however delusionary, helped me overcome my shyness when meeting new people: I had already been "introduced."

Also early in 1972, an eager young colleague offered to analyze the Erickson/Massey firm to see how its workings could be improved. We were having growing pains. I was aggressive for new design challenges, leaving Geoff to concern himself with managing the office when he too preferred creative work. And my goal was an international practice while Geoff, who had been raised in a cosmopolitan milieu, resisted its attractions. Consultants are like fortune tellers: you hang on their every word and then forget them all the next day. This was the exception. We accepted the startling conclusion that we separate our practices. Since we easily understood how our interests and ambitions had drifted apart, the split was amicable. I hoped that a couple of associates would join me, but all of them seized the

*Page 90: In 1972, the Helmut Eppichs of Vancouver requested the first Erickson concrete house.*
SIMON SCOTT

*Page 91: The stage of Roy Thomson Hall in Toronto, designed in 1976, is flanked by seating.*
FIONA SPALDING-SMITH

*Facing page: The three blocks known as Robson Square, which produced a civic heart for Vancouver, began design in 1973. The glass-roofed Law Courts are a modern forum, and the provincial government offices are buried under a park.* EZRA STOLLER/ESTO

*Facing page, top: The Government of Canada building was a 1977 proposal for a key site on the edge of downtown Vancouver. The building's mass is raised above a small park and mall of public facilities, including a government information centre, children's museum, library and National Film Board exhibition space. The six-storey steel-truss pods each contain 250,000 square feet of office space. For symbolic impact, the pods sit on 80-foot-high piers, with rounded exoskeletons that lighten their presence.* SIMON SCOTT

*Facing page, middle: The 500-bed British Columbia Medical Centre proposed in 1973 is diagonally oriented to the existing Shaughnessy Hospital in the background. In the centre is the "health mall," a glass-covered grade-level concourse for outpatient services. With the patient rooms on garden terraces, the overall theme of an open, healthful atmosphere relating to nature and the surrounding community is achieved. Laboratories and operating rooms are below grade.* SIMON SCOTT

*Facing page, bottom: A representative section of the British Columbia Medical Centre shows its low form and the order of functions: parking in the base, the diagnostic and treatment units below grade with light wells, the administration offices and outpatient clinics opening off a public concourse at grade, and the separate pods of patient rooms above, with mechanical space topmost.*

moment to go off on their own, leaving me with the office building and a staff of four.

Then in August, the theoretically leftist New Democratic Party won control of the provincial government and plunged British Columbia into a short, vigorous interregnum of reform. A few months later, a new, nonpartisan reform coalition took over the Vancouver city government. In Canada as in Europe, the issue is not government guidance, but its quality; not whether, but what. Government spending is crucial to our society, supporting everything from jobs and health to cultural expression. The taste and cultural level of politicians and top bureaucrats can have real impact. We can only hope for a leadership sympathetic to our interests. As it turned out, the new government attracted academics, and Bob Williams, a friend of mine from teaching days, became the province's minister in charge of development. Through his commendation and the support of his colleagues, my new firm was given the design of three downtown blocks in Vancouver to be known as Robson Square.

When we were asked to prepare a master plan for Robson Square, we took the initiative and did an urban design study of the whole downtown area. The Robson Square project was to fit with the future character of Vancouver. This hopeful view of the future context, made possible by a clear understanding of the city's goals on the part of public and private interests, dictated the eventual scheme for the complex of a courthouse, provincial government offices and the city's art gallery.

By the end of 1972, everything seemed possible from the drawing board of our urban study. Commissions followed in a heady progress and my new practice took off. I hired young recent graduates, frequently from the recession-ridden United States, and my office became as large as it would ever be, reaching a hundred persons in Vancouver. (Nowadays it seems that everyone I compete against in western Canada at one

time or another passed through my office.) After the Robson Square commission, large-scale proposals for Vancouver seemed more attainable. I felt I finally had a role in the destiny of my hometown. Whether it has responded or not, I have always given Vancouver my best effort — or perhaps being my home, it has given me the necessary complexity of motives that makes for the best creative work. As close to my heart as it is, Vancouver is also that close to the edge of my temper.

Large buildings can take years from their conception to approach their final form; until then, a client has little to reflect on other than a small model. He needs a willing eye to visualize the miniature, crudely detailed craftsman's product as a full-sized, permanent presence whose construction will devour a great deal of money. When the design of the building is a departure from stereotype, however confident the architect may be about the outcome, the client is asked to take a brave leap of faith. Not only must he believe, but for the vision to be brought to reality, the client must carry its standard. The best buildings rise only when the client couples his confidence with the active backing of his architect.

My proposal for Robson Square asked for a radical departure from a traditional building type, but the provincial minister and his colleagues stood behind me, as did Chief Justice Nathan Nemetz, representing one of the main users. When the New Democrats were precipitously swept out of power, the project still could have been cancelled. But the new government appointed the former chancellor of Simon Fraser University, Gordon Shrum, to examine the three-block development. He backed our scheme. Chief Justice Nathan Nemetz and Bob Williams had given us their trust initially; Chancellor Shrum's contributions were his understanding of our objective and his fearlessness in helping us to gain it. Without the protective force of these strong individuals unselfishly standing off bureaucrats, corralling funds and shooting down critics, nothing striking or unique could have been achieved. It is only through good patrons that good architecture is born. Unfortunately, many projects that do not have such strong backing are stillborn.

One project for which I had the highest hopes was the Government of Canada building in 1977. The site, key to the expansion of Vancouver's central business district, was flanked by the city's theatre complex and the Canadian Broadcasting Corporation building. I argued that contrary to the federal government's instinct to put down an imposingly rooted presence, it should recognize western Canada's traditional antipathy towards distant Ottawa with a lighter form. I proposed that the large areas required for administrative offices be housed in a structure set some ten floors above the site. The central government would take on a remote but protective guise hovering overhead. The long truss support necessary to span widely separated pilings would be externalized as a kind of exoskeleton in order to diminish its size as much as possible. The entire ground level would be a parkscape where there could be a children's centre and an educational exhibit facility for cultural agencies such as the National Film Board and the Canadian Broadcasting Corporation. Contact between the public and the government would be perceived as an interchange.

The British Columbia Medical Centre was a second unbuilt project of the 1970s. While the federal building dealt with an image, this huge hospital was to ameliorate a horror of reality: illness. The ancient Greeks believed that healing came through a renewed harmony with nature and a renewed faith in oneself through one's culture. That holistic sensitivity found its expression in Greek Asia Minor at Pergamus, which was built in a beautiful vale among springs and pine trees and including theatres, baths, a gymnasium and a library. With Pergamus in mind, I kept the complex low, with balconied patient

Child & Maternal Health Unit

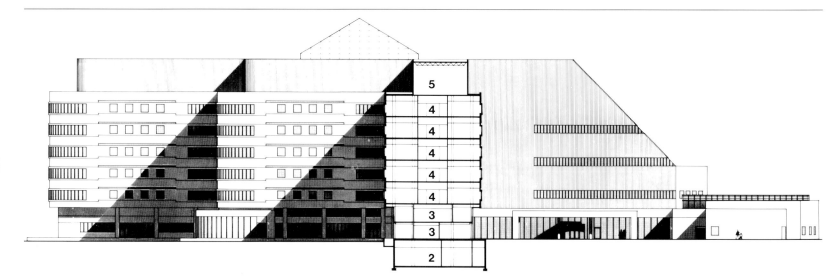

*Top: Section of the 482-bed Saskatoon City Hospital: design, which began in 1984, reflects changes in hospital building philosophy since the 1970s. The diagnostic and treatment facilities, which require interstitial spaces between floors and flexibility within them, are separated in the right wing. Across a high public atrium — a welcome space in the prairie winter — is the less costly patient wing. New economies of construction have enhanced the fulfilment of the old aim of making a pleasant environment for the patient.*

*Bottom: The patient wing of Saskatoon City Hospital is folded to give most rooms a park view. The form also decreases distances of rooms from the nursing stations, which are located at the folds. The trapezoidal diagnostic and treatment section is covered with painted corrugated metal, the patient wing in ceramic tiles. An atrium joins the two parts.* CHRISTOPHER ERICKSON

rooms looking into gardens. We planned for patients' families to be housed nearby. The technology of health care such as the operating rooms and radiology laboratories were underground, leaving the main floor as a mall of health education and preventive medicine. When the government in power changed, the medical centre was taken away from my office. The project went forward incorporating only the low scale of our design. Not until 1984 were we were able to start work on our first medical centre, in Saskatoon, Saskatchewan. There, working from a less idealistic program, we were nevertheless able to isolate the patient

rooms. We arranged them for a park view in an undulating wing that was connected with the rest of the hospital by an atrium.

Conceived in 1971, before the federal building and the medical centre, the Christ Church project was the third Vancouver project that succeeded in capturing memorable creative energy but failed to be realized. It was a prototype model for a few important ideas that were about to show themselves in the work of others and that I would use later myself. One was the use of a reflective glass skin. Light is the essence of life and representative of its mystery, so it is particularly important to religious buildings. Nowhere would it have been so integral as in Christ Church Cathedral in downtown Vancouver. The dwindling congregation could not support itself, and at the same time was confronted with the pressures of real estate development. It seemed likely that the church itself would be torn down — it was an undistinguished structure. My proposal was to bury the church in the plaza of an office tower, something that was achieved in Manhattan a few years later by Hugh Stubbins with Citicorp Center. The church would be entered from the sloping side of the site. Rising above it several storeys would be a simple three-columned tower with a giant crystal suspended in it. The crystal would

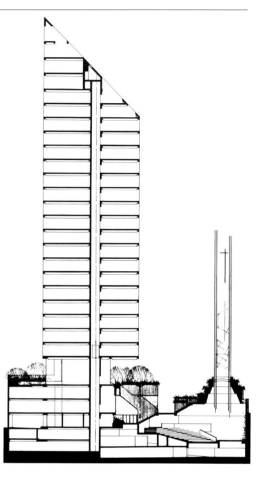

*Left: The Christ Church Cathedral redevelopment project, presented to Vancouver in 1971, anticipates the Manhattan concept of using the airspace of a downtown religious building, as well as the idea of burying a church below a plaza. The liquid-filled glass prism is suspended on stainless steel pillars, its form reflected in the bevelled glass-covered office tower behind.*
SIMON SCOTT

*Right: A diagonal section through the 22-storey office tower of the Christ Church proposal shows a pedestal on the sloping site composed of parking levels, planted terraces and commercial spaces. The crystal reflects light down into the sanctuary on the right.*

Left: A model of the Waterfront Centre in Vancouver, a 1980 proposal, consists of two towers linked by a tall glass-roofed galleria. The towers, one 16 storeys and the other 33, form a gateway from the harbour to the city and frame the city's northern mountain view. The combination of the floor space program and city requirements for view protection dictated the tapered forms of the glass-sheathed towers, which also continue the design theme set by the Christ Church proposal. JOHN FULKER

Top right: The 1980 Sun Life Assurance proposal was for two lots on either side of a prestigious downtown Toronto street. The large space requirements — a total floor area of over 1,400,000 square feet — suggested the extended lower floors. A concern for energy conservation led to an innovative atrium system for

heating and cooling. Under the clear glass slopes of the east and west façades, five-storey enclosures form intermediate climatic zones: the buildup of excessively warm or cool air is exhausted or transferred by fan to the opposite side. PANDA ASSOCIATES

Bottom right: The Harborplace Square proposal for Baltimore, Maryland, in 1982 dealt with the problem of a multi-use project on a constricted site by stacking the different functions and giving each part a separate material identity within a single tower. The lowest level is organized around a five-storey atrium with planting, small shops and a large department store. The punched window façade is for a 400-room luxury hotel, while the office tower is sheathed in glass. The taper gives an illusion of height and soaring motion that recalls sky-scrapers of the 1920s and 1930s. PANDA ASSOCIATES refract light from the sun and the mirrored walls down into the sanctuary in a prism of colours. The plaza itself would be a haven from the busy intersection. The bevelled shape of the building was a distinct departure from the glass box of the time, and seemed to predict where the modern tower form was about to go.

I continued for the next decade to use bright glass skins for dramatic and functional effects in my tall buildings. For the unbuilt Waterfront Centre in Vancouver in 1980, we proposed twin towers, which to the thousands of tourists who sailed into the harbour each year on cruise ships would be a gateway to the city. The paired buildings would also act to frame the spectacular mountain view that rises above Vancouver's downtown, north-south streets. The buildings were to be simple sheaths of steel, one an office tower, the other a hotel, their floors ranging from twenty-five thousand square feet in the lower sections to eleven thousand square feet at the top. In between was to be a galleria of restaurants and entertainment facilities covered by a tall arching glass roof. Another twinned building of the same year, also a potential landmark, was our competition submission for the Toronto office building of the Sun Life Assurance Company. Sun Life had twin properties on either side of the foot of Toronto's broad University Avenue. Two buildings could be put up with one, slightly diminished, echoing the other. A 1982 competition entry for a Baltimore harbour project elaborated on the canted and tapered form as a solution to the problem of mixing and placing a range of functions on a tight site. The program included a major department store, a variety of small retail outlets, a luxury hotel and an office building. We simply stacked them up in that order, using the exterior treatment to discriminate each functional level, starting with a punched wall at the base and ending with a size-reducing glass-curtained office tower at the top.

Just as Simon Fraser University had lifted Erickson/Massey from the ranks of regional architects to a national practice, Robson Square gave my new firm the credentials — along with an introduction of publicity — to compete outside Canada. As the project moved to completion in 1979, I began to seek commissions in the Middle East and the United States. The Americans had expertise enough for universities and office towers, but what they lacked was the experience in mixed or multi-use development that Robson Square represented. Until the 1970s, American urban law and American mentality were against the concept of multi-use since it could only be realized with close government supervision or funding. As they began to question their own conventions, American city planners became susceptible to the broader strokes by which Canadians were sketching their cities. Why not pile offices and housing together? Why not stratify property rights? Why not require a developer who is jumping the population of a neighbourhood to provide for new public spaces as well? Why not bridge a street or abolish vehicles in favour of a healthy pedestrian traffic?

As the decade passed, it became apparent that Canadians had the answers. Canadian developers set their sights on the United States; they proposed large, mixed-use projects, facilities that came naturally to them to conceive and played to their architects' special skills in fitting all the pieces together. Cadillac Fairview and Olympia and York among others met with astonishing success. It was their vision as much as their capital that put them over.

With Robson Square as an apprenticeship, Canadian developers began to involve me in American proposals, beginning with the California Plaza competition in Los Angeles in 1980. And that success opened the way to my own new field of clients among American developers, officials and architects.

# THE EPPICH HOUSES

*Facing page: The Helmut Eppich house in West Vancouver, designed in 1972, has a concrete frame. This night view shows its layered organization: obscured on the left and above the top level is the garage; the top level is the entrance and children's bedrooms; the second has living, dining and kitchen with a swimming pool to the right; on the lowest level, the master bedroom looks out on a pond.* SIMON SCOTT

*The roof/site plan of the 5,500-square-foot Helmut Eppich house shows how its concrete retaining walls span the draw of the shadowed one-acre site, opening it up to the sun as a series of terraces. The drop to the pond is 40 feet. The sliding rectangles theme is echoed at the top by the driveway.*

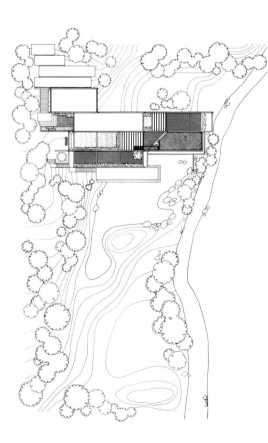

Helmut and Hilda Eppich came to me in 1972 with the usual doubtful building site in West Vancouver and an unusual question for that place and time. Would it be possible to build a house of a more permanent material than wood? Wood seemed flimsy and temporary to these immigrants from Europe. I was delighted to have clients who would allow me to try something new, and whom I did not even have to educate to get permission. Their house became my first in concrete. It is a real bridge, with design elements dating back to the second Smith house and detailing linked to all my later concrete houses. The house steps in terraces held by concrete retaining walls; flying concrete beams and columns support the roofs and trellises. It extends laterally across the site like the Hilborn house of the same year, but the mild West Coast climate allows the design a greater openness.

The property itself was a fill dumping ground, in shadow most of the time and with an easement splitting it in two lengthwise. There was little to recommend it except a stream running down one side. As so often the case, the landscape concept emerged before the house. Part of the stream was diverted to form a pond at the base of the house, providing an intimate focus and bringing reflected light into the middle of the dark lot. Then I developed a design that placed the house on the worst part of the property as a retaining structure for the dump, leaving the rest to be enjoyed.

The house descends through four levels from the roadway: garage and storeroom are at the top; children's bedrooms and main entrance on the second level down; living room, dining area and kitchen-sitting room, and swimming pool on the third level; den, master bedroom and basement are on the fourth, pond level. The swimming pool extends to the edge of the stream and overflows its walls into the pond below.

At every level you are aware of the reach of the house into the landscape, of the incessant but quiet rhythm of column and beam. Rough-sawn fir left in its natural state covers the ceilings and some walls. The board pattern is even picked up in the furniture. There is a subtle tension between the rough wood and raw concrete, and the fineness of the workmanship. Here was a precedent for the domestic use of such a powerful material as concrete.

A few years after Helmut Eppich's house was finished, his twin brother Hugo came to us with his lot. It was also a steep tuck of land, but it was high on a mountain slope in West Vancouver with extensive western views. Hugo may have expected a house similar to Helmut's, my first in concrete. It would have fit the site and reflected their shared value for a permanent construction. However, I came back with another suggestion; since the family owned a steel mill, why not build a house of steel? Wonderful clients that they were, the Eppichs accepted the idea enthusiastically. As the parts were to be machined in the Eppich's shop, I could give them ductile shapes to express the malleable nature of metal. Hence the house steps down its hillside in large arcs. A house of steel is unique if for no other reason than that no one but a millowner could afford to build it.

The south face of the Helmut Eppich house during the day has a structural cadence of flying concrete beams and columns on stepped terraces that extend laterally across the site. All walls, lattices and beams are rough-cut fir to contrast with the smoother concrete.
DICK BUSHER

Hugo's house shares with Helmut's a similar form in spite of the curved edges, and a similar allocation of space. Each level has a different function, but this time the parents' quarters are at the top and the children's on the bottom, with the common areas on the middle, pool level. At the base of the lot is a pond, as in his brother's house.

The hillside exposure is not all view; to either side there are houses which are ordinary and close. The L-shape could be angled to restrict the outlook but in order to admit light, the ends needed to be of glass. The solution was a wall of glass block that follows the curve of the custom-made steel I-beam

for each level; opaque for privacy and colourless for a natural light. On approach it looks like a cascade.

Like his brother, Hugo chose to act as his own general contractor and attend to the details himself. Both houses benefited from the attention of skilled craftsmen, special German stone and a deliberate construction schedule. Designed in 1979, the building was not launched until 1985 by the financially cautious Hugo. Yet he refused to let me change any of the original concept.

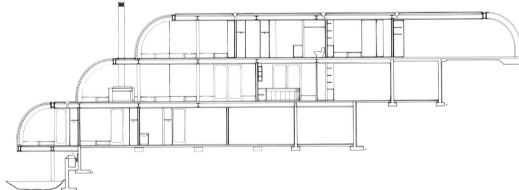

Top: In 1979 design began on a West Vancouver house for Hugo Eppich, Helmut's brother, using curved steel beams fabricated in the family plant. The most striking feature of the house is the luminous cascade of the curved glass-block end walls, which increase light but ensure privacy. The house is set into the fold of a slope with a swimming pool and pond below. Construction of the 6,000-square-foot house began in 1984 and was completed in 1987. RAYMOND LUM

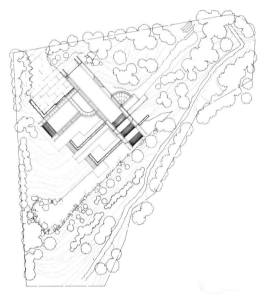

Bottom left: In some ways the Eppich houses are different sides of the same coin: the structure of Hugo's house is of curved steel beams, rather than angular concrete, and the order of the levels is reversed, as this section shows, with the master bedroom on top and the children's rooms at the bottom over the pool.

Bottom right: A swimming pool wing balances the main floor plan of the Hugo Eppich house. The kitchen is at the axis, followed by the dining room, the entrance and the living room.

# FIRE ISLAND HOUSE

This Fire Island house, a 1977 project, was originally going to be an addition to a rundown beach house, set in a string of vacation homes along the brow of the ocean shore. There is a certain inevitability about additions, however. Either the new or the old structure is going to look out of place, so after initial statements of good intentions to the client, the former shell disappears altogether and at a much greater cost than if the house had been started from scratch.

The house is finished in cedar boards, the only nod to the vernacular of the area. Corrosion attacks everything else, even aluminum and glass. The luminous salt air and ocean swells are the reason for being here but the nemesis of investing in the place.

Two mechanical devices add to the enjoyment of the house. The fences are hinged, so that the house can become something like a private barge on the sea: the barriers are like ship's gunwales when they are upright and the house seems ready to take off on the open waters. When the beach is empty, the fences can be lowered, and the house is then open to the view of the breakers. The other extravagant touch is the living room roof, which slides open at the touch of a button. Summer evenings, people sit around the fire under the stars.

Tall wooden piers, cut angularly to frame the view, engage the sloping cornice of the house in an intentional parody of the lines of a stately mansion. During the day, the white walls and white glazed tile floor set off the ocean's blue and like a camera register every subtle change in the marine atmosphere. The neighbours like to call it the White House.

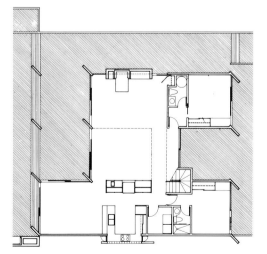

*Top: The living room interior of the Fire Island house, built in 1977, has a low ceiling over the fireplace and a high, double-storeyed one which slides open, making an internal court. EZRA STOLLER/ESTO*

*Bottom: The two-storey Fire Island house has two bedrooms with decks and dressing areas upstairs. The ground floor plan shows the house surrounded by decks on three sides. A guest bedroom and servant's room are at the rear.*

*Facing page: A dusk view of the Fire Island house; the retractable roof of the living room is open. The primary design element of this simple vacation house are the giant wooden piers, angled towards the ocean view. The siding is weathered cedar. EZRA STOLLER/ESTO*

# PACIFIC NORTHWEST HOUSE

*Top: A clearing in the forest is the theme of the 1979 Pacific Northwest house near Seattle, Washington. The rectangular meadow was cut out of the thick forest of the nine-acre site and given a slight rise towards the end to increase its apparent depth, then planted with wildflowers.* TIMOTHY HURSLEY/THE ARKANSAS OFFICE

*Bottom: Three sketches trace the emergence of the Pacific Northwest house. Its three major zones run north-south: the master living quarters on the west; the gallery in the middle, with formal dining room and swimming pool; the guest quarters on the east.* COLLECTION CENTRE CANADIEN D'ARCHITECTURE/CANADIAN CENTRE FOR ARCHITECTURE

Very special clients in 1979 wanted a house that would be at once a gallery for their important collection of contemporary art, a work of art in itself and eminently livable. Their Pacific Northwest site was nine heavily forested acres in a private residential enclave north of Seattle, Washington.

During my introduction to the clients, their art and their property, we visited the family estate on nearby Bainbridge Island. There I saw a remarkable string of gardens wrested from the glens, meadows and swamps of a similar forest property. Traces of Italianate, Japanese, English and Northwest American landscapes could be glimpsed among the firs. One image remained with me when I approached the clients' own site. It was that of a clearing rigidly framed by a tall yew hedge. Within it, a long rectangle of water reflected the surging, waving forest above. Although I typically aim at preserving natural features, this time there were too many trees and one could not, as it were, see the forest for them. In the Northwest, you either savour the melancholy of the light or offset it by every device you can. The clearing on the Bainbridge Island estate suggested a solution that would bring in light and at the same time bring out an awareness of the forest itself.

My scheme was to fell a rectangular clearing extending back into the property from a bluff that glimpsed a dramatic view of Puget Sound. Instead of a hedge of yew, a wall of fir and cedar was exposed, reaching 150 feet up and converging slightly towards the far end to give an illusion of even greater length than its six hundred feet. By adjusting the contours of the clearing, the illusion of depth was further enhanced. The clients gained a huge forest room, whose floor is a meadow of wild grass and flowers on which to place their large sculptures.

Early sketches show how the clearing was echoed in the house itself: a large skylit central space (the gallery-meadow) flanked on either side by living quarters (the forest). The clearing flows through the middle of the house to connect the meadow with the outlook over the distant salt water. At either end of the central space, water contained with surface level edges keeps the sweep uninterrupted to the eye: on the land side is the swimming pool, on the view side a shallow sculpture pond.

Because of the overall exacting detailing and the special demands of the art collection, the house was a long time in construction. Everything had to be tested or mocked up whenever we broke new ground. A computerized atmospheric control system was developed to supply ideal conditions for the

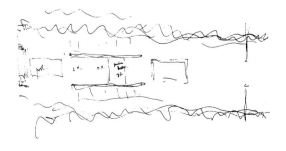

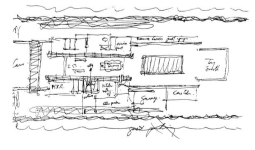

*The pool area of the Pacific Northwest house. A five-part piece by Tony Smith sits in a moss garden before the pool. The structurally decorative H-shaped elements attach the heavy house horizontals to the livelier verticals of the bordering trees.* TIMOTHY HURSLEY/THE ARKANSAS OFFICE

Anthony Caro's Riviera *sits on the living room terrace at one end of the Pacific Northwest house. The terrace is cantilevered over a ravine, and the slate-lined reflecting pool makes a visual connection with the distant ocean. The "hockey sticks" support plexiglass skylights. To the left is a small Joel Shapiro piece.* TIMOTHY HURSLEY/THE ARKANSAS OFFICE

*Facing page: The large art pieces on the walls of the living room/gallery are part of a contemporary collection that dictated the two experimental engineering features of the Pacific Northwest house: for protection, a computer-controlled heating and cooling system; for viewing, the gallery roof of sand-blasted glass-block panels on a steel structural grid. Finish*

*materials are toned with the primary structural material, a parchment-coloured cast-in-place concrete. Kasota sandstone pavers cover the outdoor terraces and extend into the interior. Beige carpeting is used in the main living spaces.* TIMOTHY HURSLEY/THE ARKANSAS OFFICE

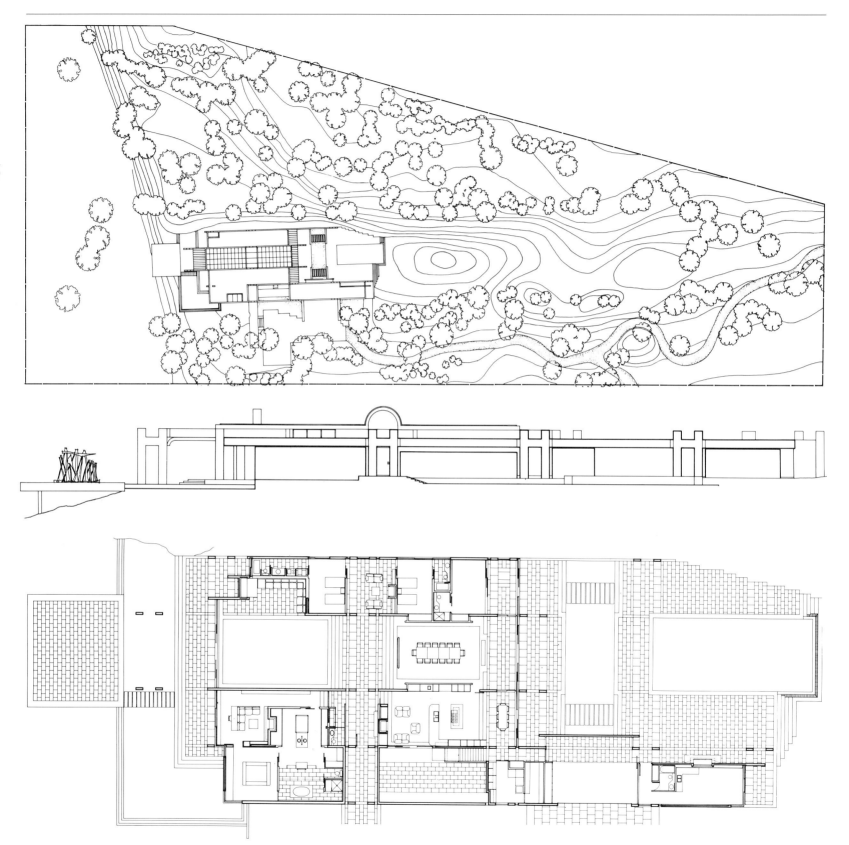

paintings, which are in continual rotation from warehouses. The stone floor is built over a continous heated plenum that exhausts heat beneath the windows out either end of the house. Thermal sensors enable the system to automatically adjust itself to extract or supply heat where needed. The basement is so full of heat pumps, heat exchangers, compressors and so forth that it looks like the inside of a submarine hull and requires an engineer to service it.

The most experimental feature is the glass roof running the length of the dining–living room–gallery. There were no precedents to guide us, but glass block was the only type of construction that promised to hold up against the impact of falling branches and give the right quality of light into the interior: an evenly diffused natural glow. To achieve this, the glass block was sandblasted on the outer surface. To protect the blocks from the stress of direct sunlight, a shading device of white painted steel fins was erected. After two years of experimentation and testing, the gallery roof went up. With custom architecture, the famous leaking roof is assumed as a breaking-in feature of the building. The more creative the structure, the more it asks for untried solutions, and hence the chances rise for nature to find seepage points. Contrary to expectations, the unique glass roof worked well from the beginning.

No photograph can do justice to the tawny parchment hue of the concrete walls. It even changes under the moving light of the day. As a rule concrete should never be painted and never finished. With a strongly tactile surface of pits and streaks, in situ concrete stands a chance of being as interesting and beautiful in its effect as natural stone. Concrete's neutral colour lets the building express its form and unites it with the landscape. I have called it the twentieth-century marble. But for this house we needed a warmer background both for the paintings and to offset the dark forest wall, so I found myself experimenting with dyes. The out-

come was one of the most beautiful concretes I have been able to use and a completely successful match for the art.

To marry the strong horizontals of the house with the overwhelming verticals of the forest, I came up with an H-shaped series of portals. They give the centre a strong cross-axis and frame a second cross-axis linking the kitchen, the dining room and the conservatory. They also embrace the pools and give a distinct sculptural suggestion to the whole. My irreverent staff called them "rabbit ears" in their tiny mockup form, but even the clients' magnificent Anthony Caro sculpture must have looked like a tinkertoy as a model. The proof is in the placement.

The large glassed areas at either end of the house have overhanging glass "eyebrows" that soften the transition from interior to exterior lighting. With no solid edge to stop the visual flow, their curved white painted steel "hockey stick" supports suggest containment and release at the same time.

Ordinary doors and doorjambs would have been inconsistent with the massive frame and walls, so we developed sliding and opening doors of an appropriate scale without jambs: full height, three inches thick, with rounded, lacquered black stiles. The gutters and electrical switchboxes are also black, the latter cannily suspended in the gaps between columns and walls. Minimalist detailing followed through on shelving, dressing rooms, kitchen cabinetry and dining room tables. We installed only those lighting fixtures necessary for the paintings. Night illumination is augmented by uplights on the columns. At night the glowing house takes on a presence of its own and asserts its independence from the black forest.

*Several frames march along the transverse axis of the Pacific Northwest house under a vaulted skylight, beginning with an opening to the entrance court, then the frameless glass front door, and on through the gallery and den to the forest floor. A 2,000-square-foot glass-block roof covers the central section.* Timothy Hursley/The Arkansas Office

*Facing page, top: The site plan of the 9,000-square-foot Pacific Northwest house shows how one end of the house sits on the edge of a ravine looking north. The 600-foot-long meadow was carved out of the thick forest.*

*Facing page, middle: A north-south longitudinal section shows that the Pacific Northwest house, like the Museum of Anthropology, was designed with major sculptures in place. From the left are the living room terrace and reflecting pool, the living room gallery with an alcove and a fireplace, and steps to the formal dining area.*

*Facing page, bottom: Floor plan of the Pacific Northwest house: the central gallery space is divided between the living room and dining room. More intimate areas are provided by the fireplace nook and the kitchen seating space.*

# ROBSON SQUARE

*Facing page: A view of Robson Square south over the roof of the Vancouver Art Gallery and provincial government offices towards the Law Courts. Robson Square also includes several restaurants on the lower level and a media centre two floors below street level. An urban context study began in 1972, and project design started in 1973; the government offices opened in 1978, the Law Courts in 1979 and the Vancouver Art Gallery in 1983. The three blocks were planned as an integrated whole, in a climate of co-operation between provincial and city governments. EZRA STOLLER/ESTO*

*The Robson Square site plan covers three blocks in downtown Vancouver. On the right is the old courthouse roof. A street bridges the sunken plaza, which has two plexiglass domes over each end of a skating rink. The centre block houses the provincial government offices under long horizontal supports that provide brows and planters over the windows. The stairs incorporate ramps and lead to an upper level crossing of a second street to the glass-roofed Law Courts.*

For many years city fathers had promised Vancouver a central square as a public focus for its overbuilt downtown, but all attempts to claim such a space had succumbed to the more powerful grab of developers. In the late 1960s the last vacant blocks available became the site of a grandiose scheme for a fifty-five-storey tower that would contain a courthouse and provincial government offices as well as private rental space. The Erickson/Massey proposal called for the most dramatic statement possible: an H-shaped tall building straddling a street, with the other preserved as a needed open public space. When the opposition party gained provincial control in 1972, they saw any tower as a political monument and responded to local cries for something on a different scale. The problem of new housing for the courts and provincial offices was handed to my firm under the working name of the Three Block Project: officially, Robson Square. The site included the block containing the original courthouse and two precious blocks in a line behind it.

When my firm was asked to prepare a master plan for Robson Square, we asked to contract first for an urban design study of the downtown area. Our study looked to the whole downtown peninsula so that we could understand its structure, growth trends, traffic needs and different character areas. We discovered which streets were edges separating one character area from another and which were bridges linking two like areas; that certain key intersections were vital nodes in the urban network and could be designed to emphasize this quality. Trees and street lighting, curbing and paving could make the definitions of street function and character even more effective.

Having recently returned from my first tour of China, I thought Vancouver's street planting could be more generous, especially considering how the climate would encourage it. We proposed a street planting for the

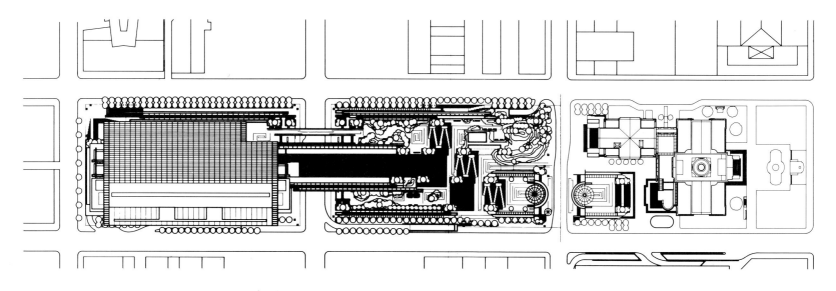

Left: The double allée of trees on the streets bordering
Robson Square. ALAN BELL

Right: Street planting shades a skylight into the lower
floor of the government offices at Robson Square.
The rose-planted brow above also shades the skylight
behind. "Flying planters" are a main architectural
element for the government offices and Law Courts.
DICK BUSHER

whole downtown but first of all insisted that twin allées be used to define the new government precinct. Managing to get them in place over the objections of the city engineer was the kind of vivid experience that made me think the Americans were right in their suspicions of city hall. However, in the end we compromised — the engineer rejected our choice of the plane tree but accepted the double planting arrangement. The trees remain my favourite design contribution to the city's streets.

Finally, our report proposed density, heights and massing for the blocks around Robson Square. The low-rise profiles of the courthouse Law Courts, and provincial office buildings connected to each other over and under the existing cross streets, as well as to the courthouse. The law would be at one end, government in the centre block, and the Vancouver Art Gallery in the old neoclassical courthouse building at the opposite end. Law, government and art would each benefit from proximity with the other, sharing a public image, public patronage and their own employees' interactions.

The historic courthouse was inviolate and the new courthouse had intricate space and heavy security requirements, so the only possibility for a focal public space was the central block assigned to government offices. If the centre block's main floor could be set one storey below grade, relieved by a series of skylit courts, we could develop Vancouver's civic square on its roof. By playing with the traffic alignment, closing one street and bridging another, pedestrians would be welcome to circulate all through the city's new heart.

We spent months analyzing the government's departmental layouts to produce a multilevel structural configuration that could support a public garden on its roof. We used water in a bold way. The top level of the government office segment carries a three-hundred-foot-long flowing pool that begins

*Top: The "stramps" leading from the sunken plaza of Robson Square to the Law Courts are an integration of ramps with stairs that allows disabled people to enter by the "front door" instead of the "back door." Lights are set into the interrupted steps.* EZRA STOLLER/ESTO

*Bottom: The sunken plaza of Robson Square includes a canopied ice-skating rink. In summer the plaza is animated by outdoor restaurants and performances.* ALAN BELL

at the terrace of the adjoining courthouse restaurant, cascades down over windows to conceal the offices behind — a romantic backdrop for the Marriage Bureau — and flows over glass decks to produce shimmering light in the halls below. The lowest sunken level connects with a public courtyard that holds a collection of restaurants and a skating rink; it also gives into the government media centre, which consists of a large exhibition space, a theatre and a conference centre. Grand stairs that connect each level of the complex are crossed rather cunningly by ramps. Developed through much thought and study, these unique devices were dubbed "stramps" by the design team and are an early built-in accommodation for the disabled that allows them front door rights.

Landscaping has an essential role in the architecture of the provincial government building. Plants that cling naturally to cliff faces in the Pacific Northwest spring from

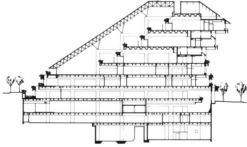

the piers that flank waterfalls and stairways. The landscape consultant, Cornelia Oberlander, had the inspiration of having roses spill out of the hanging planters. The heavy horizontals begin with laurel at the street edges, then move to terraces of pine and bamboo groves, maple and dogwood, and are topped with juniper along the long pool, giving the impression of altitudinal plant changes. As the landscape approaches the neoclassical art gallery, it forms a soft hill of rhododendrons, pines and maples, which from a distance frame the building's portico in an eighteenth-century manner.

*Facing page: The roof structure, "knee frames" and flying planters of the Robson Square Law Courts.* EZRA STOLLER/ESTO

*Top left: The main gallery of the Law Courts is frequently used for public events.* ROB MELNYCHUK

*Top right: The three 350-foot-long upper galleries of the 12,000-square-foot main hall of the Law Courts.* HORST THANHAUSER

*Bottom: A transverse section of the Law Courts: transfer areas, parking and the heat-storage tank are in the base; administration and library are two floors near grade, beneath the main gallery, into which the courtrooms open.*

*One of 35 courtrooms, which are purposefully light to ease the sombre mood of the proceedings, with red carpeting, brass rails and pale brown elm wood. Ceilings are coffered for added height and to diffuse the direct downlight. Many courtrooms have skylights, and the ones at the end of the building have full-height windows.* EZRA STOLLER/ESTO

Some may consider such a structure covered with prodigal growth in the heart of the city to be very unurbane. Certainly it is different from, for example, the beautiful hard-edged space of the Italian or Spanish square. The building in a way is merely a container for a classic, bushy Olmsted park, and in that sense is more landscape than architecture. Its composition follows landscape as much as building determinants precisely because we set out to place the promised city park on the block between the art gallery and the Law Courts.

When I came to the realization that the law is simply another aspect of our culture, with no independent existence or inflated status, I could proceed with the shaping of the new courthouse. Certain impressions fed my determination to challenge accepted preconceptions for an archetypical neoclassical structure or a modernist monolith. I asked former Chief Justice J. V. Clyne how he viewed the trappings of law. He replied, ''Arthur, as far as I'm concerned, the last time justice was carried out effectively was in the streets of London in the seventeenth century.'' I recalled that in my own experience in Saudi Arabia, you could leave your wallet in the street and find it there the next day. It seemed that their justice system, carried out in public squares, encouraged a remarkable honesty. I concluded that justice had to be seen to be appreciated. Our law courts should be less a house of ominous retribution than a civics lesson in community standards. So aside from a layout for normal security precautions, we decided our mandate would be to open the courthouse to the public and to the street.

Sheltered under the courthouse's great glass roof are terraces of galleries adorned with plants, providing a place that eases tensions and encourages visitors. The burden of heating and cooling such large open spaces would have defeated the concept entirely but for the contribution of our mechanical engineer. He suggested that the sloping roof could capture solar radiation and that a natural stack ventilation system would keep it comfortable. Air under the roof is heated by the sun — even on cloudy days — and then rises to escape through vents at the top. The upward draft of heated air draws cool air in through vents at the bottom. In the winter, the vents can be closed to conserve the absorbed heat. In order that the glass roof read as one large panel, we managed to have the panes butted and caulked without upstanding mullions.

The interior heating and cooling system is also a marvel of simple physics. Three-quarters of a million gallons of water are in a basement tank, part heated, part chilly, separated by their differing densities. The heat for the building is drawn from the stored heat of the water. The energy for heating the water is drawn from the outside provincial hydroelectic grid during offpeak hours when rates are significantly lower. It is also drawn from the excessive heat of the building's lighting fixtures. In the summer, the subterranean vault of water is a source for cooling the building. The 150,000 gallons of water for the separate waterfall system are but a drop of what a regular cooling system would need, but it too is turned to practical use: its rooftop tanks feed the fire sprinklers. Even after ten years, these heating and structural innovations remain state of the art.

Nevertheless, my first design priority was manipulating space and light under the special conditions of the moody climate. Translucent glass and reflective water are my natural tools. As at Simon Fraser University, I was providing a giant daylit shelter at the major conjunction of public traffic. The entire three-block complex is linked by a pedestrian spine, which begins at the old courthouse and ends accommodatingly under the wide glass roof before spilling out to the street below. With so many people gathering and passing by in their role of citizen, the whole reads like a new Forum

Romanum with the raised, columned and stepped great hall of the courthouse recalling the Temple of Jupiter.

When the Robson Square planning began, I opposed retaining the old landmark courthouse's legal function as the judges initially wished. The complex was heavy enough with law, and if it was to serve as a focal point for the city, then the enlightening presence of art in the vacated courthouse would be a wonderful addition. The dignity of the beloved neoclassical building and its key location would give the art gallery a prominence that it had never enjoyed before.

Setting an art gallery in a former palace of justice is an exercise you might see in Europe. It was instructive to us for both halves of the problem: the design of a public art space itself, and the conversion and preservation of an older building. The tight budget was severely tested by the heavy cost of bringing the 1910 structure up to code. This required a basic reconstruction of the foundation and bearing walls just to meet earthquake standards. While the exterior was given over to careful restoration, the new internal functions completely invalidated most of the interior structure, except for the rotunda that had to be preserved at great cost. As a result of these first calls on the moneys, gallery finishes had to be kept as simple as possible while meeting standards for security, atmospheric control and lighting.

The program requirements for a secure entrance and exits forced us to abandon the grand front door, which is opened under guard only on special occasions. My answer to disappointed strict preservationists would be that traditionally many great neoclassical villas were entered from the rear and the grand portico looked out over the garden. Indeed, just such a garden is suggested by the large fountain and flowerbeds in the "front." The new entrance is at ground level

*Top: Design of additions and renovations to turn the old courthouse into the Vancouver Art Gallery began in 1979. The main entrance faces south onto the pedestrian mall of Robson Square and is composed of a sculpture terrace supported on simple columns that frame new at-grade entrance doors. The new construction had to be modestly made of concrete, but the colour was carefully matched to the stone of the original building. Very little of the heritage structure's exterior appears changed, though in fact the entrance lobby and terrace were added, the chimney and some windows were altered.* JIM GORMAN/VANCOUVER ART GALLERY

*Bottom: The rotunda of the Vancouver Art Gallery needed extensive reconstruction to preserve it as the focal space of the circulation pattern. A grand staircase was added to connect the new entrance at grade with the original first floor; new balustrades had to match the originals of the three upper storeys. The wired glass dome of the original skylight was replaced by a smooth, clear plexiglass one. All surfaces were refurbished and painted in soft tones.* JOHN FULKER

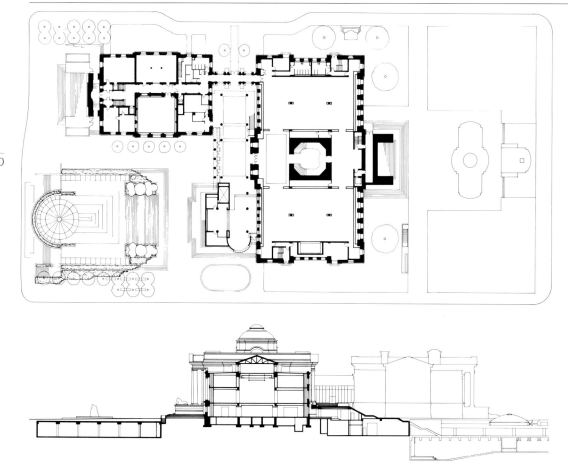

Top: Ground floor plan of the Vancouver Art Gallery:
the walls of the new internal structure fit within the old
exterior walls, so that the windows keep their depth, if
not their function. The new space of the south entrance
becomes a juncture of the administration, galleries and
shop, as well as an easy, at-grade entrance for the
disabled.

Bottom: Section through the old courthouse, which was
gutted in order to create high, open and flexible gallery
spaces, as well as to meet fire and earthquake standards. Only the rotunda and the ornate upper walls and
ceiling of the fourth floor remain. The exhibition space
totals 41,390 square feet.

at the ''back'' and is the only external addition to the structure. It contains the lobby,
information desk and shop, and its roof is a
sculpture terrace. We gave it a stairway, engaged pilasters and pediment that echo the
''front.'' We were careful to free the added
facility from the original, linking it only by
linear skylights that light the rusticated
stonework of the old basement in high relief.

One of the causes of gallery fatigue, aside
from the surfeit of things to look at, is the
feeling of being lost in an endless passage.
In all the galleries and museums I have
planned, the question of orientation and
visual contrast has been the generator of the
design. In our competition entry for the
National Gallery at Ottawa in 1975, we had
all the rooms fanning off a large central lobby
and sculpture court that was flooded with
light and looked down to the river. For an

addition to the McLaughlin Art Gallery in
Oshawa, Ontario, one long skylit corridor
served as the organizing principle. For the
Vancouver Art Gallery, we used the existing
central rotunda. The escalators are placed on
either side of it, and its skylit, vertical space
is an intended refreshment after the long,
artificially lit galleries. We gave it a simple
but elegant Adam treatment of white, green-
grey and china blue.

My design strategy for adapting stylized
buildings like the old courthouse is to make
them look better than before by emphasizing
the spirit and line of the original model and
minimizing the more recent cheap particu-
lars. One way I have found of compensating
for these small betrayals is to play them
down. We painted out the clumsy wooden
windows of the old courthouse so that they
do not read as prominently and offset its
rather mean entrance by a more appropriately scaled treatment of stairs and planting. We
made the old backside, with its engaged
pediment and pilasters miserably perched
on a rusticated base punched with windows,
much more gracious by the addition of a
terrace and broad stairs. Future generations
should comment only on the poverty that
had us doing it in poured concrete instead
of stone.

The true scale and meaning of Robson
Square are just coming clear today as the
property values around it rise and tall buildings begin to fill in the cityscape. Hemmed in
by a threatening forest of the towers of private interests, the three blocks are a meadow
sanctuary of civic and communal values: the
law courts open to all witnesses, the government offices wrapped in nature's nurturing
guise, and the arts dancing once again in
their old Grecian robes.

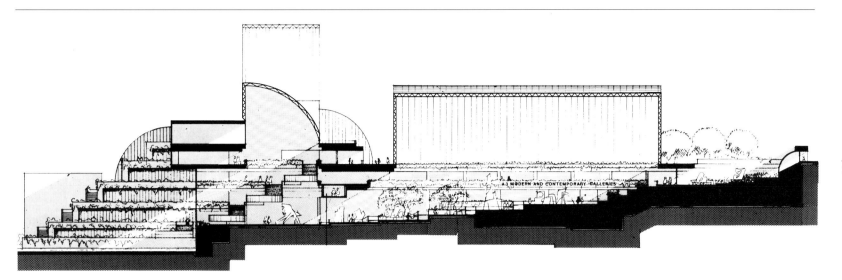

*Top: Section through the National Gallery of Canada: a long sculpture garden, the base of a T-form and covered by a half-vaulted glass roof, leads from the street to the central orientation space above the split bluff and the river. The main circulation space is given a taller half-vault, and its juncture with the exhibit wings is open to the view and to the galleries on either side.*

*Middle: The National Gallery of Canada in Ottawa was given a crowded riverbank site closely bounded by a steam plant with a tall stack, a ravine and government buildings. Instead of actively engaging the built context, the 1975 competition scheme is buried in the bluff and oriented to the river.* DEREK GRIFFITHS

*Bottom: An expansion of the Robert McLaughlin Gallery in Oshawa, Ontario, triples the existing space for a total area of 38,000 square feet. The 1984 design organizes circulation along a central corridor-spine with a vaulted skylight. Over the main entrance, the glazed bowed front holds a 55-seat restaurant.* CASIMIR BART

# WATERFRONT SITES

King's Landing is a horizontal development wedged between Toronto's waterfront freeway and Lake Ontario. It is within a complex of yacht basin, office buildings and condominiums designed by different firms, with our housing block the centrepiece. We won the commission in 1981, when Harbourfront, as the downtown lakeshore parcel is called, was in the first stage of being converted by a public corporation from deserted railway sidings and storage silos to residential use. Such development was difficult, for however much urban values had changed to make lakeside living desirable, the last great corruption of the whole area remained in place — a wide, raised freeway cutting off the scant shoreline from the city.

At the time, the Harbourfront authorities would not allow high-rise buildings on the site, removing the easy option of upward escape from the steady, intrusive stream of traffic. Instead, we were given a perimeter, a height, a rounded edge for each corner and a requirement for a covered colonnade. Of course, the more impossibly strict the design conditions, the more there is to grapple with and turn to advantage. Fortunately, the program was luxurious enough to support athletic facilities and generous decks. We put the swimming pool and tennis court at the back, against the highway, and opened the apartments fully to the lake and light. Steel and glass conservatories help to exploit the balcony spaces, which are subject to bitter winter winds.

King's Landing actually benefits from the height restriction that was subsequently removed from the rest of the Harbourfront properties. As the shoreline becomes lined

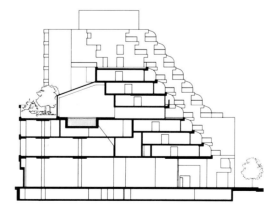

*Facing page: Looking down the face of King's Landing in Toronto, designed in 1981 and completed in 1984. The solaria are a solution to enjoying the lakefront view and sun year round. All the outside metalwork is painted nautical white.* CHRISTOPHER ERICKSON

*Top: King's Landing contains 320 residential units and an arcade retail floor at ground level. Because of the cant, some upper floor apartments have almost as much terrace as enclosed space.* CHRISTOPHER ERICKSON

*Bottom: A section showing the canted form of King's Landing: the building leans against Toronto's lakeshore highways. The highway side contains the recreational facilities, which include a swimming pool, tennis court and planted decks.*

Top: The 1978 Evergreen building in Vancouver is another stepped, terraced waterfront project. The small, mixed-use concrete building of 10 floors, 10 000 square metres, sits on an exposed corner lot in the downtown area. There was a view to capture and a developer's desire to attract prestigious tenants who wanted small, balconied offices. WILBERT BRUEGGER

Bottom: A view of the angled balconies of the Evergreen building: their alternation creates an interesting light-shadow arrangement viewed from afar. Plantings overflow the concrete brows into which the railings are set. WILBERT BRUEGGER

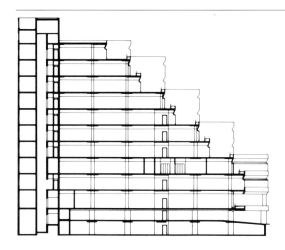

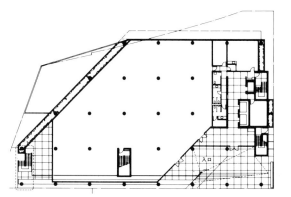

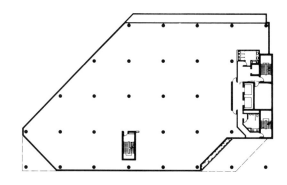

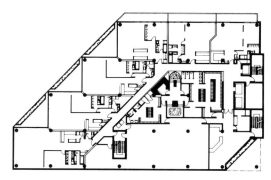

with towers, King's Landing's low scale and sunny nautical aspect become all the more distinctive, recalling as I intended the waterfront lodgings at Brighton or the long eighteenth-century terraces on Regent's Park.

A waterfront predecessor of King's Landing was the Evergreen building in Vancouver, designed in 1978. It had to balance inexpensive construction and standard detailing with the client's desire to provide for individual professionals that special kind of office space which would grant them the pleasant image of success — a view and a balcony opening to it. The property was confined and difficult, with a diagonal side that looked northwest over a yacht basin and to the mountains beyond. So we cut the building along that line and stepped up from there in a series of receding balconies. As a result, the building accommodates a variety of office sizes as well as a mix of other uses, with a residential floor and health club. The concrete Evergreen does fall into the "Queen Anne front and Mary Jane behind" category, for from the water side it opens in a decisive pattern of balconies, while the only distinction on the street front is the ivy spilling over the edges of its sawtooth profile.

The Laurel Point Inn sits on a point at the entrance to the harbour of Victoria, British Columbia. Our 1987 addition to this fine hotel greets incoming ships with a reflecting profile. Removed from the older, busier part of the city, the hotel is backed by other modern structures and in front enjoys a broad lawn prospect down to the water. A water garden protects the hotel from the public shoreline walk and enhances the water element of the view. Although the climate is temperate, the wet weather still dictates some protection for the balconies and the central, enlarged dining areas.

125

*Left: A longitudinal section and floor plans of the first three storeys of the Evergreen building show its mixed-use nature. The plans show (top to bottom) the first, second and third floors. The first floor is an open lobby. The second floor has an offset service core to allow for a flexible office plan. The third floor has a health club and residential units on the view side. The pattern of the angular balconies alternates from one floor to the other.*

*Right: A 1987 addition to the Laurel Point Inn, a 120-room hotel at the entrance to the inner harbour of Victoria, British Columbia, consists of a wing of 76 rooms. A winter garden connects the original and new wings. The balconied face of the addition looks west across ocean straits, the upper floors on the other side look to the city. The new wing is terraced like King's Landing so that the balconies can have better views and light, and it also has white trim to complement the marine context.* PHILLIP VAN HORN

# NAPP LABORATORIES

*Napp Laboratories in Cambridge, England, was designed in 1979. The entrance lobby is located between the administration (right) and the manufacturing (left). Bridges span the lobby to link the two sections, and a visitor's gallery spans the manufacturing wing for viewing without risk to the processes.* TIMOTHY HURSLEY/THE ARKANSAS OFFICE

*Facing page: Illumination streams through the concrete columns over the moat and bridge of Napp Laboratories. The moat is a reservoir for the sprinkler system and a reference to the historic canals of the area. The bridge crosses to the lobby. The glass curves back in stages at the top, letting the bents stand alone as flying buttresses.* TIMOTHY HURSLEY/THE ARKANSAS OFFICE

The remarkable Sackler brothers, who commissioned this English plant for their pharmaceutical company in 1979, have matched their great success in business with their interests in art and architecture. Their plants in Germany and France are designed by Marcel Breuer and their offices are furnished in superb Chinese antiques. Wings of the Metropolitan Museum in New York and the Smithsonian Institution carry their name. We worked directly with Mortimer Sackler, whose individual style made it a glamorous association. Meetings were held at the Café Royale in London, in historic rooms at Trinity College in Cambridge, at Mortimer's houses at Cap d'Antibes or Chester Square in London, and at his offices off Central Park in New York. The experience was the closest I have come to moving in the world of the Medicis.

Napp Laboratories is located in Cambridge Science Park, where it can relate to the neighbouring academic and research community. We were to provide accommodation for three very different functions: warehousing, manufacturing and research laboratories, and administration. As with most industrial buildings, the solution had to be a repetitive structure and a universal space that could house each separate use with a minimum of modification. Initially, we explored exoskeleton structural systems to produce column-free spaces. But we knew that our competition for the commission, Piano and Rogers, were much more accomplished with that kind of structure.

Eventually we adopted a simpler form and a straightforward use of elegant materials. We presented a structure of repetitive simple steel bents with mirrored glass block infill

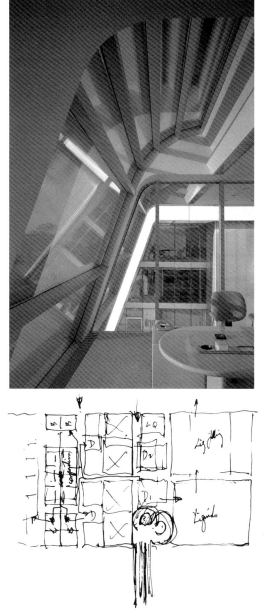

*Top: An upper office in the Napp administration block looks out through mirror-coated double-glazed windows where they wrap to the roof. The glazing is installed using a structural silicone technique that leaves the outer surface free of mechanical fixing in order to achieve a continuous glazed surface.*
TIMOTHY HURSLEY/THE ARKANSAS OFFICE

*Bottom: A plan study of the ground floor of Napp indicates a close attention to the complex functions and procedures of the laboratory with arrows, linked lines, captions and abbreviations. Two rough circles for the lobby mark a terminus for an entry bridge.*

and framing clad in lead, in reference to the lead roofs of the Cambridge chapels. Responding to the drab English weather, we arched the glass block wall inward at the top in order to bathe the interiors in light like that provided by the glass of King's College chapel. From the outside the mirrored block would break the hard silhouette of the roof against the white sky by guiding the shimmering light down its face between the leaded bents, in a reverse effect of the jutting spires and pinnacles of the nearby Gothic colleges.

Mortimer had always favoured concrete and resisted the lead and mirrored block scheme even at a mockup on site. He asked us to look at alternative ideas in concrete. However, we continued to work from the original profile which is naturally bulkier in concrete and thus breaks the enveloping surface rather than fitting flush with it. Instead of the mirrored glass block that transmitted an amber glow to the interior, we used large sheets of mirrored glass, butted and siliconed so as to provide an uninterrupted slick reflective surface flowing skyward between upstanding bents. The bristling yet regular repetition of these white concrete fins standing at a 70-degree angle on the white concrete podium gives it a classical sense of repose. The complex includes one block of offices — three floors with a restaurant and lecture hall at grade, connected by a full-height lobby to a manufacturing wing with an interstitial space for services and laboratories above. The warehouse is a separate block, connected through a mechanical core to the manufacturing, and is open at either end for future expansion.

The building sits in a field crossed by hedgerows, and we repeated their long parallel lines with plantings of poplar and hawthorn. Parallel grass berms and hedges of gorse conceal the parking lots. A grove of oaks that survived the Cambridge bog lines the driveway, and a canal was cut along the building to grace the entrance. The canal is an aesthetic reference to other ancient canals of the area but also has a utilitarian role as a reservoir for the fire control system.

In a factory building the key to success is not the outward architecture but how well the manufacturing process is accommodated. All design is subject to the process, and the building is merely its envelope. Nevertheless, after creating the best working environment, the building can also act as an advertisement for its product. Our "universal section" scheme seemed to express appropriate scientific, rational values. Each section could serve for manufacturing, warehousing, laboratories or offices. Of course, each demanded a different ceiling height and had distinct servicing, ventilation and lighting requirements. The ideal width for manufacturing became the standard for the floor plate, and the best height for the warehouse the other standard. The latter happened to give room for three office floors and so worked without adjustment for the administration block. The laboratory fit over the manufacturing component, separated by an interstitial service "floor" with ducts and services for both.

Instead of selecting among antiseptic colours as I would have for the plant's necessarily sterile environment, our interior designer, Francisco Kripacz, chose rich deep plums and cream. The colours give the building a majesty suited to the headless statue of Aesculapius, god of medicine, which surveys the lobby, and to the Sacklers as well. Remarked Mortimer, "It's the most glamorous warehouse in England."

Over the years, Francisco's work has fleshed out my architectural bones without in any way denying the thrust of the design. Long ago I concluded that the architect's mind is more suited to envisioning space and structure than the subtler materials and colours that adorn interiors. Preoccupied with the purity of our spaces, we tend to overlook them. And when an architect does attempt an interior, the result is always recognizable

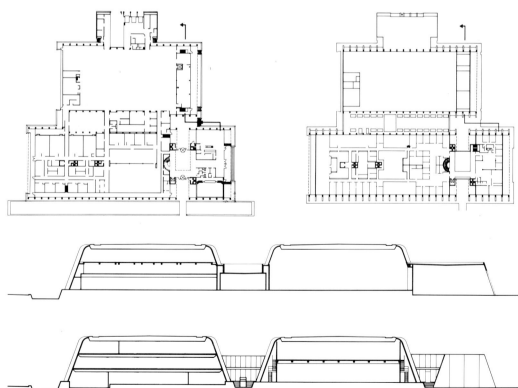

Top: A view of Napp Laboratories: the administrative and manufacturing block is at the left, the warehouse block is behind. Dining and meeting rooms look out the nearer face. The facility was completed in 1983. TIMOTHY HURSLEY/THE ARKANSAS OFFICE

Middle: The program for Napp called for approximately 100,000 square feet of offices, laboratories, manufacturing facilities and warehouses. The ground floor plan (left) indicates the general division: dining and auditorium to the right of the lobby, manufacturing and laboratories to the left of the lobby, and the column-free warehouse behind. The second floor plan (right) has a library and laboratory on the left, with offices on the right.

Bottom: Two sections contrast the twin units of the Napp complex. The upper section, through the middle, has a wide interstitial floor necessary for supporting mechanical services of the environmentally controlled laboratory and manufacturing floors. Next to it is the warehouse, a single high support-free space. The lower section is through the administrative end of the units. An auditorium and cafeteria are on the first floor, with offices above.

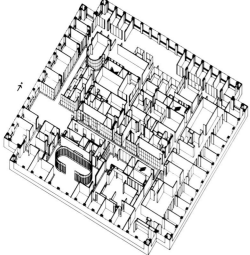

for its lack of that final, complementary step of definition — the tying together on the intimate level dominated by furnishings and their details. At the same time, the architect with no control at all over his interiors finds his work more often compromised than enhanced by the work of the interior designer, for whom a set of rooms may be but a stage for presenting a quite unrelated visual order. It takes a sure affiliation of purpose and spirit between architect and interior designer to achieve that rare building that is a conceptual unity throughout. As an associated partner, Francisco has given my practice this added strength.

I could never have taken a practical client like the Teck Mining Group to the heights of design that my associate did with our commission for the interiors of its offices in a Toronto tower. In a nation whose economy is founded on resource extraction, Teck Mining is one of the largest mineral combines. Happily for us, like the Napp Pharmaceutical Group, it is run by an individualistic rather than corporate type in Dr. Norman B. Keevil, Sr. His offices, however, expressed his field-work background more than his present eminence and tastes. Still, I would not have predicted the degree of our transformation after being shown its display ranks of mineral col-

lections and paintings of beloved mineshafts.

As we left, Francisco declared to me, "I won't use a single rock." Subsequently the paintings were replaced by Lichtensteins, Kellys and Stellas, and the board room became a tour de force with polished steel doors, a purple leather table and classic Mies chairs in plum velour. Nevertheless, we dressed the walls of the lobby and secretarial stations with stone and then lavished stainless steel on the fittings, so that the whole office became a display of the company mission, but in a subtle, more authoritative and entirely impeccable manner — although some irreverently call it "Star Teck."

*Facing page, top: The reception areas of the Teck offices use the firm's geological interests as a leitmotif. The kasota stone walls set at an angle at the back suggest the form of a mineshaft — and recall the powerful base of the MacMillan Bloedel building. Shining metal ceiling panels heighten the drama of the arrival moment. The entrance hall proceeds between a bank of stone secretarial stations and a sandblasted glass office wall. An Ellsworth Kelly is on the right.* NORMAN MCGRATH

*Facing page, bottom: The oval board room stands out in an axonometric plan of the Teck offices. Behind the board room are the elevator banks and central hall. Executive offices ring the exterior.*

*Stainless steel doors slide open electronically at the touch of a button to reveal the board room of the Teck Mining Group's Toronto offices, designed in 1980. The circular wall is perforated by translucent glass panels, and inset lighting encircles the wall like a jewelled chain. The bright metal ceiling picks up on the wall and the Mies chairs.* NORMAN MCGRATH

# YORKDALE SUBWAY STATION

*Top: The Yorkdale Subway Station in Toronto is a 1974 project. Light floods into the platform area through its long glass roof, supported by steel versions of the structural trees found in the Erickson Vancouver office and the Bank of Canada building.* SIMON SCOTT

*Bottom: The Yorkdale Station takes the form of a whole subway train, including rounded top and windowed steel sides. Total building length is 600 feet.* SIMON SCOTT

*Facing page: The Yorkdale Station features artist Michael Hayden's computer-controlled neon sculpture, installed in the skylight. The colours are deep blue at one end and graduate through the spectrum to red at the centre, returning to blue at the other apse.* SIMON SCOTT

There have been too few opportunities to collaborate with an artist, but at least we had a truly spectacular success with the Yorkdale subway station in Toronto, commissioned by the Toronto Transit Authority in 1974. The structure is just a tube of space in concrete and steel, duplicating the subway train in its overall shape. It sits at grade level on a highway median strip, and its form is actually appreciated best from a moving automobile. The roof is a skylight covering the five-hundred-foot-long centre platform and extending out about a hundred feet at each end in glazed apses over the passenger exits. We invited Michael Hayden, a Toronto artist, to help us, and he saw it as a chance to work on an idea he was developing for the application of computer controls to coloured neon tubes.

Hayden gave us a grand electronic sculpture consisting of hundreds of neon tubes marching down the length of the station's ceiling. He called it *Arc-en-Ciel*, and indeed it was an electronic rainbow, starting with deep violet at one end and graduating through the spectrum to red at the centre, returning through yellow and green to blue at the other apse. As trains enter and leave the station, the whole work pulsates to a computerized rhythm in the direction of the incoming train. While passengers wait for a train, a random pattern plays over the ceiling.

The station would have been a pleasantly designed structure without the installation, but the artist took it much further by his interpretation. Working with us, he clarified our idea of the train in motion and took it into another realm. In a similar way, Renaissance artists worked with master builders to extend the space and heighten the meaning of the chapels and palaces their work adorned.

# ROY THOMSON HALL

The concert hall is another archetypical building that can benefit from a "rethink." What was once grandly conceived has come to insult our sensitivities for artist and music: huge balcony spaces are unpleasantly impersonal, stressing anonymity, and interior surfaces are too often false plasterwork entirely shaped by acoustical needs and devices into strange, nonarchitectural forms. When not in use, such halls become dumb masses brooding over their surroundings.

In designing a new concert hall for Toronto in 1976, I began by re-examining the classical models. The oldest opera houses with their tiers of boxes and small orchestra floors made the musical experience intimate and immediate. The nineteenth-century houses added the visual delights of painted ceilings and brilliant chandeliers. I wanted to recover those degrees of intimacy and spectacle.

The hall was part of a large office development called Downtown West to be built on railway land just west of Toronto's downtown. Initially I thought of burying the hall in the great complex of offices and shops. With all the space a hall encompasses, including lobbies that extend to the topmost balconies, its structure can become oafishly large.

The hall's board of governors wanted an identifiable building, a symbolic jewel for which they could launch a funding campaign; and it turned out that the rest of the development was not to immediately proceed. Nevertheless, the placement and footprints of its buildings were fixed and dictated that an independent hall's envelope become one side of a large court that they formed. I saw that this small park, protected from outside noise, could be distinguished by its

*Top: The design of Roy Thomson Hall in Toronto began in 1976, and it opened in 1982. Since trolley lines prevented the hall from facing onto the main thoroughfare, an important grand entrance was impossible. Instead, the lights and crowds visible through the glass canopy act to draw in people through two low sets of doors.* TIMOTHY HURSLEY/THE ARKANSAS OFFICE

*Bottom: Roy Thomson Hall was to be part of the 1976 Downtown West development that fixed the footprints of the office buildings. The complex is united by a three-acre music theme park in the centre with the concert hall on 2.5 acres along one end.* FRANK GRANT

*Facing page: The lobby of Roy Thomson Hall is designed to impart a sense of occasion. The structural steel and glass canopy that forms the lobby ceiling is reflected in the mirrored walls, and the stairs curve widely to make inviting promenades.* FIONA SPALDING-SMITH

Left: The acoustical, lighting and mechanical requirements of Roy Thomson Hall are integrated in the ''bicycle wheel'' chandelier with artist Mariette Rousseau-Vermette's fibre tubes which are raised or lowered for reverberation control. Below, acrylic discs direct and distribute sound. The acoustical design was by Theodore J. Schulz. TIMOTHY HURSLEY/THE ARKANSAS OFFICE

Right: The Roy Thomson Hall auditorium was developed over 32 study models, resulting in a shield shape formed by poured concrete slabs, from which the balconies are cantilevered inward. Although it is a large hall, holding 2,812 seats, none is more than 107 feet from the stage. TIMOTHY HURSLEY/THE ARKANSAS OFFICE

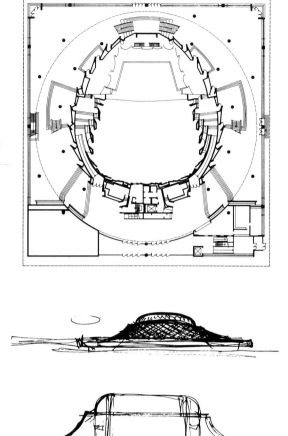

*Top left and right: The lobby level floor plan* (left) *of Roy Thomson Hall shows the space capturing the advantages of both box and circle. The mezzanine level floor plan* (right) *shows the series of "pods" cantilevered from the walls.*

*Middle left: Two early sketches for the hall. Finally a circular, tapered 39,000-square-foot canopy was erected.* COLLECTION CENTRE CANADIEN D'ARCHITECTURE/ CANADIAN CENTRE FOR ARCHITECTURE

*Bottom left: A section of the 20 000-square-metre hall conveys its mass. By designing the auditorium as a hall within a hall, the exterior structure could be devoted to visually reducing its size.*

*Bottom right: A ring beam ties the base of the canopy to the structure of Roy Thomson Hall.* FIONA SPALDING-SMITH

musical orientation. We proposed a tiny lake for its centre with an island bandshell. By putting the stage of the concert hall well below grade, it could be opened to the outside in the summer as an amphitheatre and second musical stage, the steps of which I saw as doubling as a fountain when not in use. Through the music park concept, the concert hall was integrated into and set the "tone" for the whole development. Ultimately, however, Downtown West was cancelled, and the hall may always live in a somewhat stranded state.

Ed Pickering, chairman of the board for the concert hall, gave a felicitous design instruction: "Nature abhors a straight line." Therefore I could concentrate on softer lines for achieving my goal of a low-set massing. Through seemingly endless trials we arrived at an elegant steel mesh that swept from the top of the oval auditorium to a low canopy at street level, squared to the shape of the property. The external roof would be a net of glass, making the hall a crystal pavilion in a garden for music. Such a roof would require thousands of distinctly sized panes of glass. Unfortunately, the Toronto glass industry was unfamiliar with butt glazing such as we had used for Robson Square. This and other problems regrettably priced the idea out of the budget by a million dollars, so we simplified the roof to its present form, retaining the concept though blurring my vision of its sweeping grace and facetted sparkle. Nevertheless, the glass net casts its elegant spell on the interior lobbies that extend around the hall. The balconies exit onto two series of descending landings, the majestic terraced stairs ending with views over the park.

We chose soft grey carpeting to complement the bare concrete, and offset it in the lobbies with mirrored walls and a cream colour for the steel mesh and leather seating. There were some questions about such a neutral colour scheme: what about good old red? During a board meeting, with the men sitting about in their good grey Toronto business suits, I pointed out how it would enhance rather than compete with the richness and glamour of evening gowns. It was a design judgement that the women on the board grasped instantly.

The interior of an auditorium is an acoustical problem that follows its own rules independent of site, and the acoustician is responsible to the client, not to the architect, with whom he is a design equal. To establish the hall's shape, we went through some thirty-two exercises, each with its own model. Our resolution had to provide a degree of intimacy with clear sight lines and acoustical warmth and fidelity. At the same time, I wanted the walls and ceilings to be not only the true structure but also the true acoustical shell. The balconies as well should be pure in their structure. I would have nothing false in this hall. The only configuration that met all these expectations was oval, shaped by a series of standing convex concrete piers. From each of these hung individual balconies that cantilevered inward like petals in an inverted flower. These could be entered separately, effectively dividing the audience into small groups. The closest balcony seat in Boston's famed 2,631-seat Symphony Hall is 104 feet from the stage. Although Roy Thomson Hall provides 2,812 seats, none is farther than 107 feet from the stage.

Above, the ring of walls supports concrete ceiling slabs by means of a steel structure that looks like a bicycle wheel. The slotted spaces between the slabs are used to feed in the fittings for air conditioning, light and — most interestingly — acoustics. I saw here an opportunity to bring the extremely complex requirements of the ceiling together as a work of art, a splendid ceiling like those of the Baroque opera houses. While the bicycle wheel with its rings of catwalks could be an effective chandelier, the need for adjustable acoustical banners called for the craft of an artist. Mariette Rousseau-Vermette, a renowned fibre artist also aware of design in the largest sense, worked with lighting,

acoustical, mechanical and structural engineers in realizing a consummate work of art. Her contribution consists of three rings of tapestries amounting to two thousand tubes of wool hung about a central oculus. The two outer rings retract to give the hall a selection of reverberation times that ensures clarity for early music and fullness for romantic. The tubes range in hue from ivory to concrete grey, interspersed with scarlet, purple and burgundy. As the lighting sparkles from the inner and far outer rings, great portions of the tapestry slowly move out of sight or descend into the hall to signal the next orchestral number. Against a quiet background of unfinished concrete, the hall is thus focussed, given contrast, scale and a heightened dramatic sense.

In 1981, I saw the virtue of height for a hall on the flat Alberta prairie. The Red Deer Arts Centre, a teaching theatre with attached gallery space, had to stand tall and stark in order to withstand the sweep and scale of the landscape and relate to its elemental architectural vocabulary of barns and silos.

*Top: The Red Deer Arts Centre, designed in 1981 and opened in 1986, has the opposite profile of Roy Thomson Hall: it breaks the horizon of the broad prairies of Alberta with the regional language of vertical grain elevators. Although in a northern latitude, the land and sunlight evoke the lightly carved surfaces of Islamic architecture in the slight cornice line, achieved by angling the bricks.* CLYDE S. McCONNELL

*Bottom: Red Deer's skylit lobby contains a 600-seat theatre, teaching spaces and provision for an art gallery. It shares with Roy Thomson Hall a sincerity of structure: interior walls are true to the exterior and the structure itself is clad in a single material — in this case, brick.* CLYDE S. McCONNELL

139

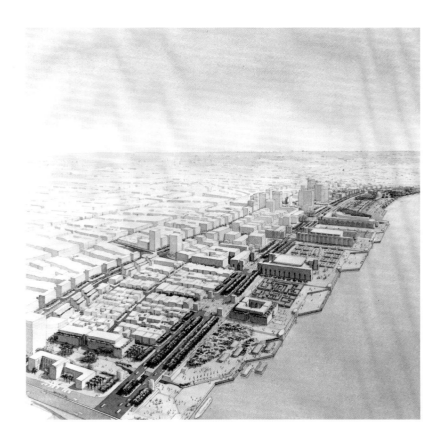

PART IV

# COUNTERPOINT

# COUNTERPOINT

The reasons that a foreign developer or public corporation might have for hiring a North American architect are not the same I might have for responding. The client may be attracted by North American leadership in design or command of modern building techniques. Or he may want some one thing an architect has done, done for him. Published projects become specialty advertisements, and the client in effect might be seeking merely a prosaic, offhand variation on an architect's Western building. For myself on the other hand, while the opportunity to work abroad is undeniably a call to my inherently restless nature (given that foreign commissions are scarce, gruelling to serve and financially extremely risky, how can they be rational business choices?) the deeper appeal lies in the match of creative wits with an utterly different physical and cultural environment. Thus the client often gets more than was bargained for in my determination to be expressive of the context — and original. First in the Middle East and then in China, Japan and Southeast Asia, I have pursued my muse.

In the Middle East, much is projected, much less realized. For all the creative energy I have invested, only a temporary structure and a single tall building have so far seen the bright light of the desert day. Working in this part of the world amplifies the built-in frustration of the design profession wherein so little of what is attempted is actually accomplished. The energy that drives me is my general conviction that I can transform something trifling or mundane into a thing of distinction and meaning. The normal pride of an architect with a small practice begins to appear as hubris in one who challenges the world in all its diversity of climates and cultures. So here in the Arab countries the gods take their revenge, and the sands lay undisturbed. I am left to observe philosophically that in creation there is growth, and even in these distant unbuilt projects there are acts of learning, development and honest assertion of ideas that are part of me.

I first visited the Middle East in 1964, on one of my customary annual ''architectural anthropology'' expeditions. Years later I had an unexpected call from Kuwait about a new university and spent a week there preparing a proposal, only to lose the scheme to a Spanish competitor in the political fallout of the 1973 Middle East war. By this time I was completely intrigued by the stark dry terrain, the impassive sun-drenched walls and the dignity and courtesy of the Arab. So later still, when I was called back by the same Kuwaiti friend to do a housing project, I was more than anxious to try my hand. Opening up a new field of prospects fit well with a business strategy that grew out of my experience with Canada's regional economies: when it was busy in the west, it was slack in the east, and vice versa. The only way I could guarantee a steady flow of sustaining projects was by having an office in each. The Arab states became another support for the practice and served us well, particularly for a time in the early 1980s when the whole of North America was in a recession.

The Middle Eastern cities have had a troubled, complicated history in their progress from appealingly simple agricultural communities or fishing and trading ports to

*Page 140: View from the north of the final scheme for the Abu Nuwas Conservation/Development Project, begun in 1981, in Baghdad, Iraq.* MICHAEL MCCANN

*Page 141: The SANCST Science Halls, designed in 1982, in Riyadh, Saudi Arabia.* SIMON SCOTT

*Facing page: A technical university in central Saudi Arabia gathers its contained desert form under shading, arched water towers.* NELSON PAU/APPLIED PHOTOGRAPHY

sprawling modern metropolises. In most you can see evidence of three succeeding waves of foreign consultants, beginning with the French and British early in this century. As the European hegemony broke up after 1945, Egyptian, Indian and Palestinian architects had their day. The British returned for a brief spell, and then the tidal crash of American skills and values swept all before it to leave its definitive mark.

The nomadic peoples of the Arabian peninsula, with no architectural tradition other than very simple domestic structures, had no clear bridge into twentieth-century architecture. Instead, they found themselves in possession of a hundred bridges, none of them compelling or secure. When I first observed the sorry transitional dilemma, I was ashamed of the way Western expertise had perpetrated such abominations on the ancient, fragile settlements. The Saudis at least have since become wiser in their selection of foreign consultants and have acquired a handful of brilliant buildings for their billions of petrodollars. But from the beginning of my experience there, I believed that Western architects must more sympathetically fulfill the needs and feelings of the local culture. I deplored here as I do in North America the tendency to simply lift from history. Modern building technology requires different responses to climate and customs than mud-brick construction.

All the great monuments of the past have their precedents in the simple vernacular of the village cultures from whose midst they rose. How else could the glazed domes of Iran have evolved, except from the round mud roofs of its villages? How could one perfect further the geometry of a mound of sand than in the pyramid, or glorify the wooden porched shepherd's house except in the Aegean temple? If the vernacular is the basis of the formal language or high style of a particular architecture, it is in turn the fruit of a people's successful solution to the basic problems of shelter through generations of

experimenting. The solution is the product of three variables: the materials at hand and the tools for working those materials, the local climate and the myths and customs that became attached to the original successes.

In attempting to design for an alien context, you must study its vernacular, not to copy or bowdlerize it, but in order to attempt to answer the same practical, aesthetic and cultural needs with fresh, insightful designs based on today's techniques and materials. You take the first of the three variables, materials and techniques, as the point of your departure and work towards an expression of the needs of the latter two, climate and culture.

The difficulties are great and the pitfalls are many. Whether by native confusion or foreign opportunism, in the Middle East the vernacular has either been ignored altogether or been treated as a source to imitate cheaply. The great historic examples of high Islamic style are unworthily vulgarized by hands too heavy to uncover the carefully worked-out truths behind their appearances. Yet the devastation that some have seen as progress and some as inevitable, I began to view as an opportunity.

The Japanese experience was a hopeful example. Japan had made a successful transition from tradition to modernity under the guidance of a few sympathetic European practitioners who had weaned its promising young architects while encouraging loyalty to original values. The result for Japan has been an explosion of creative, vital and unique architecture. In all modesty, I have hoped that in the Middle East, home to a great history of art and architecture, I could contribute to such a transition. I never expected my efforts would lead to changes in my own work.

When I began designing for the Middle East, I immediately became aware of the strength of my predilection for structure and my need to express the bones of a building. The Northwest had confirmed my modernist training, for the mild light of the region called for a bare structure and walls of glass, the better to capture its weak drift. Only in the sunny Mediterranean regions has Western architecture extolled the wall: the inviolate wall of the Romanesque monastaries, the monumental wall of the Renaissance palaces, the sweeping wall of the Baroque churches. But nowhere is the wall more sacrosanct, more subtly modulated, more dedicated to the resources of art than the walls and surfaces that defy the desert. I early realized that here was an obvious aspect of architecture that I had never really explored.

As with Japan, in the Middle East I had to give up a preconceived sense of form and space. Even though early Islamic architecture had built on Roman or Christian antecedents, their dynamic spaces became tranquil and nondirectional in Arab hands. Churches express a hierarchichal approach to God, who exists beyond the limits of the building. But in mosques, the goal is the space itself, making its peristyle prayer hall serene, democratic, nondirectional and nonhierarchical. The undue striving for an axial composition and symmetry were unknown except in Zoroastrian-rooted Iran and Iraq. The exterior is only the featureless defence against the desert and the protector of the privacy of the household.

Architecture begins at the portal, and how you move inside from space to space, so important to the Christian world, is of no consequence, for each space is a static world complete unto itself. Each is an arrangement of rooms around an inner court, a cool refuge from the unremitting desert and, when large enough to contain a garden, a token of paradise. The innermost sanctuary is the harem for women and children, and, historically, it is here that the art of decoration reaches an aesthetic intensity unequalled in the Western world. Nothing rewards the eye like the harem's arabesques, mosaics, patterned carpets and carved surfaces, and the play of light and shadow complemented by the

sound of water and the scent of flowers. It is a feminine, delicate architecture associated with the pleasures of female and family comfort, whereas the harsh, stark world outside is the world of men.

In project after project I struggled to reflect a truer sense of Arab values. I see now the brashness of early projects and their pretentious monumentality, qualities that Arab palaces and public buildings historically avoided in the warrens of their cities. I had to surmount the problem of the wall and the formless exterior in order to get into the interior and let it speak for itself, and such a confidence came only with continued practice. An early attempt was a quickly rendered competition scheme for the Ministry of Public Works and Housing in Riyadh, solicited from us by one of the deputies of the department. It was a light screened structure under a roof shade supported by immense stepped columns recalling the *muqarnas*

*In the Ministry of Public Works and Housing headquarters for Riyadh, Saudi Arabia, the 1977 competition scheme shows the office floors lifted on immense stepped columns to provide shaded public space beneath.* MICHAEL McCANN

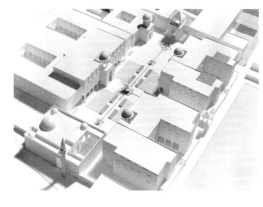

*Top left: The Ministry of Foreign Affairs 1978 interim headquarters building in Jeddah, Saudi Arabia, was intended as a simple building, quickly erected. The teak screen, hung before a glass curtain wall, is an appropriate climatic response and regional architectural reference.* LASZLO LESLIE SOLTER

*Bottom left: A 1983 competition-winning scheme for the Al Falah School in Makkah, Saudi Arabia, groups the students by age in different buildings around a central courtyard. Freestanding pavilions mark the entrances to buildings, several of which have smaller courtyards within. The socially and climatically appropriate courtyard is used to organize the complex into a formal order. Façade articulations — a ground floor arcade, punched windows for the second floor, and a partly screened third floor — refer to the traditional houses of the ancient city.* CHRISTOPHER ERICKSON

*Right: The 1983 Kuwait Insurance Company building was to be one of four inward-facing buildings, each with a corner cut away to create a partially vaulted central space suggestive of the* muqarnas, *the geometric masonry form used in Islamic architecture to support a vault over a square space. The interior is facetted with a suspended structure of mirrored glass.* JOHN FULKER

form of bracket supports for domes, but on a ponderous, exaggerated scale.

Our first real contract in Saudi Arabia was to undertake programming and predesign studies for the Ministry of Foreign Affairs building in the capital. This led to the commission for the design of an interim office building in Jeddah for the same ministry, a hasty but successful job. The ministry put the permanent headquarters building out to an international competition and asked us to be their representative for the competition and project managers for the construction of the winning scheme. The winner, Henning Larsen of Denmark, gave Saudi Arabia one of its most distinguished buildings. If there is such a thing as a professional client who brings out the best in professional services, the Ministry of Foreign Affairs was one.

Throughout our years in the Middle East most of our proposals and commissions were for public institutions. Only a few, like an

apartment-hotel complex in Madinah and the Al Falah School in Makkah, were for private interests; and a few were for corporations, like the Kuwait Insurance Company, and an office tower in Abu Dhabi. But all of these designs remained on paper, at least as far as we were concerned, for we never supervised their construction.

Ironically, where climate and culture least justify the tall building, and after more than a decade of work, an office tower for Etisalat (the Emirates Telecommunications Corporation) in Abu Dhabi promises to become our first major project to be built. It is a building with a constricted site and a single technical purpose that allowed for very little design license. We started out with the huge microwave receiver and ran it up from the ground the number of floors necessary to hold the equipment and the attendant bureaucracy. Naturally, I still tried to distinguish it from similar structures elsewhere and ended up

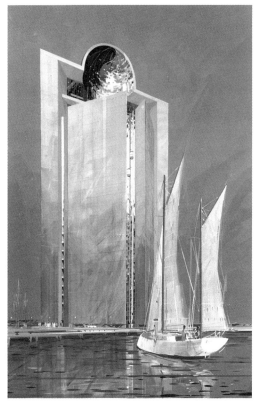

with subtle differentiations that tie it to the Middle East. Its success led to a commission for another one in Dubai.

The demise or indefinite postponement of many of our Middle East projects were due to lack of a funding allocation from a government treasury or the intervention of rival interests or the catastrophe of war. But often the cause was one common to our world as well: the scarcity of human resources, of one or a number of individuals possessing the sophistication and determination to guide the project through the besetting hazards. There are remarkable men in the Middle East, particularly in Saudi Arabia, and our most promising projects were led by them. But in a small population only recently introduced to the modern world, they are rare. It seemed that whenever we were rejoicing in the stewardship of such a person, he was moved away to head some other desperately needy government concern.

*Top left: A regional facility in Dubai for Etisalat, the United Arab Emirates' communications agency, was commissioned in 1986. The generous site is given extensive landscaping.* Dennis Hall

*Top right: A 1975 competition entry for an office tower in Abu Dhabi in the United Arab Emirates. The form is, of course, alien to the region, but extravagance is not: the tower is topped with a mirror-tiled iwan, or apse, while a waterfall streaks down the centre.* Stuart Connally

*Bottom: The 1985 competition-winning scheme for the headquarters building of Etisalat in Abu Dhabi is a 24-storey tower with adjacent parking. The exterior is clad in granite, and green-tinted mirror glass is arranged in a facetted curtain wall. At night, the teflon-coated sphere, housing communication dishes and antennas, becomes an illuminated landmark.* Lenscape

The main differences between the Middle East and Southeast Asia are simple opposites, beginning with climate, the desert versus the rain forest; and predominant way of life, migrant versus settled. The historical architecture of the first is a deceptively bluff vernacular with one strong intent, to shelter against the unrelenting sun. If a foreign architect wishes to graft onto it, he has to make himself aware of its underlying sensitive arrangements and quiet details by an absorptive, almost Zenlike study — an exercise threatened by the clients' very worldly wealth and tastes. The architecture of East Asia begins as a range of well-developed vernaculars on which artists, priests and rulers have erected classical traditions. Here, the foreigner is faced with the more intellectual task of sorting and learning while — in China particularly — the client has to be coaxed from an attitude of renunciation of the past to let architectural richness be revived.

The two cultures meet at the farthest eastern point of significant Moslem influence, the Malay peninsula. It was here that I had first entered the East in 1945, and it was here that we got our first opportunities to work in the region in 1983. At the time, Malaysia was in a boom cycle, and numbers of schemes and dreams were being floated towards realization. Some made it before the next economic downturn, but of our several ventures, only a single condominium project was built, and that without our supervision.

The Moslem influence on local architecture was necessarily decorative rather than structural, for the humid climate required that walls be abolished to let air pass through. On the other hand, the superbly adaptive tribal houses, with their open platforms and high pitched roofs, were also reduced to decorative status in the new era of crowded cities, cars and air conditioning. In our brief consultancy in Malaysia, we applied two salient regional elements, the sensuous

*The 1983 Prince Courts condominium project in Kuala Lumpur, Malaysia, was intended for a Moslem clientele and uses elements, especially in the central courtyard, transposed from Islamic architecture elsewhere. The curved balconies and lush planting are a local touch. Some 555 units are organized around a central pool. Two pavilions that accommodate recreational facilities make an elaborate, needed focus on an otherwise barren site.* Tog Tan

curving form for repeating terraces and balconies, and the lush native plantings. We added a third for one project, the large open courtyard.

In Southeast Asia, the compound with its collection of structures replaced the enclosed courts of the Middle East, but since this suburban Kuala Lumpur multiple-housing project could provide neither private family courts nor bordering jungles, a large courtyard seemed to be a useful feature. We adopted the classical Moghul version and incorporated Islamic forms in the recreational facilities about the pools. The space provided a distinguishing element for a very undistinguished site, as the area around the capital where I had stalked tigers during my army service was now denuded and scarred with housing. The marketing literature for the Prince Courts condominiums in Kuala Lumpur took full advantage of this picturesque, original aspect. We were on to a pertinent idea: it soon turned up in other projects around Kuala Lumpur and Singapore.

Our client for Prince Courts and other condominium projects was Datuk Dr. Chen Lip Keong, who asked us to ''play'' with a house for himself while we were doing his condominium project. The house also was to be in the suburban hills surrounding Kuala Lumpur. Datuk Chen's property straddled a deep draw of tall trees. Following Chinese custom, he wanted his house to look down on the neighbours, and he proposed filling in the canyon to get an adequately high foundation. I elected to preserve the jungle by intruding on it as little as possible, putting everything the house required on concrete caissons holding aloft a series of ''trays'' — seven in all. The Malaysian household customarily keeps family, servant and guest areas quite distinct from each other. What could be more fitting than for each to have its own tray with its own yard and garden, set one above the other, and reached by stairs and elevators concealed in the caissons? The only other structure on the site would be an

arrival platform with a garage. From it a bridge, suspended through the treetops, would reach an entrance foyer. And so on: a grand stairway descends to the main platform, which houses the main reception rooms and a garden with swimming and reflecting pools and pergolas. Lavish tropical plants spill over the edge of the trays and hang into the ravine below. Overhead, family quarters and master suite also have pools spilling over, one into the other. The topmost private keep is crowned by a helipad. The client liked the concept so much that he announced he would find a hilltop to put it on.

It was very well for the honorable Datuk to proclaim his precedence over his suburban neighbours, but with the Canadian Embassy development project in central Tokyo the neighbour was a royal prince. His palace could not even be touched by shadow except very briefly. The grand seigneur of Japanese architects, Kenzo Tange, invited me in 1984

149

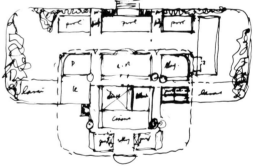

*Top: Datuk Dr. Chen, a Malaysian developer, desired a tall house with views and a commanding presence for his ravine site. A 1984 scheme of seven trays cantilevered off ten giant caissons leaves the forest relatively untouched, achieves the required heights. Of the total area of 60,000 square feet, 25,000 are enclosed.*
CHRISTOPHER ERICKSON

*Bottom: An early sketch of the main entertainment level of the Chen house shows its open planning with shaded lanais, large terrace area, planting and three pools. The next level is noted with a dotted line.*
COLLECTION CENTRE CANADIEN D'ARCHITECTURE/CANADIAN CENTRE FOR ARCHITECTURE

*The 1984 Canadian Embassy redevelopment project in Tokyo was a collaboration with Kenzo Tange. His tower at the site's edge is connected to the sloped, planted chancery by a high lobby that runs the length of the complex. The proposal also includes six townhouses and a recreational building for the embassy staff, designed with reference to the original residence. The chancery roof garden, a sloping plane of maples, visually extends a small public park. Computer modelling was the key to the massing, which by law could cast only minimal shadow on the park as well as the palace grounds across the thoroughfare. OSAMU MURAI*

to participate with him in a Japanese developer competition for the embassy site. It was a rare parcel untouched by the postwar boom. The comfortable Regency-Colonial residence was set back on a drive bordered by its own park on one side and a small public garden on the other. But the demands of the times had caught up with it, and Canada's Department of External Affairs sought a formula for paying for the expansion of the official space by including commercial rental space in the project.

The embassy required more than ten thousand square metres for the chancery section and thirty-five hundred square metres for a residential and recreational component. The amount of rental space that could be squeezed onto the site after meeting the embassy needs would determine the time required to amortize the developer's costs before the property and its income reverted to the Canadian government. Our developer did close legal investigations as

well as a computer sun-shadow study to determine the possible parameters for a revenue-producing office tower and in this way enabled us to go too far — and too confidently, perhaps — in solving the problem for the benefit of the other developers. Tange designed the tower, and I designed the chancery and linking sections as well as a set of townhouses and pool house that fit beside the old residence. We worked together by phone and telefax on matching models to get a cohesive design.

The embassy sat opposite a public garden. I had always been interested in how the Japanese mind separated the realm of nature from that of man, the better to counterpoint them. Plant material had no urban use, unlike European cities, aside from enclosed miniaturized gardens. I thought that using plants in an architectural way would challenge traditional conventions in Tokyo and be a marked demonstration of Canada's presence. By means of stepped planted terraces set into a sloping roof frame, I could give all the offices a pleasant prospect and at the same time figuratively carry the garden up onto the roof for a particular Canadian identity. Maple trees in regular modules emerging from the roof of a building might be noted anywhere, but in Tokyo, they would startle. I could imagine the maple leaf–viewing crowds in autumn.

Japan has become the friend of my youth, distanced by the changes that its wealth has brought. I find its old charms in China now: the rich heritage, the innocence before the West, the lure of the unexplored. My first visit to China coincided with that of Canada's Prime Minister Pierre Trudeau, several months before President Richard Nixon's vaunted opening in 1972. It was a dramatic occasion; an exciting adventure mixed with high ceremony, and an opportunity to discover a new and different architecture that I was not shy about capturing with the help of my heavy Hasselblad camera. By 1979, I was seeing the familiar problems a country has when making the transition to modern building technologies. China was opening to foreign businesses, and I was eager to help find ways to extend the lives of its great architectural traditions into the new era, rather than see them replaced by concrete boxes or some imported language.

Over the years, I was hopefully involved in several development proposals to the Chinese government and competition projects in Hong Kong. We won the most exciting one, a 1987 international competition for the Shanghai Culture and Arts Centre. And later that same year, the Chinese government took the initiative and invited me to make a long tour of provincial tourist cities and survey sites for small hotels. This was the first concrete step in realizing my dream of contributing to a renewed Chinese architecture founded on the local vernacular. At these important destinations, a chain of small facilities — rather like the Spanish government's *posadas* — should offer besides their comfort their attraction as contemporary interpretations of regional architecture. In the northwest, a nod at the cave dwellings; on the north central plains, the pit houses; in the southwest, thatched reeds and wattle or the elegant black-tiled farmhouse roofs of Suzhou. The romance that surrounded a visit to China when she first opened her doors to tourism has long since waned for many Westerners who no longer care to overlook the hardships and monotony of the great Soviet barrack-hotels the Chinese have had to work with. Nor do discriminating travellers relish the sterility of the standardized Western model now being introduced. The purpose of my trip was to select good sites, which often were not the first to be shown. Nevertheless, my hosts were open to the idea and fed my enthusiasm.

A country that so strikingly taps the individual energies of its citizens should recognize the individual beauties of its regional architecture. I lectured students in Beijing, Shanghai and Hangzhou to avoid the formal language of Western architecture as they learned about modern techniques. I told them to also avoid their own great buildings and return to the source, the simple peasant house. There they would find economies and adjustments, values and spaces worked out through time immemorial. Let this knowledge of the old be joined with new materials and tools to give a new direction to architecture in East Asia.

*The 1987 competition-winning scheme for the Shanghai Culture and Arts Centre arranges three performance halls in a row so they can share backstage areas, workshops and support facilities. Audiences enter via wide steps past a park with restaurant pavilions scattered through the landscaped terraces. A hotel stands at one end. Only the halls are enclosed; in order to reduce their mass, lobbies have low glass roofs.*
P & T ARCHITECTS

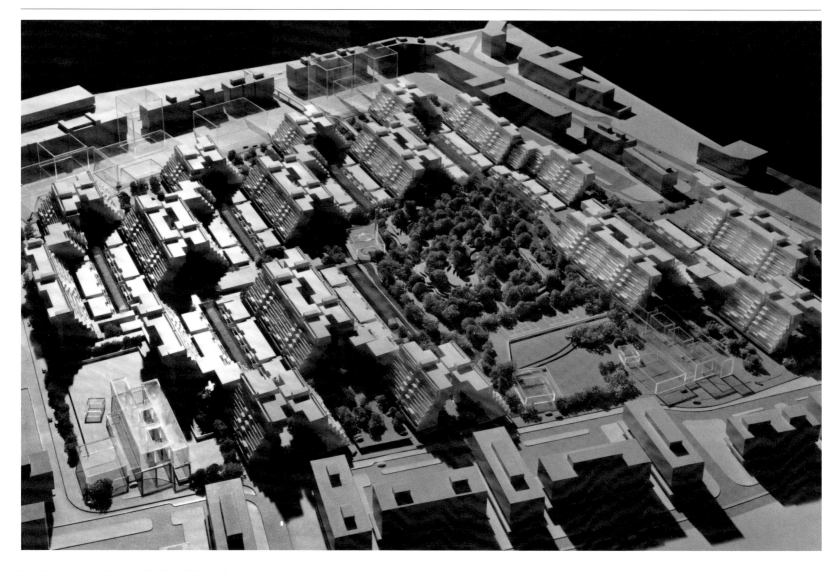

Top: An overview of the model of the 60-acre Sawaber downtown housing development in Kuwait City, Kuwait, designed in 1976. The mounded park, built over a disused cemetery, provides an open space for the entire community and links its common facilities. The buildings are aligned to respond to the climatic factors of sun and prevailing winds. SIMON SCOTT

Bottom: A hotel/residential complex in Madinah, Saudi Arabia, is a modified, 1978 version of the Sawaber prototype but has a simpler form, since the stacked blocks are connected at the top. The plan view shows an irregularly shaped site filled in with planting and trellis-covered parking. A mosque is at the lower left. PANDA ASSOCIATES

# SAWABER HOUSING DEVELOPMENT

The Sawaber Housing Development, on an unusually large sixty-acre downtown parcel, was initiated in 1976 as a political gesture intended to draw back a native Kuwaiti presence to the capital's centre. The government's program called for a luxurious complex to match in multistorey form the pseudo-palaces that private Kuwaiti fortunes had built in the suburbs. It had to overcome the Kuwaitis' natural aversion to apartments, which endangered privacy through overlooking neighbours and the lack of a family courtyard. Our innovation was to treat the nine hundred large units as stacked villas. The stepped profile accommodated traditional enclosed courtyards admitting light and air from above. This unusual configuration, leaning inward as it went up, also provided a completely shaded and naturally ventilated inner street, like a souk, where we had places for the men to sit and talk and for the children to play.

Each structure was designed as a neighbourhood and carefully aligned to counter the harsh effects of the summer sun and sandstorms. They were grouped around an abandoned cemetery developed as an internal open space for the community. Covered walks laced across the property to a new shopping and recreational club common to all. Unfortunately, the government lost sight of its original objective when it put the project out to bid. As a result, only the unique outline was vaguely ours, and no Kuwaiti of means would live there.

The Sawaber project was an important break for us as our first commission in the Middle East and led to even larger urban projects in Kuwait and Baghdad.

Saudi Arabia was the prized client but difficult to obtain for a relatively unknown architect without a corporation behind him. Our first design work there was in 1978, at the holy city of Mohammed's birth, Madinah. Our client was an eminent Iman who wanted a hotel/residential complex. He showed us plans and photos of a piece of property inside the city, which as infidels we could not enter. We simplified and refined our Sawaber prototype for him, incorporating a mosque already on site. The souklike street became a grand lobby and shopping concourse for the hotel and a meeting place and playground for the apartments.

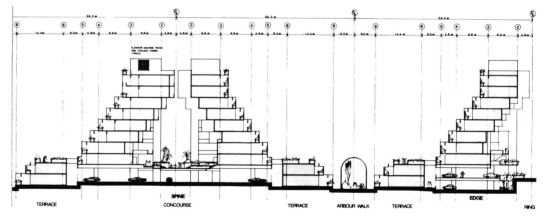

*Top: A perspective of the shaded community space in the paired Sawaber stacked villas shows windows placed for privacy.* RON LOVE

*Middle: Section of the stepped residential blocks of Sawaber: The mass is articulated by pulling out the first two floors as garden townhouses and the top two floors as penthouses.*

*Bottom: An interesting pattern of light and shadow for the Madinah project is created at the ends of the blocks by the articulation of the individual room units.* PANDA ASSOCIATES

# FINTAS TOWN CENTRE

*Top: A 1979 centre for the new town of Fintas, south of Kuwait City, Kuwait, had to accommodate four million square feet of retail and commercial office space, as well as public facilities including clinics, government offices, cinemas and related parking. A section of the air-conditioned mall shows shops around an atrium. On the left is the botanical garden.*

*Bottom: An elevation of Fintas shows, from left to right, the botanical garden, the air-conditioned shopping mall with its evocative gateway office building and fortress-like parking structures, the entertainment complex, a bus station within the bridge structure, and the souk market of the eastern block.*

Fintas, a new town on the coastal corridor south of Kuwait City, was to serve an anticipated 250,000 population. In 1979 we were asked to design its centre. For this assignment we wished to find a twentieth-century equivalent for the walled and towered Arab town, giving it a new relevancy and configuration. The western part of the centre was to be an enclosed, air-conditioned mall, colourful enough to fulfill the need for the primary recreation enjoyed by the Kuwaiti family as a whole — shopping. We wrapped the mall in a wall of parking garages simulating the walled city with its turreted corners. The spiral entry and exit ramps became the portal towers of the main gates.

Following the traditional town layout, we placed four gates at the cardinal compass points, two as facetted, mirrored and screened entrances punched into the base of low-rise office structures, a third giving into a conservatory area surrounded by a hotel, library and a theatre, and the last opening off a bridge across the main motorway to the capital. This bridge linked the western half of the centre with the eastern, more traditional shopping area of the souk. The bus station fit within the bridge structure, and its upper deck was lined with shops and restaurants and provided a clear view to the gulf.

The natural slope of the one-kilometre site was only ten metres. By maintaining a constant level through each half of the centre, we created a dramatic fall where the two halves met. At this point one descended by a series of stepped gardens and water basins, modelled after the gardens of Moghul India, to an open plaza. Here was the Friday mosque, a food market and beyond that the covered souk, cooled by the natural circulation of air. The souk led to civic administration and service buildings at the town's edge. In surrounding blocks we designed the higher density housing, additional offices and a park that used the interesting forms of some abandoned gypsum pits.

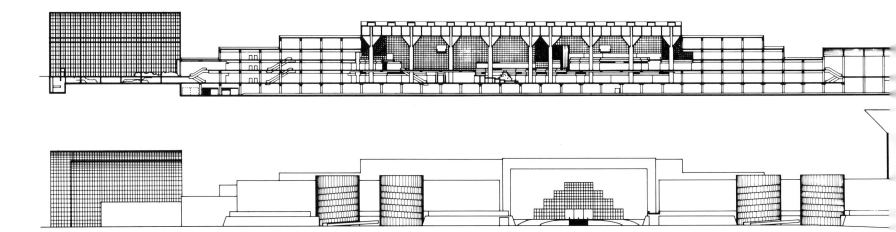

Top: An overall view of the model of Fintas shows the multilevel, Western-style shopping complex flanked by four large parking structures, each for 1,300 cars, with their circular ramps. Additional offices, housing and a regional park are to the right. A traditional market is in the distance. In the foreground, plexiglass volumes of suggested additional buildings for a hotel and cultural centre flank a multivaulted botanical garden. SIMON SCOTT

Bottom: The eastern block of Fintas centre is given over to a traditional souk market of many small shops. The cellular structure of its precast roof encourages natural ventilation. A plaza is flanked by the Friday mosque, a fresh food market on the right, and the gated souk itself. SIMON SCOTT

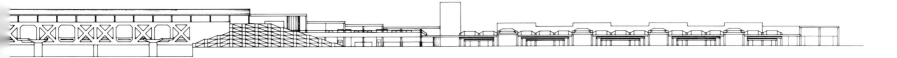

# AN ADMINISTRATIVE HEADQUARTERS

A 1978 administrative ministry headquarters in Riyadh, Saudi Arabia, became a favourite early experiment with desert forms. The two branches of the ministry were housed in the wings with the executive offices in the centre. The building's height was limited by the flight path of a nearby airport, but we gave it a presence by lifting it off the ground on its wings, with offices hanging from them as mirrored glass prisms, and setting its gardens and entrance well below grade. I was inspired by a royal diwan at the head of a garden in Shiraz; it had facetted mirrors in its great vault that scattered the cypresses and pools into myriad reflections. In this case we placed an oasis of date palms that would reflect cooly in the shaded mirrored office cubes. The roof was a stepped concrete shield covering the whole complex. An inner garden, in keeping with Moslem tradition, was sheltered by a pyramid that could take fullest advantage of desert light and shadow through its simple geometry. This winning competition scheme was never built.

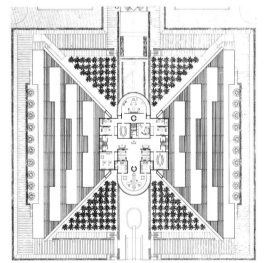

*Left: The floor plan of the administrative headquarters in Riyadh, Saudi Arabia, shows the configuration accommodated within the pyramidal form.*

*Right: The entrance to the administrative headquarters in Riyadh is thickly planted. The hanging rooms are mirrored to enhance the shaded oasis effect. The chief executive's office is in the top juncture. The 225,000-square-foot building is clad in buff-coloured limestone.*
PANDA ASSOCIATES

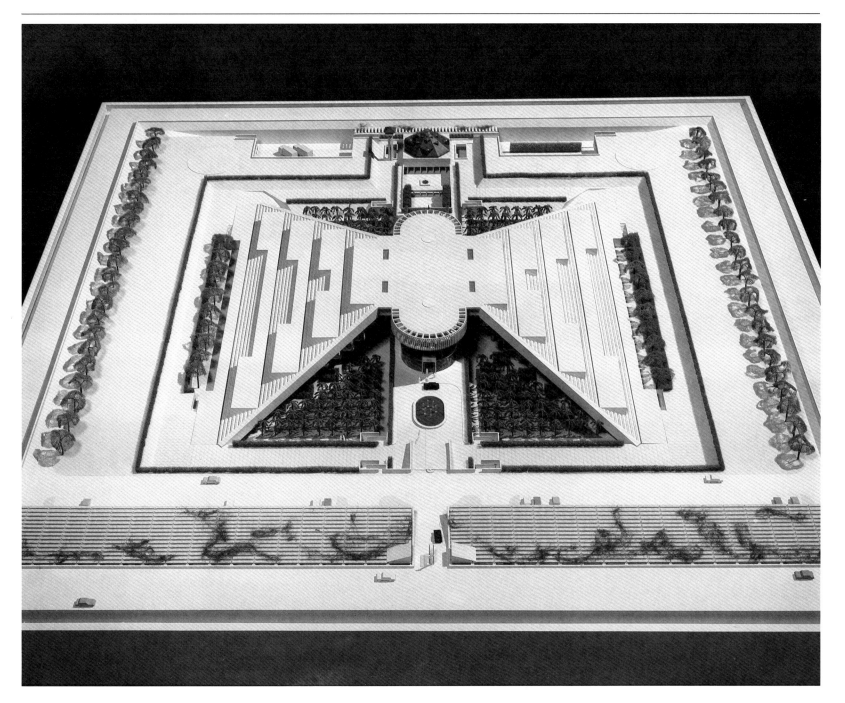

*An aerial view of the administrative headquarters in Riyadh shows the low pyramidal form with two sides cut away to expose the office floors and shelter the entrance and a garden. The office floors add articulation to the solid sides of the pyramid. The building is set almost two storeys below grade in response to a flight path.* PANDA ASSOCIATES

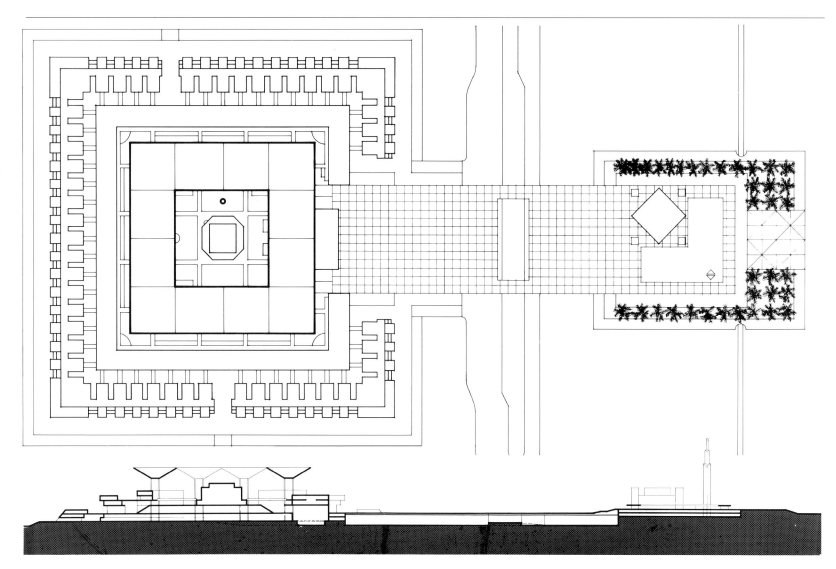

Top and middle: *Floor plan and section of a 1980 technical university near a new town in Saudi Arabia. The plan shows a wide platform leading to a Friday mosque (right). The outer ring of the square contained form (left) is student housing; within is the four-storey academic unit. In the middle of the academic quadrangle is a two-storey central quadrangle of support facilities such as the library. The early section shows water towers as a protective device over the central plaza and the Friday mosque (right).*

Bottom: *A flat shading structure replaced the water towers in the final scheme for the technical university. A view of the entrance shows the low base with limited openings.* NELSON PAU/APPLIED PHOTOGRAPHY

# A TECHNICAL UNIVERSITY

Our most distinctive solution for a desert settlement was presented for a technical university near a new town in the centre of Saudi Arabia in 1980. We simply gave it the historic compact form that the severe climate had always dictated: buildings that shaded each other and the pedestrian, and walls that defied the wind and drifting sand. As in many of our desert projects, the site offered little inspiration and functional requirements became the primary factor in giving us the design.

The campus had to accommodate a complete community for fifteen hundred students and three hundred faculty. We clustered the school's common facilities such as dining hall, library and mosque on the central uppermost plaza under the shading structures of water towers. Beneath the plaza, we put the parking, bus stop and service areas. Around this central elevated platform was a lower academic street of classrooms with offices above. Around this in turn was another street for dormitories; lower yet, but still raised slightly from the desert floor to collect the breezes.

Each residential block looked into side courts, which were shaded by concrete screens and heavily planted. The corner blocks were club facilities, and the street provided for casual recreation under bordering trees. Bridges crossed the street to tie it into lounges and the ring of lecture halls. Beneath these were the heavy laboratories serviced from the underground system. Across from the main entrance and bus stop was the sports complex that formed a tongue connecting into the nearby town, whose residents would share it. The whole college,

finished in sand-coloured concrete, would look like an enormous stepped pyramid, deceptively simple yet extremely complex, with the economy of a desert plant form and the compactness of a local village.

At the junction of the college with the town was a Friday mosque for townspeople and students alike. Its inspiration came from the very beautiful ninth-century mosque at Kairouan in Tunisia, which is a many-columned hall with an egalitarian, horizontal prayer hall surrounded by heavily buttressed walls. Constructed entirely of precast concrete, the new mosque would have a structural system of precast vaults with windows of prefabricated concrete screening inset with coloured glass, reminiscent of the carved plaster windows of traditional mosques.

*The Friday mosque of the technical university has a multicolumned hall made of modular arch elements after a ninth-century model.* NELSON PAU/APPLIED PHOTOGRAPHY

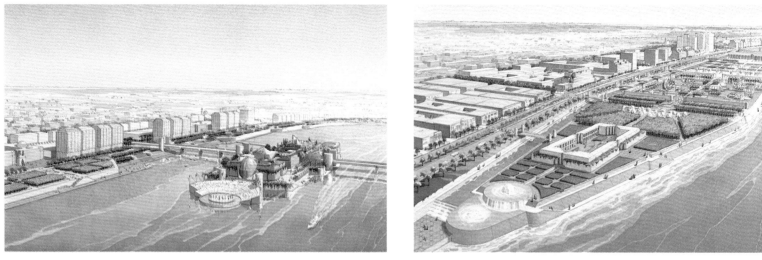

# THE ABU NUWAS PROJECT

The Abu Nuwas district of Baghdad lies just south of the centre of town and across the Tigris River from the presidential palace. Built up in the nineteenth century, the district is popular as a recreation area and renowned for the barbecued fish of its lively restaurants.

Abu Nuwas is named for a celebrated poet of pleasure who lived during the Abassid period, Baghdad's years of glory. Now it was run down, and the Iraqi government wished to revive it. Our 1981 commission was to do a master plan and overall urban design scheme for a three-kilometre section on the banks of the Tigris River that extended into Baghdad's main concourse. We developed two different concepts to focus discussion by a distinguished international panel.

One concept set an island in the river, and the other created a water garden on riverfront landfill. The island was midriver of a new bridge that had already been proposed by the government. There would be a science museum and aquarium inside the island while the outside would be a fanciful terraced Arabian *isola bella* given over to the display of Arabic scientific devices related to natural phenomena: water wheels, windmills, observatories and clocks. Our renderer, Michael McCann, gave it a delightful storybook look.

The water garden scheme was bolder, after President Saddam Hussein's suggestion to follow the eighth-century example of Caliph Al Mansour, the founder of modern Baghdad. In a tumultuous time for his country, the president wished to remind the citizens of their golden age. I needed little encouragement and grandly proposed to re-

*Facing page, top: The 1981 Abu Nuwas Conservation/ Development project in Baghdad, Iraq, required two preliminary schemes. A third, final scheme combines elements of the alternatives. It retains an island form and gives prominence to Abu Nuwas Street as the organizing axis. A series of cultural facilities includes an amphitheatre with smaller theatres enclosed in its shell.* MICHAEL McCANN

*Facing page, bottom left: In the first scheme, a proposed bridge across the Tigris River between the Abu Nuwas district and the presidential palace would serve a new island. A museum on the island would include outdoor installations similar to those of the astronomical garden of the Rajah of Jaipur — an idea later applied in the SANCST Science Halls gardens.* MICHAEL McCANN

*Facing page, bottom right: The second scheme for Abu Nuwas develops and extends the riverfront, bringing water back to its original banks with a canal. The water garden scheme offers a series of cultural buildings that grandly invoke Baghdad's golden age. A Tivoli-like pleasure garden occupies the middle distance.* MICHAEL McCANN

*This page: The model of the final Abu Nuwas scheme includes urban planning for the district. The gated court treatment of Abu Nuwas Street makes it a processional boulevard and gives the cultural facilities a complementary commercial space within the urban fabric. The facilities include a history museum, the National Library, a performing arts complex, the Science Discovery complex, an art school and theme gardens (pleasure, scented, maze and bird sanctuary).* SIMON SCOTT

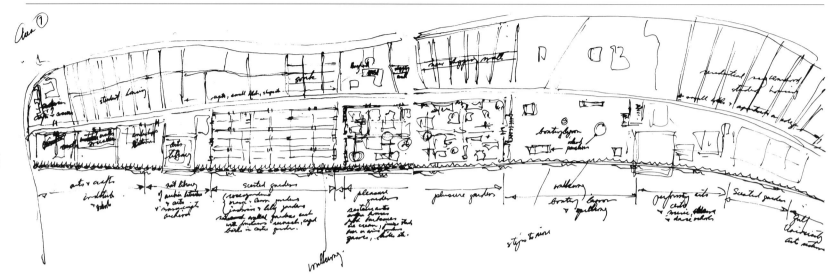

*Top: A sketch of the Abu Nuwas water garden plan, covering 2.5 kilometres of the Tigris riverfront, is remarkably detailed. From the left are the Arts and Crafts school, the National Library, separate water garden enclosures, a boating lagoon with island pavilions, a performing arts centre and gardens.*

*Bottom left: A sketch of the moated, walled Abu Nuwas pleasure garden; a grid of walkways and platforms support restaurants, rides and fantasy structures, with trees at the intersections. Food and game stalls line the wall.*

*Bottom right: The formal scented garden plays on geometry in the Islamic fashion: larger rectangles subdivided into smaller ones. Viewing platforms punctuate the riverside. The centre is a treed garden with aviaries. The scents are specified: roses, oranges, lemons, jasmine and lilies.*

*Facing page, top: The development of the riverfront district was part of the Abu Nuwas commission. The island scheme laid out a radical intrusion on an axis of bridge and island and assumed the government's desire for large new blocks of apartments. On the left is a nineteenth-century district of courtyard houses to be preserved.*

*Facing page, bottom: The final scheme provided for widening Abu Nuwas Street and was mandated to intrude one block further from the river. The pattern of streets and blocks is rationalized; at the edge of the area (right), single-family housing is replaced with multiple-housing buildings.*

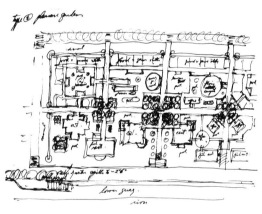

turn part of the river to its old banks at Abu Nuwas Street, let it flow through a series of walled gardens to a boating lake and then back into the river. The water gardens would express Abu Nuwas's own poetic joys, with the scent of flowers, the sounds of birds and water and the food served in pavilions. Museums, archives and theatres would be scattered through the district. Behind the gardens, the existing Abu Nuwas district was to be preserved and consolidated with added squares, gates and arcades typical of a classical Arab town.

When President Hussein and the panel met to consider our proposals, the storm of war was already breaking, and our presentation was made in the pit of the National Assembly Hall in a wild, tense atmosphere. One of the panelists, the Indian architect Charles Correa, told me he would never forget how I described the wonderful paradisiacal gardens while above and about us stood ranks of soldiers with machine guns. Neither will I. Nevertheless, our client ultimately instructed us to attach the island element to the water gardens for a final scheme — and then the awful demands of war consumed the government. This magic carpet is now stored for better times.

*Top: The broad avenue behind the gate of the Hamma Government Complex is flanked by the Assemblée Nationale on the left and the Palais des Congrès on the right. Each has an elaborate roof garden and a distinctive, patterned roof form — one in gold, one in silver — for its major hall. Ceremonial entrances to each building are marked by small pavilions.* DEREK GRIFFITHS

*Bottom: The 1984 Hamma Government Complex in Algiers provides a monumental group of government buildings as the termination of an important axis of the capital. The 25-acre complex is entered through a massive gateway building that accommodates lodgings for the deputies of the Assemblée Populaire Nationale. The gate, assisted by patterning, is an interpretation of a North African form. Through the gate can be seen a pavilion and a pair of pylons that serve to accentuate the progression of the axis.* DEREK GRIFFITHS

*Facing page, top: A rendering of the Hamma Government Complex: a slightly modified 12-storey gate now has tapered residential wings that accentuate its height. The view along the axis passes the Palais des Congrès on the left and the Assemblée Nationale on the right, then leads through the grand square between a hotel and the National Library to connect with the botanical garden beyond.* MICHAEL MCCANN

*Facing page, bottom: The elevation of the Hamma Government Complex's Assemblée Nationale building along the central axis. The top floor is expressed as a solid cap with punched windows supported by two-storey columns. Behind the colonnade is a smaller scale single-storey colonnade. Entrances are marked by pavilions. The facing Palais des Congrès would closely match it.*

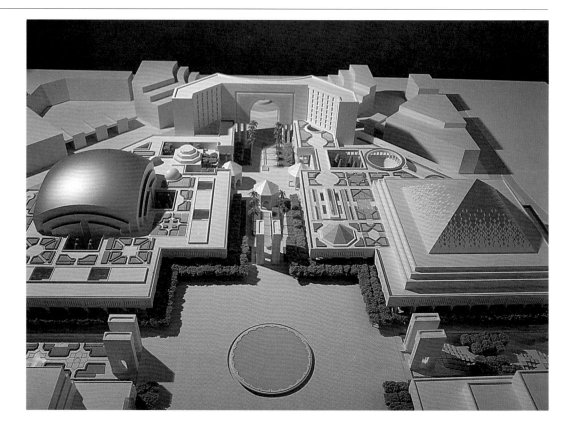

# HAMMA GOVERNMENT COMPLEX

In the capital of Algeria, we found the architectural context to be a charming and comfortable combination of Arabic and French intentions. The colonial vision for Algiers followed that of Baron Haussmann's for Paris, and the city still reveals next to its Arabic images the beginnings of wide formal avenues, *étoiles* and *carrefours*. These formal elements are taken to their conclusion in our 1984 design for the completion of the Algerian capital.

The site for the Hamma Government Complex was directly beneath the hilltop Martyrs' Monument and adjacent to a large park. The project included new buildings for the Assemblée Populaire Nationale and the Palais des Congrès, a grand square, the National Library and a hotel, the last two to be designed by others. Our task was to consolidate this rather amorphous complex and give it an appropriate dignity. On the étoile at the base of the site, we proposed an Islamic triumphal arch containing housing for deputies of the Assemblée. The arch opened to a wide avenue between the Assemblée and the Congrès which led to the main square beneath the monument. Four monumental gateways at the compass points defined the entrances to the square, and all the components open onto it. All gates, porticoes, pavilion and roof forms were to be of Arabic character. The avenues dropping down from the square would be bordered by formal parterres and water channels typical of caliphate times. Islamicized gallic urbanism would be an appropriate architectural style to symbolize victory over a colonial past.

Our happiness at winning did not last long. Other than getting a photograph of the Algerian president with our model, we heard no more. At last report, the Algerians had introduced major changes, Bulgarians were promising to execute the working drawings on the cheap, and Chinese were going to construct it.

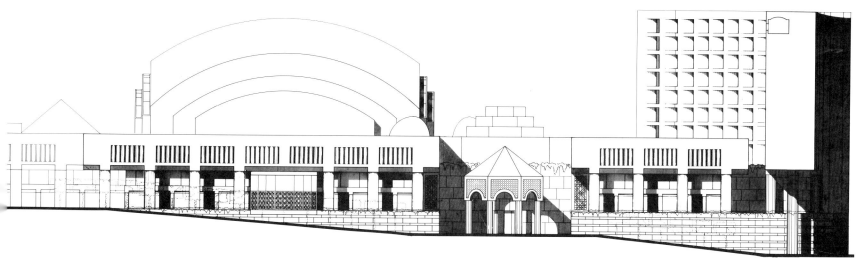

# TWO UNIVERSITIES

*Top: The residential communities of King Abdulaziz University in Jeddah, Saudi Arabia, are laid out according to traditional settlement patterns in response to both cultural and climatic factors. Mosques and the narrow, turning pedestrian streets, providing shade and short vistas, are the local orientation points. The whole form reads as a historic accretion, like many Middle Eastern cities. Design began in 1980.* LENSCAPE

*Bottom: The second, 1987 master plan of King Abdulaziz University: the academic buildings are arranged along an arcaded pedestrian street. The central facilities, including library and mosque, are at an angle to the academic core. The central, planted square picks up the two axes in a geometric play. The university will contain 17,000 students, 2,000 faculty and 5,800 support staff.*

By the early 1980s we were well enough known to successfully contract for the design of two universities in Saudi Arabia. They promised to be so vast and complex that we formed a different consortium of architects, planners and engineers to handle each of them. My design philosophy was entirely sympathetic with these new projects, for both the mediaeval college on which I had based my Canadian universities and the traditional Islamic *madrasa* — an institution that predated Europe's universities — were communities where students lived and learned with their teachers. The madrasa was physically indistinguishable from the fabric of the surrounding city, so that daily life surged below the windows of the classroom, testing and adding to the education of students.

For our first master plan for King Abdulaziz University at Jeddah, begun in 1980, we interspersed the academic facilities with the residential compounds and patterned the university organization on the Arab city as much as possible. Narrow streets with continually changing vistas combined with squares to provide the overall structure. Within each faculty there was to be a similar pattern of streets and courts on a smaller

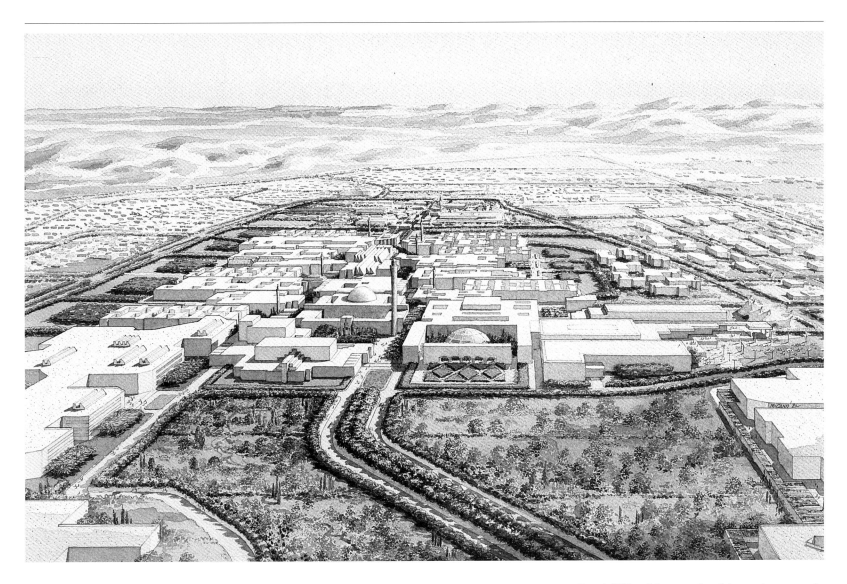

Top: A 1982 aerial perspective of the men's campus of King Abdulaziz University shows the central section of the 650-acre site. The women have their own campus. The main entrance to the men's campus leads to the spine of the main facilities, including the main mosque and central library. On either side of the spine are the buildings for the different academic disciplines. Housing is on the other side of the service road. All the academic buildings look inward around courts, with major entrances on primary pedestrian routes.
MICHAEL McCANN

Bottom: A model of the men's campus of King Abdulaziz University, seen from the opposite perspective of the rendering, shows the connection of the academic core with the housing on the right. LENSCAPE

Top: The single-student residences of the Islamic University of Madinah in Saudi Arabia are organized in clusters around courts, with small central courts in the buildings. Each cluster houses 2,000 students in four-storey blocks. Nine-person dwelling units are served by facilities on the ground floor. The semicircular structures of the stairs are organizing elements. LENSCAPE

Bottom: Design of the Islamic University began in 1983. The 1985 master plan incorporates existing buildings already on the 300-acre site and establishes a new order through the use of a strong central arcade with gates marking the faculty buildings. From the right, the entrance leads to an arrival court. Beyond is the academic core organized around a Friday mosque with another planted court. Clustered single-student housing is adjacent to the core. Beyond are sports facilities, married-student and faculty housing, and commercial districts. LENSCAPE

scale; the dormitory block was likewise organized. The identity of each faculty and dormitory was marked by definitive gates opening off the streets and squares, as in an Arab town. We followed architect Hassan Fathy's principle of "interiority," which puts emphasis on interior space — the opposite of outward-looking occidental buildings.

A new university president requested a new look at the master plan and put the dormitories in a separate village outside the academic campus. Meanwhile, temporary buildings kept springing up and the administration developed a strategy for turning the present temporary campus into a women's university and phasing the men into a new complex quite apart. The new plan to meet this strategy is a major departure from our original concept, and the fourth in the history of the university.

We were asked in 1983 to supply an overall scheme for the Islamic University of Madinah, a small religious school on an extant campus. It is littered with temporary buildings, which keep increasing in number and aspect of permanence the longer that new construction is delayed. With the jerry-built presence accepted for at least the early phases of development, a powerful free-standing shaded arcade was used to diminish its importance as much as to define the new hierarchy of squares and gates that act as the spatial grammar of the campus. We somehow carved out the major spaces that link like disciplines and used the new dormitories as major building blocks encompassing the academic heart. The new, sympathetic Arabic form was to lift the college from ignominy to some architectural distinction, but as years passed and key people changed, the ambition and ability to commit to a massive, permanent construction program have slipped away.

Top: The main arrival court of the Islamic University of Madinah with fountains and gardens is a forecourt of the main mosque, befitting the religious nature of the institution, which will ultimately serve 7,600 students and their families. The unifying motif of the arcade with gate pavilions marking entrances begins here and is repeated behind the mosque. MICHAEL MCCANN

Bottom: One of Islamic University's three faculty courts. The whole campus is organized around a hierarchy of courts. Academic buildings are grouped around the faculty courts, which are linked to the main mosque court by gateways. The buildings themselves have interior courts. MICHAEL MCCANN

# SANCST SCIENCE HALLS

A public science and technology education and awareness centre for the Saudi Arabian National Centre for Science and Technology (SANCST) in 1982 turned out to be one of the most interesting Mideast projects to go through my office, as well as the one that reached the furthest stages of design. SANCST wanted a demonstration centre of science as seen through the Moslem eye. Arabs were the progenitors of modern science, for they preserved and augmented the early Greek achievements during Europe's Dark Ages when these would have been lost to us. The Moslem view, however, differs philosophically from the conventional Western view. It sees the world as a unity, whereas our science concentrates on many fragmented categories of matter and knowledge. The SANCST Science Halls complex is about interdependencies and relationships within a unified whole.

Appreciating the sophistication of the client, we took the opportunity to propose a very different program and planning process. This is usually a fairly tedious exercise of sorting out the client's requirements for the building. I wished to substitute instead my customary method of asking enough questions so that the program and plan would emerge on their own. Science is so complex that I had no idea where to begin. The philosophy and history of Moslem science is one subject; the present body of scientific knowledge another; the best pedagogy yet another. Once the client accepted our questing stance, we initiated it with a seminar involving several extraordinary philosophers of science from the Middle East and America. We had several days of rarified

and stimulating discussions about concepts of art and science and their philosophical bases. Then we organized a tour of the world's significant science centres, from Barcelona to Toronto to San Francisco and on to Singapore.

The SANCST Science Halls has two objectives; besides expressing the Moslem perspective on science, it will make science accessible and available to different levels of innocence and learning, from the Bedouin to the graduate student. Our deliberations led us to propose a many-layered technique for exhibits. Visitors will descend through a spiral souklike street where ''demonstra-

*A view of the entrance of the 1982 SANCST Science Halls in Riyadh, Saudi Arabia, from the semicircular arrival court: the freestanding pavilion and the water channel are historical forms. The entrance is flanked by the domed theatre/planetarium and the Imax auditorium.* SIMON SCOTT

*Facing page: An aerial plan of the roof and site of the Science Halls shows, counterclockwise: main entrance at lower left, formal gardens at lower right, amphitheatre, wadi (or riverbed) garden of traditional irrigation methods, and, at top, medicinal herb gardens. The roof pattern clearly shows the traditional rotated square geometry and spiral pattern of the main circulation within. The roof between the central court and two main theatres is an interpretation of one used on Arab baths.* SIMON SCOTT

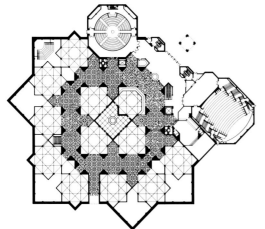

tors'' in the manner of the old market story-tellers will expound an elementary picture of science. By conscientiously adopting the oral tradition of learning, rather than the visual methods that Westerners are accustomed to expect in museums, we tailored the SANCST facility to the local culture. More sophisticated visitors will penetrate to further layers, where theatres, hands-on demonstration laboratories and displays present a deeper and more detailed level of information.

The building forms will be familiar to the Saudi, with inner courtyards and light wells capped by traditional, hooded wind-catcher forms that modulate the strong sunlight. The so-called souk street of storytellers will have many areas opening off it as it spirals down. The spiral itself reflects the unifying principle of the Islamic tree of knowledge, while the plan and the individual spaces are based on Islamic geometry. The atmosphere throughout will be contained and intimate. Imitating the striations of the rocks of the desert wadis into which it is set, the walls of the museum express the blind protective mass of a desert fortress. Other than the angular wandering of the walls to catch the changing sun and shadows, only the articulated roofscape and the entrance gallery give it a distinctive presence. The scheme was presented in 1983 and awaits fulfillment.

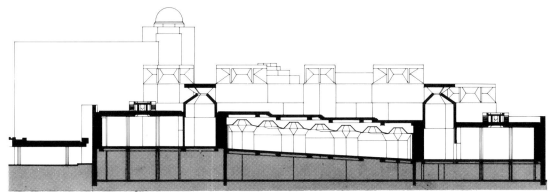

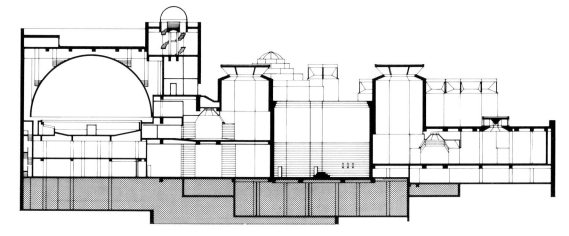

Top spread: Striated Riyadh limestone is used for the exterior cladding of the Science Halls, with varied banding depths to provide shallow relief and texture. A shaded pedestrian bridge links to the administration building of the National Centre for Science and Technology at right. SIMON SCOTT

Facing page, bottom: Plan of the main exhibit area of the Science Halls: the paving marks the spiral main circulation route (the souk street), leading down past thematic areas. In the five points are theatres. Most of the 85,000 square feet of public space is on this level.

Left: Two sections of the Science Halls. In the first (top) the souk street is indicatd by its slope and multiple vaults. It is flanked by demonstration areas under the windcatchers and laboratories at either end. The wind-catcher forms are actually skylights. The second one (bottom) shows the domed theatre (left) topped by the observatory and support space below.

PART V

# REGENERATION

# REGENERATION

A vital design is beyond style. It should be as unrepeatable and unique as the time and place of its emergence. It should embody an intrinsic idea that has been clarified through relentless probing. The process should move without prejudice. I could not be limited by a personal repertoire from engaging the Edwardian era with a pool house for an old Vancouver mansion, or providing — at the same time and less than a quarter of a mile away — a permanent backdrop for evanescent fashion in a hair salon. Much of the process consists of long observation and continuous testing of a massing model until suddenly there is a fit. But an idea can erupt with a force that overturns weeks of work on a concept abruptly made ordinary. Such inspiration has always made me trust the subconscious more than conscious thought. Not that the creative subconscious is an underground lake of still, captured water: in practice it is like a river that flows unseen below the desert floor. And so the obvious answers, the perfect solutions, drawn from quietly shifting waters, do change over the years.

One natural source of inspiration for me is the great architecture and simple vernacular that I seek out in my travels. However, such buildings often take years to absorb; at first sight they are too powerful, and the conscious mind too overwhelmed to dismantle and examine the elements that make them so. Their images take time to sink in before they can flow freely within the subconscious. Then they may appear unexpectedly as I walk onto a site or develop a space or cast about for a detail; only later will I realize where they came from. In the 1950s, I had

Page 174: The 1983 Puget Sound house on a rural acreage in Washington State has a copper-clad steeple over its entrance and a barrel-vaulted roof over its dining room. WAYNE FUJII

Page 175: A perspective of the 1980 California Plaza competition scheme looks towards the Los Angeles core: a 400-room hotel, three residential blocks, the Performance Plaza and two office towers. MICHAEL MCCANN

Facing page: The Canadian Chancery in Washington, D.C., was commissioned in 1983 and opened in 1988. TIMOTHY HURSLEY/THE ARKANSAS OFFICE

Top: The Hollies, the Edwardian-era Keevil mansion in Vancouver, began extensive renovation in 1983, including the addition of a pool house in the manner of a conservatory. The white-painted steel and glass structure is not a replica in detail; instead its style conveys a compatible spirit. RAYMOND LUM

Bottom: Suki's, a hair salon in Vancouver designed in 1986, has exposed concrete walls contrasting with high-gloss cream and black fixtures and a facetted glass façade. A similar vertical glass form will mark the entrance of the Dance Gallery in California Plaza. The angular stairwell to the left leads to a beauty college on the basement level. SIMON SCOTT

*The small, two-storey Erickson office building in Los Angeles had the immediate appeal of an entry courtyard with large shading podacarpus trees. In the 1981 remodelling, the façade was given a play of textures: raked concrete under glass panels, broken by a glass-block window.* MARVIN RAND

Europe to absorb, until in 1963 I poured much of it into Simon Fraser University — though its many impressions remain with me still. In the 1960s, Japan and East Asia acted as contradicting challenges that put me more on my own resources, so that in the 1970s, the confidence of my eye and a devotion to context dominated the source. But meanwhile, Islamic architecture was feeding the stream. Although post-and-beam architecture, the basis of our classical buildings, is an endlessly fertile medium, I felt the narrow climatic and cultural basis of my loyalty to it and grew restless, finally bringing home the interpretive experience of the Middle East in 1983, when I worked on Canada's chancery in Washington, D.C. For the massive wall facing Pennsylvania Avenue, I played with subtle, light-catching indentations and protrusions almost accidentally dispersed on the surface. The fine grillwork on the cornice was suggested by the Arab parapet more than the neoclassical Washington model.

The timing was right for change. With the California Plaza contract award in 1980, we had opened an office in Los Angeles. Here the possiblities of the wall could be explored through the context of California's Spanish architecture, which itself has Arabic origins.

From the beginning, Los Angeles was the equal of our Toronto and Vancouver offices, for an American base offered two solid advantages. First, it could fight the dim ghost that shadows wide recognition of any American professional — South or North — who is not a resident of the United States. As Philip Johnson frankly stated to Edith Iglauer for her 1979 *New Yorker* profile of me: "It's a question of acceptance. . . . Erickson's a Western architect and what's worse, he's in British Columbia, which is a province of a province to us." Second, acceptance in the American metropolis brought a potentially larger range of opportunities. Canadian projects seemed to be shrinking in size and number. Los Angeles — although still in the west — was a promising base for a strategic move into a far wider field. As it turned out, with the rules of the game shifting, it was not that easy in the United States.

The move coincided with the stimulating but risky explosion of architectural vocabulary brought about by Postmodernism. Suddenly the beaux arts was back in play, and the questions changed from functional to stylistic. Although my basic drive for cogency through clarification and simplification remained constant, I too was ready to test new directions.

While I was raising the flag in southern California, I suffered a historic defeat within my own Pacific Northwest. Ordinarily the loss of a competition produces only momentary dismay, but when we lost the Portland Municipal Services Building competition early in 1980, dismay was tinged with disbelief. Every day, good architecture is defeated by bad — but I was shocked by Princeton professor Michael Graves's winning scheme. It was not a matter of taste nor of an expensive prank being played. Graves was nothing if not serious about what he was doing, and brilliant at it. He was assaulting the aesthetic canons of the age. I had been defeated by someone who wanted to consign postwar architecture to some ''dustbin of history.'' Architectural movements are not launched into public currency by theoretical tracts or small buildings. Only a large building like the Portland Municipal Services Building can do the job. It was Michael Graves's first major work, and more than Philip Johnson's own famous AT&T building, it marked the arrival of Postmodernism.

There were two problems for an architect to consider with the Portland building. First, the budget was very limited — a fact that in the end badly affected Graves's bravura performance. Second, the building would have a certain bulk owing to its need for large office spaces. In our proposal we relegated the main mass to the upper storey, stepping it out for sculptural interest. Through its base, we made a kind of Burlington Arcade of small shops. The London original is still lively, and I believed that it would translate well to Portland, with its similar rainy climate. The arcade led out onto a grand portico overlooking the city's central park. We offered two versions for the overhanging secretariat: one of reflective glass to diminish its size, and one of precast concrete with punched windows that conformed with the adjacent public buildings. Since I was working in a familiar Pacific Northwest context, I placed a broad basin of water in front to reflect light into the portico. Having acceded the force of its originality, I would criticize Graves's building mainly for being oblivious to the crucial contextual factor of light. The exterior is painted with strong colours, including an oppressive dark green at the base. As a general rule, deep hues on buildings in the Northwest absorb the weak light without return, an effect that is downright depressing. But then, a rigorous theoretician can ignore local perception as mere opinion.

Philosophically, I found Postmodernism easy to shake off. In claiming to take up again an agenda that had been set aside after 1945 by Modernism, Postmodernism was casting us back into a world of eclecticism, which itself reflected a sad cultural insecurity in the infant North American civilization. The best design of the continent has from the beginning been utilitarian, with a beauty that comes from a purity of line and form and an honest respect for materials. It builds on that treasured American value, ''common sense,'' to give us down-to-earth solutions such as those archetypically rendered in their furnishings and homes by the Shakers. The historically opposing stream in North American architecture, nostalgic eclecticism — skyscrapers as Gothic cathedrals, houses as French chateaux or classical temples — is always a defeat of the potential of the vernacular for expressing better the sensibilities of culture, the beauties of place and the strength of native ingenuity. Modernism had

*Located between the historic city hall and county courthouse, the 1979 competition scheme for the Portland Municipal Services Building recognizes their importance by setbacks and public spaces, allowing them their contribution to a key and symbolic downtown site in the Oregon city. The bulky office spaces are lifted up to provide extensive public space around the base. A shopping arcade encourages traffic between the plaza and a transportation stop.* ALAN HICKS

Facing page, left: The four-block mixed-use Harbor Steps development for Seattle, Washington, began design in 1980. It features a 22-storey condominium tower and an 8-storey luxury hotel. SIMON SCOTT

Facing page, top right: Creating a public focus between downtown Seattle and its waterfront, Harbor Steps offers a wide stairway set with fountains and formal planting reminiscent of Baroque stairs. MARIBETH EDMONDSON

Facing page, bottom right: The Winter Garden hotel-office complex, a 1985 developer proposal for Anchorage, Alaska, consists of two 16-storey wall-like buildings, one a 440-room hotel, the other offices, placed to allow views and light to enter between them. A glass roof connects them to create a winter garden. DARYL PLATER

connected with that pragmatic sensibility. In this way Modernism addressed the present; thus, philosophically and by method, it embraced the future. One hundred years ago, the new age of iron and steel construction saw the Victorian architect fiddling with mediaeval decoration while the definitive, progressive work was being done by engineers. Given our own dynamic developments in applied science and computer technology, the postmodernists' preoccupation with recondite style seemed like a similar retreat.

Personally, the postmodernist din was less easy to ignore. The press loved it, and with its undeniable flash it took over the world with all the speed and ubiquity of a hemline change. In the hands of a master or acting as a release for new talent, artistic rebellion can always turn up innovative and exceptional work. But the effect of Postmodernism was to turn up work of an alarming banality by lesser practitioners.

In practice, when context made it pertinent to do so, the new eclecticism freed me to render more literally the classical canons that I had loved since 1950. In fact my design for the Portland building reveals a discreet awareness of the coming shift. The punched window solution does indeed draw from the neighbouring buildings, but it also shows an awareness of the one most visible feature of the new historical literalism. The arcade, of course, is an unadulterated reference to a historical precedent.

A sister city and a similar treatment, also modelled in 1980, was a downtown development in Seattle called Harbor Steps. In the last century, Seattle's harbour was lined with a high bluff, and while sluicing and filling have levelled much, the Harbor Steps site and the adjacent lively old Public Market still perch on sharp slopes that drop some sixty feet to the waterfront. During the early 1970s activist groups had fought to save the market and restore the 1890 buildings of Pioneer Square, several blocks farther south.

Now their attitude had captured the establishment, and the intervening waterfront of warehouse and factory buildings dating from the 1890s to the 1930s was being restored and converted to residential, office and retail use. Therefore the design for Harbor Steps called for solid walls and punched openings, in keeping with its neighbours, and for its centrepiece I gave it a grand stairway on the order of the Baroque Spanish Steps. Rising beside the steps is a hotel-condominium tower. With Seattle's new art museum across the street, the steps should become a new destination point in the city, an exciting stage of activity lined with shops and trees leading down to a small square. However, the crowning beauty of the steps will be their generous number of fountains.

The Winter Garden mixed-use development, a 1985 developer proposal for Anchorage, Alaska, had no such context and was on the edge of the downtown, so it had to be an attraction in its own right. To accomplish that end, I had no hesitation in returning to the period when Anchorage was a log village. Instead of tapping the local memory of crude frontier amenities, I opted to elaborate on a feature of the era's genuine elegance: at the corners of the two sixteen-storey buildings are slender shafts that evoke the grand chateau hotels erected by the railways from the 1880s to the 1920s. The buildings themselves were placed at the limits of the block, carefully positioned to let in views and light. A glass roof extends between them to create a winter garden for activities and to separate the 440-room hotel from the office building. The base of the complex and the atrium, which is one storey above grade, are given life with restaurants and retail activities.

One of our first projects in Los Angeles while California Plaza was starting up was, like Harbor Steps, also set in a neighbourhood of early twentieth-century buildings. The 1982 Crown Plaza office building was next door to the famous art deco Oviatt

Left: The nine-storey Crown Plaza building was designed in 1982 to fit into the historic business district of Los Angeles. It provides 80,000 square feet of leasable floor space. The façade, with its bay windows reminiscent of early Chicago windows, has stepped balconies for added interest on the top floors. The exterior is clad in polished light grey and dark grey granite, with polished stainless steel touches on the columns and windows. MARCELLO IGONDA

Right: The small site, special client needs and an oddly shaped lot determined the unusual form of the 1982 proposal for the Maguire/Knapp building in Los Angeles. It faces north and south, and reacts to two different energy conditions with distinct façade treatments. The south face (shown here) is a solid wall penetrated by narrow window slots, disappearing towards the top where narrower floors require light from only one side. The north face, which slopes towards the gardens of the Los Angeles County Museum and a view of the Hollywood hills, has a clear glass wall cut by the occasional balconies of the executive suites. EDWARD CONNERS

building on a narrow lot, and provided only a façade to play with. Embellished with shades of grey polished granites, stainless steel and greenish glass, Crown Plaza is elegant in detail and finish. To break a stiff façade and give it still more interest from the ground, we cut in balconies and a skylight at the top.

In contrast, the Maguire/Knapp building, also in 1982, provided the freedom to relate directly to contemporary Los Angeles. The size, the special needs of the client and an oddly shaped lot determined the curious form of this small office building. Facing the building north and south, we gave it two different façade treatments for energy considerations. To the south, a solid wall would be penetrated only by narrow window slots, disappearing towards the top where narrower floors required light from only one side. The north face, however, sloping towards the gardens of the Los Angeles County Museum and a view of the Hollywood hills, would have a clear glass face cut by the

occasional balconies of the executive suites. Modest though it is, it shows that a sleek building can still have a certain presence.

My first engagement with the new eclecticism came in 1983. I was flattered to be invited into a limited competition for a visual arts centre for Ohio State University, for an academic arts committee is very demanding, looking for the impact of absolute contemporaneity. The site included two neoclassical buildings that framed the main entrance of the centre of the university. Therefore the mass of our building, including galleries and a performance space, went underground to support a plaza entrance to the university scattered with appropriate porticoes to the various parts of the complex. An open arc of columns set in a pond at the bottom of an amphitheatre suggested in eighteenth-century terms a romantic folly. The administration building was sculpted like an octagonal baptistry to contrast with the rectilinear volumes of the existing build-

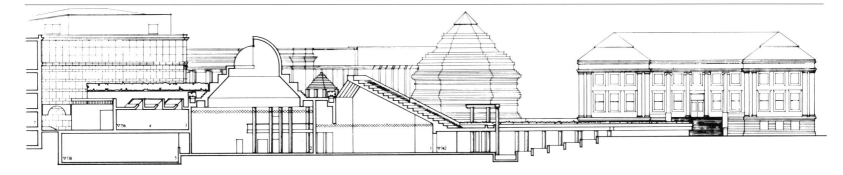

ings. However, my love of landscaping betrayed me. My main priority was to enhance and preserve the splendid oval common that my scheme now married by taking over the intervening through street. Nor, apparently, did I take the historical references seriously enough; the winner proposed to re-erect the foundations and quaintly crenellated tower of an armoury that had encroached on the oval for several decades until it burned down in the 1950s.

In a hectic two-month period in 1982, we twice attempted to work in New York at the separate invitations of two of the most famous developer personalities of the moment, Donald Trump and George Klein. Although neither took our proposals, these were memorable design exercises. The pressures were great: I was stimulated by the prospect of having a presence in Manhattan, the mood and the place were perfect for the grand gesture, the clients the most noted for seeking signature buildings, and the work was done swiftly under short deadlines.

A mixed-use hotel and condominium tower for Trump was for an East Sixty-first Street location, on the corner of Madison Avenue. I gave it a base with an ample hemicyclical colonnaded plaza for a small, exclusive hotel opening on the Sixty-first frontage. For the commercial section on Madison Avenue, I urged inviting Fortnum & Mason to have a presence in New York. It was that kind of location. The very sleek forty-one-storey residential tower was composed of two interlocking arcs. The configuration made an interesting geometry for the viewer

as well as the resident, for it attempts to relate at once to the stone façades of the street level while jutting defiantly clean into the sky.

George Klein had a sensitive site at 60 Wall Street, opposite the historic old Treasury Building. A planning committee required a polite bow in that direction. Evidently we did not bow low enough, although this time we presented two entirely different alternatives. One design was an H of slender towers reflecting the stepped profile of buildings in the vicinity, and we composed it entirely on a model that included the surrounding prewar towers. The sweeping hemicycle of its colon-

*Top: A diagonal section through the Ohio State University Visual Arts Center in Columbus, Ohio, shows how the galleries are submerged and lit by skylights. Light is admitted to the special collections gallery from the rear of the amphitheatre seating that forms its roof, and light enters the main gallery through the observatory.*

*Bottom: The 1983 competition scheme for Ohio State provides a needed gateway for the university and submerges most of the programmed facilities under terraces, creating a mall that completes and extends the oval. In the centre, an amphitheatre and pool form a performance and display place. An octagonal steel "baptistry" holds administrative offices; an "observatory" form provides a skylight for the main gallery.*
CHRISTOPHER ERICKSON

*Left: A model of the 1982 Trump condominiums and hotel proposal makes its statement on the Manhattan skyline: interlocking arcs are given a smooth skin of broad bands of glass and polished granite for the 41-storey residential tower. A department store and 128-room hotel are in the solid base.*
CHRISTOPHER ERICKSON

*Right: Two alternative proposals were quickly modelled in 1982 for a New York office tower at 60 Wall Street that would contain 1.5 million square feet and relate to the context of prewar stepped buildings and square banks. The second proposal (shown here) recalls the profile of Grand Central station, with the higher rent upper storeys larger than the supporting shaft. The entrance, like the one for the Trump proposal, is a hemicyclical colonnade and distinctly classicist. The punched window treatment is broken at the top by a panel of glass curtain wall.* PANDA ASSOCIATES

nade echoed the neoclassical splendour across the street. The façades picked up the punched window patterns of adjacent buildings and varied them with horizontal banding, disdaining, in the current manner, to rationalize a whimsical composition.

The other Wall Street scheme was a purely symmetrical composition and pursued the concept of an economic alternative to the skyscraper form. We had been asked to vary the floor area from seventy thousand square feet at the bottom to twenty-five thousand square feet at the top. This we had done in the first proposal; but for the second, since the highest rents were on the upper floors, we made those forty thousand square feet and put the twenty-five-thousand-square-foot floors rising out of the conventional seventy-thousand-square-foot base. The profile would be arresting, a contemporary evocation of the Grand Central tower, and since Manhattan is all about profile, we thought we had a winner on our hands.

Chicago has historically offered architectural substance to New York's glitz. It is a tough city, with the highest standards embodied not only in its famous buildings but in its professional community. When I was invited in 1988 to join a developer competition for the flagship branch of the Chicago Public Library, I knew that to succeed our scheme could have nothing faint or equivocal about it. The unique Chicago city-block pattern, long and narrow in a north-south direction, became the driving contextual element. One long thirteen-storey block, expanded in the middle for the needs of the language and literature division, meets the program requirement for huge spaces for the library collection, incorporates a public transportation hub — and provides a dynamic form for what otherwise might be implicitly read as a warehouse. A community library is active, not closed; I called the distinct structure for the main reading room "the athenaeum" and gave it an appropriate suggestion of Classicism. In model form, the building projects a monumental scale. But its heights correspond to adjacent buildings, and our proposal sets out the amenities that will give it a human vitality. These include the atrium between the reading room and the main body, which would have retail services and the children's library on the ground floor and information counters above, a winter garden with a restaurant off the transportation hub, and a park with an amphitheatre and fountain.

The whole of my work — the Chicago library proposal as much as any building—in some way reflects my abiding awareness of historical compositions, their numbers and range increasing with the scope of my travels. Although a thorough examination of classical and neoclassical architecture had gone from the university curriculum by the time I was a student, I was lucky that my years in Europe had enabled me to become steeped in the exemplars — their power all the greater then for sites uncorrupted by postwar development. The quality that makes a building emotionally moving is never so much a matter of decorative elements as spatial arrangements. When site or purpose are similar, I often include in my own work a contemporary allusion — a suggestive gesture — to those proven compositions that have moved me. The addition of explicit historical details is not valid except in restoration or additions where replication is necessary. I work for a contemporary evocation of the essential spirit of past experience. Frank historical copies can never project the intentions of the original; to copy is inevitably to pervert or to trivialize. Outsized replicas of the Parthenon tell you nothing of the perilous birth of democracy on the rock of the Acropolis, while they can speak openly of state tyranny. Luxurious pavilions modeled on the Taj Mahal without the embrace of its tall twin flanking mosques and huge gate tell you nothing of the cries of love and death, but something of voluptuous hedonism.

With every passing decade, our world civilization hurries faster and farther away from a period of set physical limits. The more we know ourselves to be "lost in space," the greater is our need to cultivate our communal values. Traditionally, important buildings have drawn us into communal life by their very existence. They are noble interpretations of our customs and institutions that could only come about when people act together.

And however modest or fine the structure, we can sense that the act of its building was an act of reverence. Reverence, like intuition, springs from something deeper than the intellect. Fed by dedication and humility, reverence embodies a profound respect for the task, the place and the tools at hand. Think of a small group of men and women gathered on a wilderness shore, examining trees and stones, testing the wind, attending to a rite — about to begin to build together. It should not be so very different today.

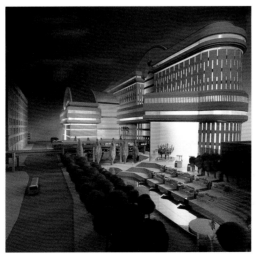

*Top: The 1988 competition scheme for the Chicago Public Library's Harold Washington Library Center evokes the classical athenaeum, the nineteenth-century precursor of the public library for the main reading room wing. The street level of the atrium and the winter garden accommodates the Children's Library, retail and food services, and public circulation areas. The long 775-foot form of the building is cued to the unique Chicago blocks nearby, which are laid out to capture sunlight and deflect wind.* LERHEUS WOODS

*Bottom: The porous walls and glazed spaces of the Harold Washington Library Center offset its monumental 13-storey presence. The winter garden juts into a small park of trees that ring a long reflecting pool.* PANDA ASSOCIATES

# PUBLIC BUILDINGS

The difference between working with a private developer and under government contract can be described in terms of trade-offs. With a developer, the emphasis is on the bottom line, and while I attempt to use that priority as just another creative stimulus, it often restricts the design evolution. The developer in most cases has a view for profits that is short-range, a keen appreciation for the proven and a belief that the unusual design feature is a financial risk. The public corporation, however, will often prove more amenable to strong design statements, then discover its budgetary conscience over issues of detail, materials and amenities. With the developer, there are clear priorities and a pace that keeps everyone in touch with reality. When the business is politically driven, the honour of being invited to compete is sometimes considered the compensation for the entry, and the project itself might drift off into committee limbo. Our recent public buildings reflect some of these vicissitudes of an architect's practice.

The Fairfax County Center was a successful competition for us in 1982 probably because it involved great ingenuity in siting, always our strong suit. In this case, the property was a piece of rural farmland well hidden by low hills at the geographical centre of an increasingly suburban Virginia county. A creek bed and wild brushy area along one side was a nature preserve.

We surrounded the building with a large lagoon formed by damming the creek and flooding the swampy area in front of the preserve. This would be a new recreational area for walks and nature viewing. A small amphitheatre was added for outdoor meetings and summer concerts. We wanted the offices to step down in terraces around its hill, hugging it and making the most of the site. The approach would be by a curving country drive with parking lots broken by planted berms. The entrance opens to a forum area, a large room of stepped seating that looks out onto the pond. Off this space are the council chamber, meeting rooms and

*The 1982 Fairfax County Center in Virginia was conceived as an urban complex in a natural setting. The 375,000-square-foot government facility covers a peninsula in a lake bordered by a nature preserve. A view from the lake side, across a footbridge, shows how the broken arrangement of the office areas lets light in and enhances views of the lake and woods beyond. On the other side of the building, a central entrance plaza becomes a ''town square'' with the addition of a clock tower. Facing it, a large, glassed lobby offers quick orientation to the visitor.*
DEREK GRIFFITHS

the municipal department service centres. On entering, visitors know immediately where to go. Our proposal capitalized on natural light, which filters down from skylights between staggered floors and viewing windows. In keeping with the setting, the roof terraces are planted with evergreens, which require a minimum of upkeep and provide at once a cool surface in summer and a warm one in winter.

We had in 1980 proposed a similar land-hugging form for a wooded hillside site in the nearby District of Columbia. With the same engineering firm that had helped us with the Sun Life towers scheme, we worked out solar heating principles in a competition for the Washington, D.C., headquarters building of Intelsat, a public corporation that handles satellite communications. Intelsat needed a facility that would have both offices and laboratories. We placed them in two- and three-storey buildings stepping down the hilly site with open courts between. Over all of it was a fitted mirrored glass canopy; it looked like a protected forest settlement on another planet, low and flowing down through the trees. Within the buildings was one climatic zone; under the canopy another, transitional one. The movement of air by

fans could meet most of the heating and cooling demands.

An independent design at least stands or falls on its own merits. I am always wary of additions to older buildings: historically, it is always the original that is more interesting, and almost without exception an ambitious addition falls short. Not wanting to venture into that trap, our competition proposal for the expansion of the Beverly Hills Civic Center in 1982 kept the attractive Spanish-style building and part of the old fire-hall intact and merely attempted to provide an appropriate setting for them. As with the Robson Square complex, this would be an opportunity for a government building to be more than a sum of its offices.

Since the complex would include a library and small theatre as part of a civic centre, it made sense to provide a pleasing city garden as well. So, again following the model of Robson Square, we buried the offices and put the garden on the roof; each department would be entered off the garden. The decorative old city hall would stand alone, unencumbered by modern alterations. By closing a street and burying the parking lot, an uninterrupted walking surface of raised gardens could connect all the facilities. Because of the

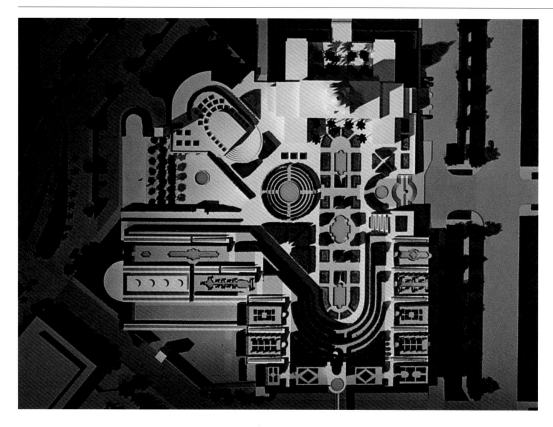

Top: A 1982 expansion scheme for Beverly Hills Civic Center in California places the new facilities under a stepped garden, setting off the Spanish-style city hall with a formal Spanish garden and fountains. The city hall's giralda-style tower acts as a visual axis. JULIUS SHULMAN

Bottom: The government offices of Beverly Hills, like Robson Square, are low-rise structures, supporting a public garden on their roofs. The civic center includes a library, auditorium, new fire-hall and parking, all kept low: the emphasis is on the garden, and the intent is to complement, not compete with, the picturesque 1920s city hall. JULIUS SHULMAN

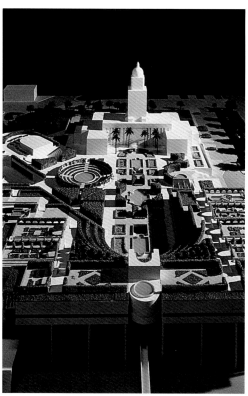

multistoreyed requirements of the police and fire stations, the gardens would be terraced and so divided. We would give each section a different predominant planting and use water as in the classic Hispano-Moorish gardens of Andalusia. At the end of the garden, opposite the tower of the existing building, there would be a tall cascade plunging into a tiled grotto, then feeding a procession of fountains.

With the Markham, Ontario, Municipal Building competition in 1986, we were back dealing with the landform. The site was next to an important suburban crossroads backed by existing school and theatre buildings. But the city hall itself was to be comparatively small. A long low structure can be dull in itself, but set along the edge of a body of water it would gain interest as a lakeside pavilion. As well, water animates the ground in all seasons, so we proposed a large artificial lake for the property — not an expensive feature for its impact. From the highway, hillocks pushed up to contain the lake also screen the view of the city hall, so it is seen in glimpses across the water, yet from the hall the highway is hidden. In winter the lake becomes an ice skating rink, in summer the backdrop for outdoor theatre.

Fresno, California, sits on the floor of the hot Central Valley, offering no landforms to play with. It badly needed a distinctive civic centre when we won its city hall commission in 1987. The elements were there, but undeveloped. The city hall site was at the end of a mall that ran between a number of civic buildings from a large courthouse. The wide public space needed a design treatment using water and additional tree planting. Meanwhile, a flat expanse of cars filled the adjacent open space where a park should go to draw the library and the town's one distinct monument, an old water tower, into a comfortable complex.

Our studies led me to believe that the new

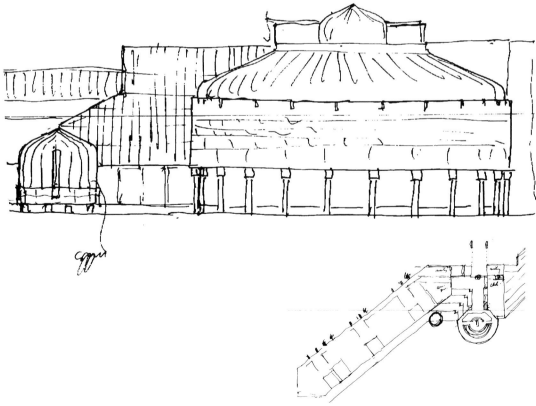

Top: The Markham Municipal Building in suburban Toronto, begun in 1986 and to be completed in 1989, uses the classical touches traditional for such a building but for a gentle rather than imposing image. The round council chamber sitting in water recalls the library at Hadrian's country villa. The artifical lake is protected from the ring highway by freeform berms. The low scale of the whole building makes invitation, not display, the theme. RAY AGUILA

Middle: The exotic cupola shape sketched for the Markham building subsequently gave way to a more classic dome form. The lines between the rotunda and the smaller copper-sheathed form of the marriage chapel indicate the glazed roof of the large public space of the winter garden. The building is reinforced concrete clad in reconstructed stone. COLLECTION CENTRE CANADIEN D'ARCHITECTURE/CANADIAN CENTRE FOR ARCHITECTURE

Bottom: A sketch study of the Markham city hall main floor has the departments spread along the wing on long floors penetrated by three entrance atriums. The result is a flexible office space configuration. COLLECTION CENTRE CANADIEN D'ARCHITECTURE/CANADIAN CENTRE FOR ARCHITECTURE

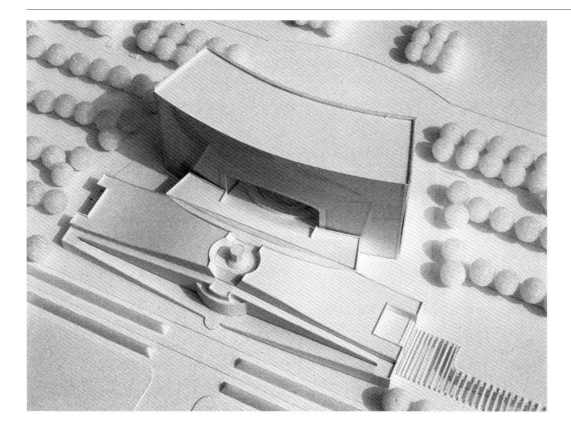

*Fresno City Hall in California anchors the mall on which it is sited by arching over it at one end. The curved block contains city offices; behind it, but part of the same 187,000-square-foot building, is the low council chamber. The chamber has a fountain on its roof and long pedestrian ramps along its low wings. The 1987 plan also provides for landscaping the mall with trees and water.* MARCELLO IGONDA

city hall should not entirely close the mall; by bridging the mall and letting it run through, the hall's image would be strengthened. But through planning studies, we found that the council chamber and the departments directly associated with it had to be linked across the first two floors. So we pushed the chamber to the back of the property and framed it with an arch, with linking halls leading back to the offices in the bases of the arch. The whole composition, clad in limestone, sets off the council chamber. Although this was just a result of working out the mall's geometry, it was a very serendipitous plan; the council members, recognizing its symbolism, readily accepted it.

Rounding out this recent trio of individually distinct government halls is one commissioned in 1987 by the Province of Ontario for Thunder Bay. The city lies at a far northwest reach of Lake Superior and is the region's port for mining and grain exports. It is, like so many similar North American cities, reclaiming its waterfront from the railways. The site overlooks the lake, a roadway and a public park built on abandoned tracks.

Government buildings usually have a public reception floor for meeting rooms, restaurants and government services. The bureaucracy goes upstairs with much smaller waiting areas. Thus the program yields a large, featureless mass. In this case, it could not be reduced in size, so I determined to give it some interesting, even fanciful touches. Because of the steep slope of the site, the entrance level was a full storey above the lake front. So we put a covered porch along the lake side to take advantage of the views. Its oversized columns recall the dominant pattern of Thunder Bay's lakeshore grain elevators.

To make the building profile interesting, I manipulated the top two storeys and their window openings. I put one storey behind a cornice at the top of the columns and incorporated the top floor into the roof as an attic storey. Three porticoes also had columns, giving me the opportunity to play with changes in scale. The moulded shapes were executed in metal to purposely avoid their reference to classical detail. The use of stone was relegated to the walls and pavement.

Prince George, British Columbia, was seeking a multipurpose community centre rather than a government one, but one that would make a similar kind of contribution to its city. Like Thunder Bay, Prince George is the hub of an extensive resource-based economic area and is also a winter-bound town. Several years ago it reserved a six-block site a short drive away from the central business district for an activities complex, which, according to the accepted design values of the time, would have been a megastructure in the unfriendly sense of the term, serving neither car nor pedestrian well. The streets stopped at its boundaries, and a library was the only built artifact on the site.

In 1986 the program called for a conference hall, a twelve-hundred-seat theatre, an art gallery, parking and administration. A slight bowl in the land allowed us to bring the streets onto the site over an underpinning parking structure and thus integrate the new facilities with the city grid. At the entrance we put a small square, given a busy life by shared automobile and pedestrian traffic. A large, skylit, covered rotunda — a painted steel structure above the brick complex — would cover the common entrance court through which all facilities are entered, although the conference wing also has a separate entrance. The rotunda, like the plaza outside, can be a stage for civic activities. Next door is a community swimming pool and nearby a hotel. The Prince George city fathers must have understood that such a range of attractions in one place — including a park and views — add up to a real alternative to the shopping mall for their children, not to mention the increase in their own pleasures. They voted to proceed with the complex in one go, rather than risk building it in phases.

# CALIFORNIA HOUSES

A house is distinguished by its small size relative to its extraordinary complexity. Because of this, it is a trying thing to design and succeeds only if you overcome the complications so that the house emerges with a sense of ease and grace. The Spanish word *gracia* captures the latter attributes in a single resonant word that conveys not just a generosity of spirit but a noble response in the face of adversity. Its application in architecture means the avoidance of meanness or fussiness in any detail, no matter how insignificant. Scale is consistent all the way through. The size of something never exempts it from possessing amplitude. The same generosity of line and gesture can be seen in the individual interior spaces as in the total look of the house. Perhaps the quickest to recognize this quality are the artistically inclined who, as clients, can anticipate from the beginning of the design process the kind of pleasures they will experience living in an attentively detailed house. Unfortunately, the whole adventure, as sure as the reward may be, seems to have its own requirements for gracia on the part of the clients. Sometimes the most hopeful scheme is stillborn when the clients' ideals turn out to be greater than their resources.

As my reputation grew in the 1970s, several such clients sought me out from California. From the Northwest to California is a relatively easy step down the Pacific coast, with people sharing the same tastes for informal living and broad views. The regions differ in intensity of light, but the California climate is, if possible, still more benign. Glass doors, large windows and generous outside living areas are sought by people who enjoy what is called the "West Coast lifestyle." I reacted by making California houses more open than my Northwest houses. In keeping with the large size of the properties, the California houses are also more luxurious.

None are highly urban sites; they all have long views of rolling hills, often with the Pacific Ocean in the distance. In the Northwest such views are broken by evergreens in the foreground or dimmed by heavy clouds, and the house clings to the site like a plant seeking light. But in the clarity of California, the sere hills become a background against which the houses are placed like fine pieces of jewellery. The simile helps to explain the importance of the base to these California houses. The setting of gems gives them their due importance when they would otherwise be lost. In the same way, strong foundations are the transition stage between these houses and their domains, rescuing them from the oblivion of their surroundings.

Spanish architectural traditions are still eminently suited to California, which shares the same Mediterranean climate, and I draw on them. White hard-plastered interior walls provide cool, glareless spaces; and with dark wood cabinetry and tiled floors, they play to the sun-and-shadow polarities. Although owing much to the Arabs, the Spanish style has its own free indoor-outdoor circulation that I also appreciate. I play, as always, with water, but use it more lavishly than ever, as you are tempted to do in dry climates. Water is less a tool for bringing in light than a way of toying with light and temperature. Finally, freed from the Northwest's common use of wood, I translated the tradition of the plastered wall to concrete, making the California houses a most personally pleasing series.

Donald and Marlene Grant's house in 1979 was an early favourite. A steep, heavily forested site on the eastern side of the Palo Alto hills called for a long, slender house set along its slope. The vegetal energy of the gnarled oak and madrona branches is tranquillized by a simple platform of concrete, topped by a vertical slab on columns like the crowning comb of a Mayan temple. The rooms run along the length of the house, with fifteen-foot ceilings emphasizing the very narrow form of the structure. The house is edged with a slender lap pool that provides a linking mirror with the tops of the trees. Mrs. Grant, an interior designer, was prepared to enhance the simplicity of their home by offsetting the unfinished concrete interiors with fine silk furnishings.

Farther south, in a more agricultural area, the Wilson Bradleys commissioned in 1979 what I call my Palladian house. From a high shoulder of land in the Santa Barbara hills, the view sweeps over avocado groves to brushwood slopes punctuated by cypresses reminiscent of the Italian lake country. With such full landscapes in every direction, it seemed necessary to survey the domain from a symmetrical belvedere on a rusticated podium like Palladio's Villa Capra. This device simultaneously removes the dwelling from the landscape yet engages it in a venerating way. The surroundings are separated into four different worlds by four twin-columned porticoes. The arrival portico looks into a court and a hillside forest. The bedroom portico looks at an abrupt upward slope of meadow grasses, while from the opposite dining room the meadow drops into a series of benchlands. Beyond the entrance, the living room looks down a broad expanse of steps to a pool, which hangs over the edge of a valley plunging to the plains below. The

193

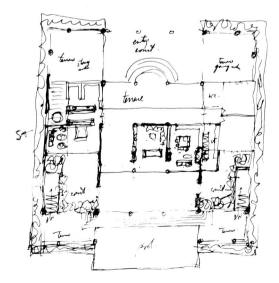

*Top: The 1979 Grant house is essentially a pair of long deep horizontal beams running above a narrow podium on a forested, sloping site in the Palo Alto hills south of San Francisco Bay in California. Fifteen-foot-high ceilings accentuate its slender form, along which the rooms are arranged in a line, separating functions with simplicity and giving each a view. The living room is in the centre and looks out over a reflecting pool. The 3,000-square-foot residence is built entirely of concrete.* SIMON SCOTT

*Middle: The 1979 Bradley House near Santa Barbara, California, adopts a Palladian approach to a country house: a rigid geometry overlooking bucolic views, a classic siting, executed in simple materials. The horizontal massing of the residence is punctuated by robust columns. Construction is buff-coloured concrete, with stone paving on both exterior and interior floors.* SIMON SCOTT

*Bottom: A sketch plan of the Bradley house places three distinct living areas in a line across the bar of an H formed by terraces. The master bedroom suite is on the left, living and dining rooms in the centre, the guest wing on the right. The covered area comprises 5,300 square feet, with 6,000 square feet in courts and terraces.* COLLECTION CENTRE CANADIEN D'ARCHITECTURE/ CANADIAN CENTRE FOR ARCHITECTURE

Top left: *The 1981 Malibu house in California is shaped like a ship's prow. The formal entrance is through an earth berm that incorporates a greenhouse.* CHRISTOPHER ERICKSON

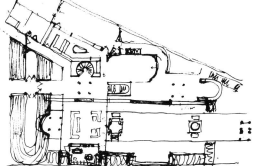

Bottom left: *A sketch plan shows how the Malibu house was sited for maximum views on an oddly shaped and harshly restricted lot.* COLLECTION CENTRE CANADIEN D'ARCHITECTURE/CANADIAN CENTRE FOR ARCHITECTURE

Right: *A 1986 sketch of the main floor plan of the Khosla house in Portola Valley, California. The living room is placed on the summit of a hill, and the rest of the house descends in two wings on either side of a stepped court, with a retractable roof, reflecting pools and a double row of clustered columns. The left wing holds the kitchen and master bedroom, and the right wing contains the children's rooms.* COLLECTION CENTRE CANADIEN D'ARCHITECTURE/CANADIAN CENTRE FOR ARCHITECTURE

pool is also a protective barrier between the flammable brush and the house itself.

We moved from the sublime to the subterranean in 1981 with a house at Malibu for a couturier and her husband. They had a narrow triangle with its apex on the ocean where naturally they wanted the widest view. In itself this would be a difficult feat, but the covenant on the lot prevented us from building more than twelve feet above the ground at any point on the view side, which perversely slipped precipitously away to the beach. It was a struggle from the beginning, squeezing, shoving, pushing and gauging all the parts so that the site and the house would work effortlessly together.

The solution, born of necessity, was to bury as much as possible. A series of belvederes over a buried concrete nonhouse emerged. The progress through the property is a structured series of events, beginning with a tunnel entrance through an

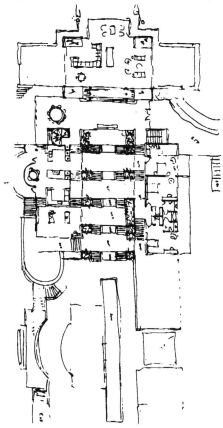

orchid house. From here stretches a long vista through an inner court and entrance hall to terraces and pool beyond. The round tempietto forms, glass domed, flood the intervals with light. Two series of these move parallel towards the water. The farthest one sits over a hot pool in the long single stretch of water formed by the swimming pool. The water spills over the edge and seems to vanish into the ocean beyond. The narrow apex is thus as broad as the wide horizon. The house was to be finished with the glistening white limestone of sun- and sea-bleached shells and to plow through the shorecliff like a prow riding the ocean.

Two clients who are pursuing their dream are Vinod and Neeru Khosla. They bought thirty acres in the Portola Valley near Palo Alto for their house as a reward for an early and extraordinary business success in computers. They came to me in 1986; I had not worked with such a young couple since I was their age. They wanted a work-free, highly electronic, pet-friendly house on a hilltop that had alternately long and short views to capture. I put the living room on the highest point, which would have a distant view of the San Francisco Bay over an abrupt drop-off. Behind, on the gentler approaching slope that ran down into vineyards through an oak forest, I placed two wings, one dining-kitchen-family and one bedroom. Between the clustered supporting columns defining the two wings, the grade was sympathetic to a stepped pool courtyard reminiscent of Moghul gardens. A glass roof covers this courtyard. Below it is the swimming pool with an infinity edge dropping into the close-in view of vineyards set in rolling hills.

Like the Khoslas, my Los Angeles client had come to the United States as an adult, and like them was charmingly direct in approaching me for my services in 1986. All were innocent of the kind of philistinism that a native might fall into through wide but shal-

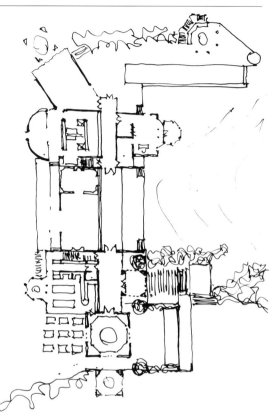

low exposure to the architectural abundance of North America. Such a person thinks that a house similar to that of an architect of wide reputation can give the same satisfaction as one created by that architect. The Los Angeles client amused me with a story about flying into Vancouver with a first-class seat-mate who, upon hearing that I was to build his new house, objected, "But he's the best!"

The house is high up a hillside looking down a valley to the towers of Los Angeles. In the neighbourhood there is scarcely a ridge that does not have some eclectic mon-strosity hunched on it, so the siting challenge was to screen this immediate view, directing the vision instead to the uninhabited slopes above the site. Once again, the landscaping preceded the building and, this being Los Angeles, the original, sprawling 1950s mediocrity was pulled down in the process. The new concrete house went to the rear of the four-acre lot, the existing flat benchland ahead was cut away and an oval pond backed

by cypresses was placed at the bottom as a screen against the nearest lower neighbour.

The owner is a connoisseur, and his pro-gram called for generous wall space for his art and various places to dine according to the occasion and time of day. A series of pavilions of Loire stone were devised, col-lected loosely about a main pavilion of structural steel. The main dining pavilion is an island in a pool, inspired by Hadrian's library at Tivoli. The roof is a long shallow pool over glass to let dappled light into the living room. Above it, we devised an enamel-striped glass shade, which will surely arrest in turn the view of any neighbours.

*Left: The Los Angeles house, initiated in 1986, has a primary beam frame like the Bradley house, but of steel. The square pavilions of Loire stone become an ordering device; the connecting house structure has a steel truss roof pavilion shaded by striated glass.* PHILLIP VAN HORN

*Right: An early floor plan study of the Los Angeles house has most of the elements of the final scheme, although the master bedroom, upper left, is angled off. A rectangular lap pool is placed on the arm of the ridge. Steps lead up to the main entrance, screened with trees. To its left is a formal dining pavilion; straight ahead is the kitchen. The living room is in the centre.*

# PUGET SOUND HOUSE

On a family vacation ranch overlooking the Puget Sound in Washington State, our clients decided to make a permanent home. Their property was a wonderfully diverse spread: grazing fields for their Arabian horses, berry patches, fruit orchards, a swampy glade, and a forest of conifers, broadleaf maples and arbutus on a cliff face spilling down to the beach. After my initial visit, I practically invented my own program, for I wanted the house to partake of all these special natural features and each room to capture a different light. The living room needed to have a view of the sound and the looming Cascade Range. The dining room

*Facing page: The Puget Sound house in Washington State, begun in 1983 and completed in 1986, affords the privacy of a large country house, with guests accommodated separately from the owners. The patio overlays the lower floor of guest and recreation rooms. But the true spirit of such a place is family enjoyment: hence, the viewing bench in its belvedere is a symbolic centre. The living room looks southeast towards the Cascade Mountains. WAYNE FUJII*

*The living room of the Puget Sound house is sited for the mountain view, with the half-vault and a crescent of end pillars framing a prominent peak. The 12-sided pillars are covered with cedar. A similar treatment is given to the master bedroom pavilion, which looks into the forest. WAYNE FUJII*

*Top: The owners of the Puget Sound house wanted to look back through a break in the trees to their farm, so the land was contoured and a small valley opened up with sides that frame the view and an artificial pond at its bottom. The meadow is planted in seasonal flowers, including daffodils for early spring and, later on, lupin.* INARA KUNDZINS

*Bottom left: The scheme of the Puget Sound house was inspired by a timely visit to the Acropolis and encouraged by a client requirement that the roofs be pitched. The result is an arrangement of separate pavilions that, while appearing loose and casual, actually follows a proportional organization based on the golden mean.* INARA KUNDZINS

*Bottom right: An early conceptual sketch of the Puget Sound house shows it as a series of ordered rectangles on a bluff over the water. The only break in the rectilinear theme is the dining room, which is given a northwestern view of the farm property down a valley, and a southeastern view of the Cascade Mountains across the water. The guest bedrooms sit close to the bluff, and the master bedroom looks south into the trees at the edge of the bluff.* COLLECTION CENTRE CANADIEN D'ARCHITECTURE/CANADIAN CENTRE FOR ARCHITECTURE

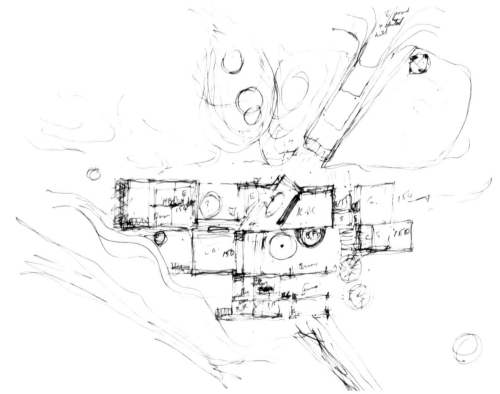

should enjoy the lowering sun over the forest meadow, and the master bedroom suite had to have intimate views of the forest floor. These priorities so scattered the rooms that it seemed impossible to tie a house of any sort together.

A loose arrangement is not easy to compose, for its exacting laws rest on an obscure geometry that defies easy comprehension. Such is the mystery of the Athenian Acropolis, with the offset angle of each of its temples. All have differing views, compositions, scales and styles yet create among them a strange and compelling tension that is fundamental to our fascination with the whole. It was 1983, and Postmodernism was swirling around with its historical contrivances. Here was also a chance to play teasingly with fashion and to show it up; so we have a house that looks like a house "should," with pitched roofs and lots of columns and slatted siding. Anybody can provide that outline. The real lesson and attraction of history's archetypes lie much deeper.

I bravely pursued the concept by making each part of the house a separate pavilion angled away from the others; their precise relationships were slow to be fixed. With no guiding geometry, we could only manipulate them until they felt right. The test was the courtyard, since it was so focussed. A greenhouse with an exaggerated, pedimented doorway of copper went at the apex. The outer edge, which was also the roof of the guest quarters, was flooded, and an open rotunda placed on it as a viewing pavilion.

The structures are unified by a simplified slat covering that is an abstract of a typical regional style. A different porch with carved cedar columns at the end of each room adds to its distinctiveness and emphasizes its outlook. With the addition of a copper-clad steeple for the front entrance, the result is a decidedly picturesque composition. It suited the informality of a country house and the clients' wish to take full advantage of the charms of rural life.

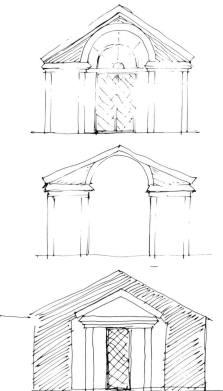

*Top: The barrel vault and apsidal end of the Puget Sound house living room focus its view. Furnishings were co-ordinated by Allen Salsbury, a Northwest designer who had worked on the Boultbee house in the 1960s and came out of retirement for this commission.* Wayne Fujii

*Bottom: Three elevation sketches for the Puget Sound house study a number of solutions in a classical vocabulary. The decision to wrap the roof and sides with cedar boards makes the forms simple and abstract, and unifies an already complex composition. The treatment each wing received was finally even simpler than the sketches show, except for the greenhouse, which opens on the central patio and is outlined in copper.* Collection Centre Canadien d'Architecture/Canadian Centre for Architecture

# LABORATORY BUILDINGS

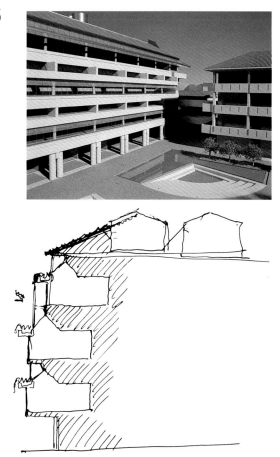

*Top: The 1985 Stanford University Biological Sciences Expansion has requirements that push a four-storey building to seven. To reduce its mass and fit into a prescribed site, the façade is broken with horizontals to match existing buildings and give a light, porous feel. The roofline encloses the attic of the upper interstitial space and has a glass eyebrow to keep the roof size constant and make it seem lower. ADRIAN VELICESCU*

*Bottom: A sketch of the Stanford biosciences building: greenhouses go behind the roofline; interstitial spaces are tucked in; eyebrow planters lower the building.*

After more than fifteen years without North American work related to my original source of renown, the university, I was surprised by a rush of campus commissions in Washington State, North Carolina, California and Arizona, all related by their specialized scientific purposes. Perhaps having Napp Laboratories or the SANCST Science Halls or the hospitals in the company portfolio helped. Indeed, special-use buildings present special puzzles, mostly having to do with the particular requirements of the equipment they contain. Having designed complete campuses may have been less relevant, for the university settings in these projects were not only given, they came with as many regulations as those in the most zealous historical preservationist neighbourhood.

Stanford University has the distinction of being laid out by Frederick Law Olmsted. His great quadrangle has put its stamp on everything built since. This splendid and vast space is dominated by the chapel and surrounded by a double-columned colonnade in a Mediterranean style that ties together the clusters of buildings around smaller courts at each corner. Its yellow sandstone — or at least concrete of the same colour — clay-tiled roofs, wide gables and simple walls have become requisite for all subsequent buildings.

When we were appointed to do Stanford's Biological Sciences Expansion in 1985, the task was far greater than a simple laboratory building. In a key corner of the campus, our building had to bring identity to the complex and yet harmonize with the two existing buildings in order to read as a cluster. The building would also be the entrance to a general sciences group of buildings, with its court serving as the forecourt for the whole.

Even though we were building only three laboratory floors and the ground level administrative floor, for a modest four storeys topped by roof greenhouses, the extra interstitial service floor above each laboratory floor would result in a seven-storey building that would tower over its neighbours. We had to find a way to reduce the apparent height and bring it into a sympathetic scale with the other buildings. Using the identical roof area and slope as the rest of the buildings brought us part of the way. The deep slope was a nice cover behind which to hide the topmost service space, like an attic, and our building then stepped up from the adjacent building the same amount that it stepped up from the next, making a correct order.

Next we had to bring our façade into line — although the floor levels would not tie in — by somehow picking up the horizontal banding of the other buildings. We emphasized the difference between the interstitial and the laboratory floors by recessing the glass of the former and extending the glass of the latter as a kind of horizontal bowed window. It has fine vertical baked enamel patterns on the upper half of the glass in the manner of lath house-shading. To lighten the impact of the roof eave, we made it of glass, at the same time keeping the tiled roof the same depth as the others. The point of the exercise was to comply with the worthy Stanford style, yet to conceive a building that was fresh and contemporary in accordance with its research use.

A second biological sciences building went into design in 1986 for the University of California at Irvine. The campus had been designed in the 1960s by William Pereira on a ring plan around a central common. The buildings are limited by their period style, with its dominant precast sun screens. I felt that as long as we could relate the biosciences building to the others in scale and general colours and refer to the vertical striations of the precast concrete, we did not have to adopt the technologically obsolete sun screens.

Aside from their exterior trim, laboratory buildings leave very little choice to the architect with their demanding layouts and technical considerations. After many massing trials with the laboratory blocks, we settled on a plan of two wings off an administrative core as being the most efficient. It remained to arrange the unit so that it tied into an existing lecture hall and properly acknowledged older science buildings arranged on the ring. We decided to invoke the spirit of advanced research and give the building a slick, laboratory-looking skin rather than conform to the heavier precast concrete around it. We gave it colours that were complementary to the southern California hills: aqua, ultramarine and deep green. The aqua of solex glass alternates with vertical panels of frosted solex and opaque fibreglas panels in deep blue or green. The base and cap of the building still pick up the tones of the precast, and the administrative block with its punched windows is entirely precast.

All of our studies, as with all of our buildings, were done with models — in this case accurately depicting the details and colours of adjacent buildings. Thus the matters of relationship and contrast to existing surroundings can be accurately gauged. If you are trying to respond to context with any degree of sensitivity, you cannot risk guessing or hoping for a fit without careful examination in model form.

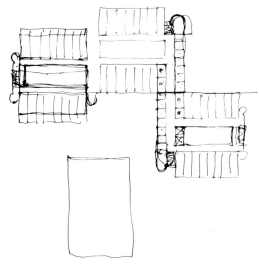

*Top: The Biological Sciences Unit 2 building at the Irvine campus of the University of California, conceived in 1986, has a bright, sleek glass curtain wall. The 1960s campus has no historical motif, but the huge new science building of 215,000 square feet could not appear out of scale with its neighbours and linking plazas. The limestone central wing, its height ameliorated by its narrow shape, is for offices; the laboratory wings, one clad in green glass, one in blue, lend an appropriately clean, high-tech character. The vertical striations of frosted and clear glass refer to the vertical precast sunscreens of the earlier buildings.*
ADRIAN VELICESCU

*Left: A floor plan study sketch of the Irvine campus Biological Sciences Unit 2 works out a functional separation of offices and laboratories that will enable a reduction in scale of the huge building. The many small offices are arranged in two rows on a sliding face, similar to the MacMillan Bloedel building.*

The 1986 Textile School for North Carolina State University's new Centennial campus is to provide a model for subsequent development. Working from the simple strong forms of local architecture — yet having to diminish a mass of 170,000 square feet of offices and classrooms and 100,000 square feet for a high-ceiling processing plant — meant making full use of the slope of the site, in which much could be buried. The remaining mass is broken by using multiple roofs, themselves diminished by being set back from the cornices. DARYL PLATER

Facing page, top left: The General Motors Advanced Concepts Center on a Malibu bluff in California encompasses 100,000 square feet of laboratories, workshops, design studios and offices. The 1985 commission had to be environmentally sensitive while expressing the building's high technology purpose. Its mass is fitted to the rugged topography, and the roof is planted in native flowers. The main roof structure consists of several long narrow convex forms with skylights running between them. The one-storey administration wing spans the structure. MARCELLO IGONDA

Facing page, top right: A detail sketch of the General Motors building shows how the columns of the studio and workshop roofs terminate in glass lenses held by stainless steel rings, meant to evoke the automotive industry. COLLECTION CENTRE CANADIEN D'ARCHITECTURE/ CANADIAN CENTRE FOR ARCHITECTURE

Facing page, bottom: The General Motors building takes the gully of its site and carries it through in the form of the building. This sketch study of the main floor places the production wing on the right and the design laboratory on the left of the "gully-plaza." The triangular pool, at the bottom of an amphitheatre, represents its head. The wide mouth is the long horizontal span between the two sections, consisting of a pool with an infinity edge that sweeps the eye towards the sea. The dotted lines indicate the administrative floor above, reached by two circular stairwells.

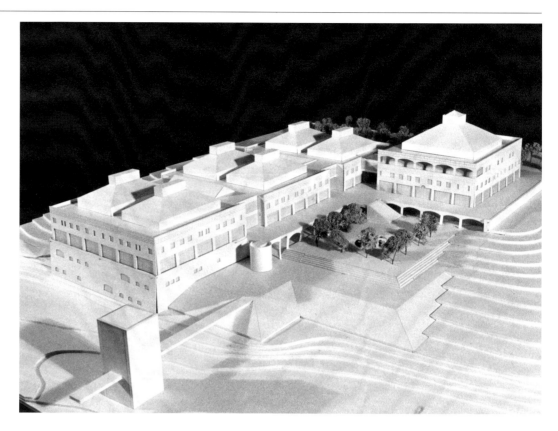

The unique feature of the new Centennial campus of North Carolina State University at Raleigh is its program to combine state-funded university facilities with extensive private research and development facilities as well as townhouses, a village and a conference centre. Acting with local firms, we were consultants on the master plan and in 1986 presented the first precedent-setting cluster of buildings for the Textile School. They are simple, strong volumes in the finite forms of the regional vernacular. Incorporating a high space for a processing plant, the buildings needed to be large. To fit into the rolling hills of the site, they needed to have their mass broken up. We were able to submerge some of the space into a hill overlooking a ravine, and then we took care to articulate the façades. To further reduce the height and prevent the group from congealing, we moved the familiar rooflines back from the cornices and doubled their number. A pedestrian-oriented courtyard is built up from the ravine and surrounded by the active elements of the complex: the library and cafeteria.

General Motors wanted its Advanced Concepts Center to be in inspiring surroundings and also to be able to draw on a pool of creative people, so in 1985 it chose a broad acreage of rolling terrain on the California coast at Malibu, directly across from Pepperdine University. So much of the magnificent Pacific coastline has been desecrated by ugly, insensitive developments that we all wanted the facility to be a demonstration of site compatibility.

Our intentions did not allow us to ignore even the sparse brush cover, which I was working into the scheme when the authorities instructed us to regrade the vulnerable slopes. The design, sensitive to neighbours' views from below and above as well as the original land form, is based on sinking the main workshop and the design studio to

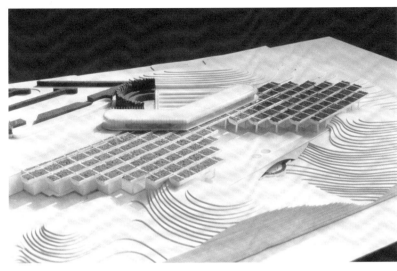

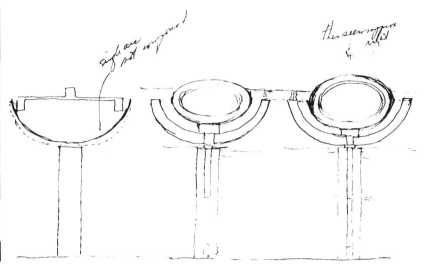

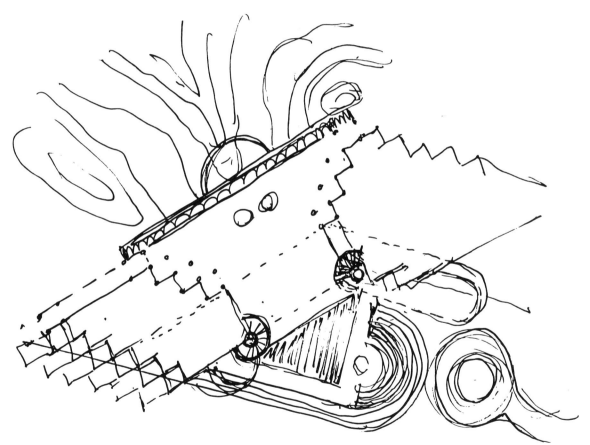

either side of a shallow depression at the head of the main gully that penetrates the site from the shore. Spanning the site on the highway side is the one-storey administrative wing. Between the studio and the workshop, a broad open terrace at the head of the trench holds a rotating stage for model display. The terrace continues under the administrative bridge to a court at the back, where a similar stage is the centre of an amphitheatre built into the slope, and on past this to join visually with the Malibu hills in the background.

In an effort to flood the studio and workshop with diffused natural light, a roof structure was devised on which sit convex shells that meet at the apex in a narrow skylight. These convex fibre-reinforced concrete shells extend out in long cantilevers from columns standing in water outside the glass walls of the studios. A glass lens held in a stainless steel oval ring terminates each of these symbolic projections of an automobile assembly. The shells' top surface would be planted between the skylights with succulents like the native ice plants. Where not planted, shallow water basins would provide a reflective surface link to the sea below.

The project was in its final working drawings when extra soil tests revealed old earthquake faults that prohibited construction.

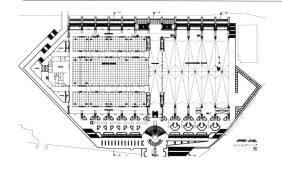

*Top left: The floor plan of the upper level of the San Diego Convention Center in California shows a series of meeting rooms, varying in size from 1,000 to 30,000 square feet. The rooms are given viewing and lounge space along either side. A food services kitchen is on the far left, the outdoor exhibit space is on the far right. A vaulted concourse bisects the top floor to connect with the city side of the building.*

*Top right: The 1984 design of the San Diego Convention Center establishes a strong identity for its function while offsetting the extraordinary size of the building and expressing the waterfront character of its site. The largest program element, the 250,000-square-foot exhibition hall, opens to street level. The semi-enclosed, tented exhibit area on the roof, shown here in night-time illumination, adds interest for passers-by. The tent structures are made of teflon-coated fibreglas cloth.*
EDWARD GOHLICH

*Bottom right: On the side of the San Diego Convention Center that faces the city, the great gantrylike structures, originally proposed of painted steel, support glass-vaulted circulation areas. The glazed vaults give the building a transparency and lightness, reducing its mass and providing a partial view within.*

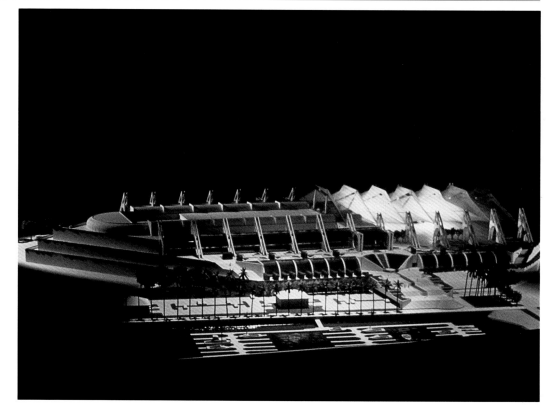

# SAN DIEGO CONVENTION CENTER

The design problem presented by a convention and exhibition hall is how to give an enormous building a mass that is not intimidating and an outline that expresses a sense of occasion. Typically there is not much joy to be found in contemplating these gigantic structures, for essentially they are nothing but great barns with tremendous delivery, service and traffic requirements. They often squat in some prime location like their notorious cousin the covered sports stadium: not, it would seem, very friendly to surrounding urban life. Their antihuman scale somehow has to be tamed. In San Diego, the context of the centre includes a fragile older downtown district and the marvellous San Diego Bay with its incessant, lively traffic of yachts and freighters, ferries, windsurfers and warships.

The San Diego Port Authority awarded us the Convention Center in a competition in the spring of 1984, but the announcement detonated a political explosion in city government that took months to settle. We were proud to have won over prestigious competitors, and we were fortunate that our structure, somewhat modified, eventually proceeded.

We started our design by submerging all those blank, introverted exhibition and meeting spaces as much as possible behind public spaces and landscaped terraces so that they would rest low, like the hull of a great ship. I've always liked to put a roof to use, so we proposed for it an outdoor gathering area covered by an all-weather tent. The tent's structure would also support the lobbies reaching up the sides of the hall, true gantries recalling the boiler plate and rivet-

ted steel of ship and dockside construction. Our proposal called for rivetted steel, but cost restrictions and fire protection ruled that out in favour of concrete. We used painted steel details on tent cables, railings and circular skylight canopies.

The nautical look was gaily enhanced by flags and the sail-like tents. Enough of the outdoor events could be glimpsed from the street so that the roof would be a constant source of interest to passers-by. With its lively roofscape, grand stairs connecting to the docks and its splendid setting by the bay, the San Diego Convention Center will be an attraction for everyone, not just conventioneers.

*Top: A section of the San Diego Convention Center: the exhibition hall, which has 27-foot ceilings, takes up the centre; beneath it are two levels of parking. In the vaults of the upper level concourse, a series of semicircles continues the arched theme of the gantries.*

*Bottom: The glazed vaults of the San Diego Convention Center develop a clear pattern of access and circulation, beginning over the lobby and continuing within the triangular structural frames.* MICHAEL GUSTSTADT

# CALIFORNIA PLAZA

California Plaza is a giant redevelopment project in the heart of Los Angeles. It consists of 11.2 acres on Bunker Hill, a master contract for a billion dollars of investment, a ten-year time line to completion, and the participation of international real estate development companies guided by the city's Community Redevelopment Agency (CRA). Our firm is in charge of overall design; we are supported by other locally based firms and see to the integration of the design of all components. The California Plaza game has many players, and they shift or change, the forces of economics prevailing. But the game has one end, which is to renew and increase residential and commercial activity at the core of the mighty Los Angeles basin.

California Plaza began with a competition. Over the past two decades the CRA had disposed sites in the area to selected developers. A last 8.75-acre piece was offered in 1980. Through the good offices of Los Angeles architect Tim Vreeland, we were invited to enter with a group headed by the Cadillac Fairview real estate company. The fruit of three months' effort on the part of our team of architects, landscape designers and developers from Los Angeles, Vancouver and Toronto was a presentation of models, reports and renderings of a single conceptual entity. And it was as such, the more cohesive vision, that in 1980 our scheme won out over the other finalist. The competing team of stellar architects followed the existing city block pattern while ours challenged it, bridging streets with plazas and even adding further property so that the whole became a link in a chain of pedestrian parks penetrating the city.

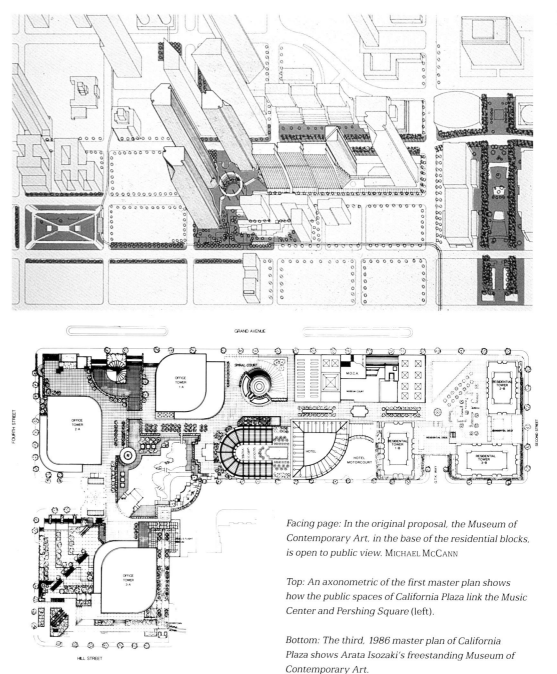

*Facing page: In the original proposal, the Museum of Contemporary Art, in the base of the residential blocks, is open to public view.* MICHAEL MCCANN

*Top: An axonometric of the first master plan shows how the public spaces of California Plaza link the Music Center and Pershing Square (left).*

*Bottom: The third, 1986 master plan of California Plaza shows Arata Isozaki's freestanding Museum of Contemporary Art.*

*Left: The lobby of One California Plaza is recessed behind a colonnade at the base of the tower. The mullionless structural glazing system of the wall curves to respond to the form of the building.* MARCELLO IGONDA

*Right: California Plaza's spiral court leads from Grand Avenue to the shopping arcade under the first office tower. The steps serve to draw people down and provide a pleasant sheltered area for eating lunch.* MARCELLO IGONDA

*Facing page, left: A view of the 42-storey One California Plaza from the central fountain plazas: the Museum of Contemporary Art in red Indian sandstone is at the right. The tower, on a base of pinkish-grey Oklahoma granite, uses both light and dark grey reflective glass.* MARCELLO IGONDA

*Facing page, right: Perspective studies of the first office tower of California Plaza explore alternative treatments of the base, cap, corner pier and patterning of the glass in an effort to determine a clearly identifiable cap and base. One California Plaza was built without the stone cornice and opened in 1986.*

I see Los Angeles as a successor in kind to London — a vast collection of boroughs without a real centre. In Los Angeles, the connecting filaments are the freeways. In London, what had originally been royal hunting preserves became a pattern of protected parks running through the city. And so, in the manner of St. James Park and Hyde Park, California Plaza's 5.5 acres of mandated open spaces would lead from the Music Center to the symbolic core of Los Angeles, Pershing Square. But in keeping with the city's history, the gardens would be Spanish rather than English, with running waters, fountains and scented courts.

We placed the office towers at the end near neighbouring towers and arranged them about a central Performance Plaza. This was a covered outdoor stage for television specials and performance events that would attract both tourists and the far-flung Angelenos. We restored the "Angel's Flight" funicular that had existed early in the cen-

tury and planned for the inclusion of the Museum of Contemporary Art, a Dance Gallery, some small museums, and a cineplex. Throughout the exercise, we stressed spaces and settings for restaurants and shops. Three low condominium slabs totalling 750 units marched the length of the project towards a 450-room luxury hotel that anchored the other end. We proposed to terrace and landscape far up the condominium sides.

Another distinctive proposal, for the Museum of Contemporary Art (MOCA), reflected my tendency to rethink accepted institutional models. At the time, the best collection of contemporary Los Angeles art resided in converted stables outside Milan, Italy. Its owner, the prescient Count Panza di Piumbo, gave each artist an individual "stall" that is entered from the loggia. With this gallery in mind, I gave the MOCA a long series of spaces that ran across the joint base of the condominums. The exhibit areas would virtually open to the street. It seemed

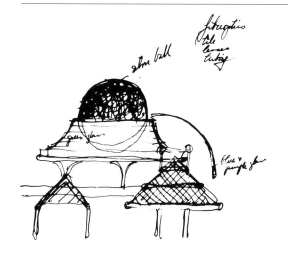

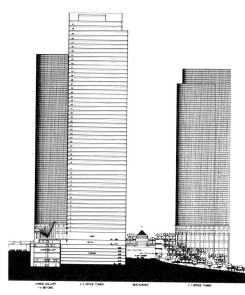

*Top left and right: In 1987 a water garden became the most recent scheme for the centrepiece attraction of California Plaza. Its location is the same as the original Performance Plaza, bridging Olive Street. Restaurant pavilions (right) are placed around and in a small lake, which will also have a performance area. Studies for the restaurant pavilions (left) explore different roof forms. To instill the pavilions with magic, they will be built of green, blue and purple glass. Fibre-optics, lenses and tubing will be incorporated to enhance the effect.* CHRISTOPHER L. HOWELL

*Bottom: A second office tower, Two California Plaza, begins construction in 1989, along with the Dance Gallery (left) and water garden (right) at its base, as indicated by this section. The third office tower is set for the final phase in 1995.*

a sensible move from the traditional art-museum-as-temple to art-as-street-scene, appropriate for contemporary art (taking it somewhat at its word) and particularly for Los Angeles, the irremediable capital of the car culture. Needless to say, my move away from the hallowed precinct idea was swiftly rejected by the MOCA board. Eventually Arata Isozaki's justly celebrated building took its place in a vastly different scheme. I like to think I played a role in the success of his building. His first proposal, a four-storey mass on a given constricted site, did not seem to help the project. Knowing his program, I had my team look at submerging the building on a slightly larger site with two one- or two-storey sections above grade on either side of a courtyard. In one day-long session I had first to get Iso's acceptance and then persuade the developer to release that much more land to him. Once it was done, Isozaki applied his art to bring off a marvellously dexterous building.

A revised master plan was drawn up within three years after the first, granting the MOCA and a first office tower their go-ahead as the first component of phase one. They were completed in 1985. A subsequent component includes a Dance Gallery, which is to be below the plaza, with only its entrance announced. Although it was difficult to squeeze into a limited space all the requirements of a theatre designed primarily for dance, even greater ingenuity was needed to bring the audience in at the top and then entice them down to the lowest orchestra level. We used a skylight to let light down the well of stairs, for the procession of the audience is as important to Bella Lewitsky, the dancer for whom the theatre was originally designed, as the movement on stage. Since the skylight would be the only visible evidence of the theatre, we developed a spiral of glass gesturing skyward with a staggered outline, suggesting the arrested grace of a dancer's movement.

As California Plaza unfolds, the degree of change seems to match the scale of the project, and none of the original plan will be seen in the built form. The second phase brings a hotel by another architect. The Canadian developer insisted on underground shopping in an odd transfer of northern ideas to the sunny south, and we spent a year cracking it open to the light to satisfy the CRA. With the input of a consulting impresario, the Performance Plaza was transformed into a modern version of Shakespeare's Globe Theatre: seats were in circular tiers above an orchestra level into which restaurants opened. The theatre could function as a cabaret by night and a market plaza by day, and the stage would be part of a huge fountain whose water spouts would act as curtains. A change of developer, a change of consultants: out went the outdoor theatre in favour of a number of informally arranged spots where ''spontaneous'' events could be staged. But the CRA pressed for a stronger locus, not willing to allow economies to cut down a program feature that would give California Plaza the feel of being a hub for the downtown.

As an alternative to an expensive major outdoor centre, I proposed turning the open plaza into a garden like Copenhagen's Tivoli, using an important artist to provide the element of fantasy. I quickly settled on David Hockney, whose magical sets for opera and ballet display a true gift for fantasy and whose fame as a painter might just help my case. I conceived of it as a water garden of wonderful pavilions, boats, bridges and sea creatures calling up a subconcious mythical world that has haunted us since the Middle Ages and before. His themes would be carried into the design of the shops and restaurant decor, costumes, and even tableware, so that all became part of a huge stage. It would be an artwork that people would move through. I was thrilled at the prospect of collaborating with the eminent Hockney. There are two ways design rises to integrity

and universal impact: one by the winnowing and accretion of the efforts of many over time, and the other by the relentlessness and genius of a single artist. Hockney's vision would provide the impetus to save California Plaza as a place, putting a ''there'' into it that mere architects could not achieve. While the client was considering the idea, we were faced with the CRA's demand for something, and proposed that garden pavilions and restaurants be built entirely of coloured glass, making at least a gesture at the bejewelled and crystal city of myth.

California Plaza's second phase begins in 1989, and the third phase will be realized in the 1990s. In the end, California Plaza will have gone up in much the same fashion as any piece of the city, in fits and starts, an essay on the art of design flexibility in a world where economics rule.

*California Plaza's spiral motif is given a sculptural expression for the entrance of the Dance Gallery. The high, structural glass work, illuminated at night, supplies the striking form needed to draw people into the underground facility. The Dance Gallery will house a 1,000-seat theatre and ancillary facilities.* CHRISTOPHER L. HOWELL

# CANADIAN CHANCERY

Neoclassical pretentions give Washington, D.C., an arcadian, dreamlike quality. The white marble monuments, the gigantic obelisk, the great open mall and overall low scale are intended to project formality. Yet there is an unintended innocence about it all, rooted in the naive belief that by imposing a city on the wilderness, a geometry on the city and Greco-Roman lines on the buildings, civic virtues and national strength will follow and a great republic be proclaimed. Today, this Enlightenment philosophy is protected with more ordinances than perhaps any other city would support.

At first glance, such rigidity might be associated with architectural sterility. But my experience in designing the Canadian Chancery proved otherwise. Someone suggested to me that in Washington we would have to go before twenty-five committees twenty-five times. In the end, we developed a genuine admiration for the necessary fences that guard the capital. The more restraints, the easier it is to design: the best of all possible worlds is when restrictions can be turned around to become sources of inspiration.

Everything was set out for us. The authorities gave us the envelope of space, the coverage and the cornice line. They mandated the use of the language of Neoclassicism with its order of base, colonnade, pediment and attic. They had already given the Canadian government an unparalleled site on Pennsylvania Avenue, the processional route between the White House and the Capitol. No other government has the privilege of such a position. Across the avenue is the grand neoclassical National Gallery with I. M. Pei's elegant, cooly modern addition, and across an adjacent park is another neoclassical building, a temple of justice.

*Facing page: The rotunda of the Canadian Chancery in Washington, D.C., finds its most immediate reference in the neighbouring Federal Trade Commission building. The chancery, designed in 1983, had to conform to strict design guidelines mandating a classical architectural order of elements from base to attic. The ambassador's office is in the attic penthouse.*
TIMOTHY HURSLEY/THE ARKANSAS OFFICE

*Washington's Pennsylvania Avenue Development Corporation required that the chancery build to property lines. On the short Pennsylvania Avenue elevation, the main public staircase to the podium level is framed by the "Rotunda of the Provinces" and the grade-level entrances to the art gallery and theatre.*
TIMOTHY HURSLEY/THE ARKANSAS OFFICE

More than any other building of mine the chancery was designed from the outside in. It was a pleasure to abandon the more difficult task of marrying the interior needs to outside determinants and instead to sculpt the building solely to fit the site, then to fit the program to the envelope. We worked almost entirely from models, beginning in 1983 with an early site model in styrofoam that determined the initial massing of the building against its neighbours, and moving to larger and larger models that in the end almost filled the studio as we studied the details of parapets and cornices.

A cornice and base line had to be present, and a columned face at least inferred. We had to build to the height required and fill out all corners of the site; this scheme left a hole between two wings containing a large inner courtyard and suggesting a U-shaped building. Washington required the completion of the pediment across the fourth side, and doing so gave us a strong horizontal to set off a grand entrance facing the green park space. I pulled back the stately row of columns that would normally support the heavy architrave, so that they support nothing but a skylight; then I made them of aluminum in an irrepressible tweak at the restrictions. A rotunda seemed to echo the classical porch of the landmark Federal Trade Commission building down the street, but its circle of twelve pillars number the ten Canadian provinces and two territories, an element of symbolism that a building of this kind can sustain. After all, a chancery inevitably conveys an image to its host country.

*Top: A model of the chancery conveys a sense of the interior court as an extension of the park. The court contains a pool of water, in which will ride a monumental sculpture of a Haida spirit canoe. The architrave span closes the fourth side of the chancery to provide a proscenium for the VIP entrance.* PANDA ASSOCIATES

*Middle: The longest side of the Canadian Chancery faces John Marshall Place Park, a space it adopts as its broad front yard. The Pennsylvania Avenue diagonal runs on the left of this aerial view of the presentation model. At this point, the ambassador's suite on the attic floor is expressed as a "villa."* PANDA ASSOCIATES

*Bottom: At this key location along the processional route between the Capitol and the White House, the area surrounding the chancery has a concentration of official Washington architecture. A federal courthouse sits across the park from the chancery and behind it are two District of Columbia government buildings; opposite is the National Gallery. The lot beside the chancery remains vacant. This axonometric shows how the chancery's angled corner lines up with I. M. Pei's uncompromisingly modern East Wing.*

Given the highly visible site and the importance of the Canadian-American relationship, the key design consideration was how to represent Canada appropriately. We could not flaunt some national distinction as we would in a completely alien country, for in the larger cultural picture our countries are indistinguishable. Politically, however, the relationship is full of complexes and complexity. In the end, I wanted the chancery to

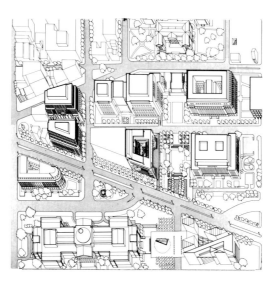

express an image of Canadian reserve and good manners, coupled with a characteristic gesture of openness and invitation, to affirm our similar heritages and at the same time project an element of freshness and forgivable naiveté. As for more specific readings, these will be found in the long horizontals that suggest the breadth of Canada, or in the ample courtyard with its light and spaciousness. In the middle, a large pool symbolizes our ocean limits. Standing in it is what I believe to be Bill Reid's finest sculpture, a bronze spirit canoe filled with legendary Haida figures, an eighteen-foot-long work that will delight children and philosophers alike. Of all the top sculptors in Canada, his work would be the most distinctive in Washington.

The chancery was an opportunity for me to experiment with the juxtaposition of dramatically different scales moving from the outside into the courtyard area. After the soaring opening onto the park, you see in its shelter the smaller rotunda and setback colonnade. Through these in turn appear the miniature entrance porch, the balconies and the domestically scaled penthouse of the ambassador. Conforming with Washington's classical architecture formula, set back from the building's edges, this last touch recalled Pliny's villa on its promontory over the Mediterranean.

The first compositions were much too complex; the balconies in the courtyard, the differing scales and treatments of the windows, the many shapes and sizes of columns betrayed the simplicity I needed to achieve. But in every design I tend to move from the complex to the simple as the form becomes clearer. What began to emerge was a gigantic sculpted form, cut away from the outer layer to reveal succeeding layers of inner strata, each different but of the same genre. Earlier punched windows were difficult because their strident beat diffused the clarity of the succeeding planes, so we abandoned them for long, more rhythmic bands of glass

A skylight behind the chancery's 160-foot architrave vaults to a colonnade of cast aluminum columns. These nonstructural members tease a city of impressive columns, but more importantly they initiate the play of scales that are a primary feature of the building.
TIMOTHY HURSLEY/THE ARKANSAS OFFICE

215

repeating a hooked pattern that seemed to pervade the composition in both two and three dimensions. A bold bulging cornice line was replaced by a subtler incised line in the stonework of the façade, and a sculpted railing at the top of the building by a quieter pierced one. These details and the occasional miniscule punched light in the hanging architrave served to emphasize the surface solidity of the cream and grey streaked Adair stone and the clarity of its planes.

The relationship of the three faces of the building, each of which had to have solid edges and top but be cut out between, were critical. The Pennsylvania Avenue side where the architrave spans from a relatively solid west corner, housing the art gallery and ministerial offices, to the slender triangular pillar — the only reference to the angularity of I. M. Pei's gallery across the street — is a dramatic entranceway. The John Marshall Park side, which is the VIP entrance, has the more expansive porte-cochère: a broad stairway leads between the soaring colonnade to the courtyard where the Bill Reid sculpture sits. This side also has its more solid corner to

the north end, from which the hanging architrave spans to the same triangular column. It houses the immigration department with its modest entrance played against the grand opening of the portico. The north face is the duty entrance for personnel and goods: mostly blank, it plays on subtly receding and advancing planes intimating the theme of the receding strata of the other façades.

The relatively new and enthusiastic Pennsylvania Avenue Development Corporation did have some comments as we went along. One was a reservation about an early asymmetrical composition of the art gallery façade, which to me introduced a degree of dynamic tension to that face. I had to bow to a more mundane punched window, which may be calmer in the total composition of the building. Objections to the polished stainless steel fence posts also prevailed, since they are not found elsewhere on the avenue. I thought they would reflect the surrounding planting intriguingly, disappearing into the shrubbery and not seeming a barrier at all.

We also went through prolonged discussions with our own Department of External Affairs over the interiors. At the beginning it was agreed that the department's own interior designers would handle the internal nonpublic office areas and that we would be responsible for all the areas which had to do with public information or reception. However, there was some contention about who should do the ambassador's suite — in my mind the most significant reception area of all. I had hoped that the chancery could be a showcase for Canadian design, with furniture and finishes from our top designers, but by the time the suite was conceded to us, it was too late to arrange the special commissions for the opening in 1988. Our own lobby design, with its cream and grey stone colours broken by vermilion furnishings, was carried to the dining suite and lounge. Department staff found this a bit strong, as well they may. My view is that, properly practised, design is nothing if not a courageous adventure.

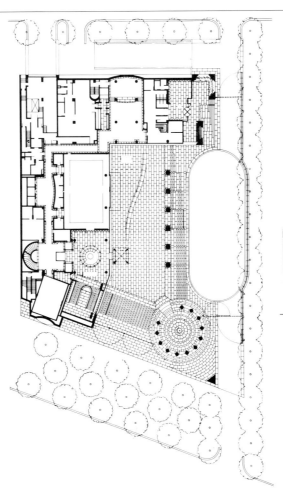

When Philip Johnson phoned to congratulate me on receiving the 1986 American Institute of Architects Gold Medal, he praised the chancery as the best building I had ever done. I put down the phone very pleased with his words. Then a thought occurred to me: you always hope that your last work is your best, but here was Philip speaking from his revivalist mood, and I working to subvert the historicist scheme with the virtues of modern Classicism. If the chancery ''fit'' in this most self-consciously historic city, did that mean I had succeeded too well?

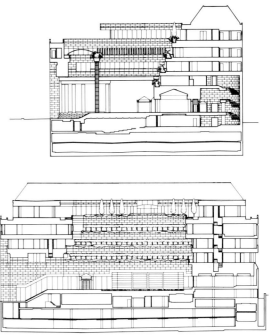

217

*Facing page: a single angular column supports the long horizontals that define the volume of the building. The chancery is clad in Adair limestone from Ontario.* TIMOTHY HURSLEY/THE ARKANSAS OFFICE

*Left: The podium or entrance level plan shows the public spaces of the 226,000-square-foot chancery. A large general-purpose room in the centre faces a rectangular pool in the court. The rooms at the upper right are the immigration offices, which have their own entrance off John Marshall Park.*

*Top right: In a section cut parallel to Pennsylvania Avenue, the planters step back to open the central space. The tall columns support a glass vault and a planter. In the centre of the podium level is the small entrance pavilion.*

*Bottom right: A section through the chancery, cut parallel to the park, reveals the horizontal planters that articulate the court space and recall Canada's wilderness.*

# PROJECT CREDITS

Projects are listed in the order in which they appear in the text. Dates given are for the start of design on each project. The following abbreviations are used to indicate the responsible offices:

AE      Arthur Erickson independently
AEGM  Arthur Erickson and Geoffrey Massey
EMV    Erickson/Massey Vancouver office
EMM   Erickson/Massey Montreal office
EMT    Erickson/Massey Toronto office
AEAV   Arthur Erickson Architects Vancouver office
AEAT   Arthur Erickson Architects Toronto office
AEAL   Arthur Erickson Architects Los Angeles
        office

For each of the projects illustrated, the architectural and landscape design direction was established by Arthur Erickson and his team.

Individual credits are given for Erickson staff members, assistants or collaborators who played a major role in the design, documentation and execution of each project.

For projects with a large team or long time duration, the credits are grouped according to the level of responsibility or type of professional involvement.

The credits for joint venture partners, major subconsultants and other associated firms are limited to the firm name, even for projects on which principals and staff of the other firms were integral members of the design team.

## P A R T  I

ERICKSON GARDEN, Vancouver, B.C., AE, 1960

SMITH HOUSE I, West Vancouver, B.C., AEGM, 1953

KILLAM-MASSEY RESIDENCE, West Vancouver, B.C., AEGM, 1955

GRAUER GARDEN TERRACE AND CABANA, Vancouver, B.C., AE, 1957

BOULTBEE HOUSE REMODELLING, Vancouver, B.C., AE, 1960

DANTO HOUSE, Vancouver, B.C., AE, 1961
*Leo Ehling*

DYDE HOUSE, Edmonton, Alberta, AE, 1960

FULDAUER HOUSE, West Vancouver, B.C., EMV, 1963
*Gary Hanson, Bob Easton*

THOMAS HOUSE, West Vancouver, B.C., AE, 1960

LAXTON HOUSE, West Vancouver, B.C., EMV, 1964
*Gary Hanson*

BALDWIN HOUSE, Burnaby, B.C., EMV, 1963
*Gary Hanson, Vagn Houlbjerg*

BAYLES HOUSE, West Vancouver, B.C., AE, 1963
*Arthur Boyd*

LLOYD HOUSE, Vancouver, B.C., AE, 1962
*Gary Hanson*

POINT GREY TOWNHOUSES, Vancouver, B.C., EMV, 1963
*Fred Dalla-Lana, Fred Olin, Bill Tong*

SHANNON MEWS, Vancouver, B.C., EMV/AEAV, 1971
*Ken Burroughs*
*Tom Robertson, Barry Simpson,*
*Freeman Chan, Harry Haid*
Structural: *Tamm Engineering*
Mechanical: *J. D. Kern & Company*
Electrical: *Arnold Nemetz Engineering*
Landscape: *Don Vaughan & Associates*

FILBERG HOUSE, Comox, B.C., AE, 1958
*Leo Ehling*

SIMON FRASER UNIVERSITY, Burnaby, B.C., EMV, 1963
*Geoffrey Massey, Ken Burroughs, Ron Bain,*
*Bruno Freschi, Rein Raimet, Leo Ehling,*
*Genje Ogawa, Bing Thom, Fred Dalla-Lana,*
*Dan Lazosky*
Structural: *Otto Safir (Central Mall & Transportation Centre); Bogue Babicki & Associates (Classroom Block & Married Student Housing); Swan Wooster Engineering (Women's Residence & Water Tower)*
Mall Roof Consultants: *John Kariotis, Jeffrey Lindsay*
Associated Architects: *Zoltan Kiss (Academic Quadrangle); Rhone & Iredale (Science Complex); Robert Harrison (Library); McNab Lee & Logan (Gymnasium & Theatre)*

## P A R T  I I

CENTENNIAL MUSEUM COMPLEX (proposal), Vancouver, B.C., EMV, 1965
*Andrew Malczewski*

PROJECT 56, Vancouver, B.C., AE, 1956

CITÉ DES TERRASSES, Montreal, Quebec, EMM, 1968
*Dan Lazosky, Nick Bawlf*
Joint Venture Architect: *David & Boulva*

FISHERMEN'S QUAY, Vancouver, B.C., EMV, 1969
*Rein Raimet, James Strasman*

SIKH TEMPLE, Vancouver, B.C., EMV, 1968
*Ken Burroughs, George Bradburn*

VILLAGE LAKE LOUISE, Banff National Park, Alberta, EMV, 1969
*Rein Raimet, Ron Bain, Geoffrey Massey, George Bradburn*

ERICKSON/MASSEY (ARTHUR ERICKSON ARCHITECTS) OFFICE, Vancouver, B.C., EMV, 1968
*Paul Rust, Bruno Freschi, Gary Hanson*

CENTRE DU PLATEAU BEAUBOURG (competition), Paris, France, EMV, 1971
*Rein Raimet, Andy Roost*

GRAHAM HOUSE, West Vancouver, B.C., EMV, 1963
*Gary Hanson*

SMITH HOUSE 2, West Vancouver, B.C., EMV, 1964
*Gary Hanson, Mo Van Nostrand*

MONTIVERDI ESTATES, West Vancouver, B.C., AEAV, 1979
*Eva Matsuzaki*
*Arthur Yesaki, Rick Clark, Joachim Halbach*
Structural: *C. Y. Loh*
Mechanical: *Park & Djawa Engineering*
Electrical: *R. J. Wong & Associates*
Landscape: *Cornelia Hahn Oberlander*

CATTON HOUSE, West Vancouver, B.C., EMV, 1967
*Gary Hanson, Nick Milkovich*

HILBORN HOUSE, Cambridge, Ontario, EMT/AEAT, 1970
*James Strasman*
*Walter Porembski, Khaja Vicaruddin, Ciro Polsinelli*
Interiors: *Francisco Kripacz*

MacMILLAN BLOEDEL BUILDING, Vancouver, B.C.,
EMV, 1965
*James Strasman, Geoffrey Massey*
*Gary Hanson, Proctor Lemare*
Structural: *Otto Safir*
Mechanical & Electrical: *Reid Crowther & Partners*
Lighting: *William Lam*
Associated Architect: *Francis Donaldson*

UNIVERSITY OF LETHBRIDGE, Alberta, EMV, 1968
*Ron Bain, Gary Hanson*
*Rein Raimet, Tad Young, Andy Roost,*
*Byron Olson*
Structural: *Bogue Babicki & Associates*
Mechanical & Electrical: *Reid Crowther & Partners*
Mechanical: *F. S. Dubin Associates*
Lighting: *William Lam & Associates*
Associated Architect: *Robins Mitchell Watson*

BANK OF CANADA, Ottawa, Ontario, EMT/AEAT,
1969
*James Strasman*
*Keith Loffler, Fred Allin, Pui-To Chau*
Joint Venture Architect: *Marani Rounthwaite & Dick*
Structural: *C. D. Carruthers & Wallace*
Mechanical & Electrical: *ARDEC;*
*Brais Frigon Hanley*
Lighting: *William Lam & Associates*
Landscape: *Emiel van der Meulen*

CANADIAN PAVILION, TOKYO INTERNATIONAL
TRADE FAIR, Japan, EMV, 1964
*Ron Bain*

CANADIAN PAVILION, EXPO '67 (concept),
Montreal, Quebec, EMV, 1964
Associated Architect: *Evans St. Gelais*
Special Consultant: *Jeffrey Lindsay*

MAN IN THE COMMUNITY (AND MAN AND HIS
HEALTH) PAVILIONS, EXPO '67, Montreal,
Quebec, EMV/EMM, 1965
*Ron Bain, Michael Miller*
Structural: *Baracs & Gunther*
Mechanical & Electrical: *Bouthillette & Parizeau*
Landscape: *Harper-Lantzius Consortium*
Special Consultant: *Jeffrey Lindsay*

CANADIAN PAVILION, EXPO '70, Osaka, Japan,
EMV, 1967
*Bruno Freschi, Ron Bain*
*Vagn Houlbjerg*
Associated Architect & Engineering: *Nikken Sekkei*
Special Consultant: *Jeffrey Lindsay*

HABITAT PAVILION, Vancouver, B.C., AEAV, 1975
*Bing Thom, Alberto Zennaro, Freeman Chan*
Structural: *Bogue Babicki & Associates*

GATHERING PLACE, EXPO 86, Vancouver, B.C.,
AEAV, 1983
*Rainer Fassler, Eva Matsuzaki*
*Paul Berthon, Bruce Trewin*
Joint Venture Architect and Engineering:
*Phillips Barratt Engineers & Architects*

MADRID FAIRGROUNDS (competition), Spain,
AEAT, 1985
*Yasuo Muramatsu, Wyn Bielaska, Diana Lilljelund*
Engineering: *Hispana Alemana Construcciones*

MUSEUM OF ANTHROPOLOGY, Vancouver, B.C.,
EMV/AEAV, 1972
*Ron Bain, Alex Kee*
*Freeman Chan, Barry Simpson, Nick Milkovich*
Structural: *Bogue Babicki & Associates*
Mechanical: *Mechanical Consultants Western*
Electrical: *W. T. Haggert & Company*
Landscape: *Cornelia Hahn Oberlander*
Exhibits: *Hopping Kovach Grinell*

# P A R T   I I I

GOVERNMENT OF CANADA BUILDING,
Vancouver, B.C., AEAV, 1977
*Eva Matsuzaki*
*Wilbert Bruegger, Larry McFarland, Paul Berthon,*
*Kiyoshi Matsuzaki, Dave Osborne*
Joint Venture Architect: *McCarter Nairne*
*& Partners*
Structural: *Bogue Babicki & Associates*
Mechanical: *Reid Crowther & Partners*
Electrical: *W. T. Haggert & Company*

BRITISH COLUMBIA MEDICAL CENTRE,
Vancouver, B.C., AEAV, 1973
*Russell Vandiver, Richard Blagborne,*
*Milton Gardner, Peter Petrall, Bob Billington*
*Che-Cheung Poon, Bob Hoshide, Larry McFarland*
Structural: *Bush Bohlman & Partners*
Mechanical & Electrical: *D. W. Thomson*

SASKATOON CITY HOSPITAL, Saskatchewan,
AEAV, 1984
*Bruce Trewin, Kiyoshi Matsuzaki*
*Rick Clark, Melanie Marchand, Kon-Hee Ho,*
*Gerry Eckford*
Joint Venture Architects: *Billington Poon*
*Associates; Folstad & Friggstad Architects (City*
*Hospital Architects Group)*
Structural: *Cochrane Lavalin; Fenco Lavalin*
Mechanical: *McCartan Gaudet & Associates;*
*D. W. Thomson Consultants*
Electrical: *J. J. White & Associates*
Landscape: *Hilderman Witty Crosby Hanna*
*& Associates*

CHRIST CHURCH CATHEDRAL DEVELOPMENT,
Vancouver, B.C., EMV, 1971
*Ron Bain*
*Tom Robertson*
Structural: *Bogue Babicki & Associates*

WATERFRONT CENTRE, Vancouver, B.C., AEAV,
1980
*Kiyoshi Matsuzaki*
*Paul Berthon, Bruce Trewin, Alan Bell*
Structural: *Jones Kwong Kishi; Severud Associates*
Mechanical: *Vinto Engineering*

SUN LIFE ASSURANCE COMPLEX (competition),
Toronto, Ontario, AEAT, 1980
*Alberto Zennaro*
*Ralph Bergman, Peter Clewes, Richard Coombs,*
*Anne Vezina*
Structural: *Robert Halsall & Associates*
Mechanical: *R. David Mackay Engineering*

HARBORPLACE SQUARE (competition), Baltimore,
Maryland, AEAT, 1982
*Ralph Bergman*
*Richard Coombs, Barbara Vogel, Peter Clewes,*
*Oscar Pereira*
Structural: *Robert Halsall & Associates*

HELMUT EPPICH HOUSE, West Vancouver, B.C.,
AEAV, 1972
*Nick Milkovich*
Interiors: *Francisco Kripacz*
Structural: *Bogue Babicki & Associates*
Mechanical: *J. D. Kern & Company*

HUGO EPPICH HOUSE, West Vancouver, B.C.,
AEAV, 1979
*Nick Milkovich, Inara Kundzins*
Structural: *C. Y. Loh & Associates*
Mechanical: *J. D. Kern & Company*
Landscape: *Cornelia Hahn Oberlander*

FIRE ISLAND HOUSE, New York, AEAV, 1977
*Nick Milkovich, Francisco Kripacz, George Hunter*

PACIFIC NORTHWEST HOUSE, Washington, AEAV,
1979
*Nick Milkovich*
*Inara Kundzins, Allen Cheng, Bob Hoshide,*
*Sandra Fraser*
Structural: *Bush Bohlman & Partners*
Mechanical: *D. W. Thomson Consultants*
Lighting: *Incorporated Consultants*
Landscape: *Cornelia Hahn Oberlander*

ROBSON SQUARE (Provincial Government Offices
& Law Courts Complex), Vancouver, B.C., AEAV,
1973
Co-ordinators: *Bing Thom, James Wright,*
*Rainer Fassler*
Structural: *Bogue Babicki & Associates*
Mechanical: *Reid Crowther & Partners*
Electrical: *W. T. Haggert & Company*
Lighting: *William Lam & Associates*
Landscape: *Cornelia Hahn Oberlander, Ken Morris,*
*Robert Zinser, Raoul Robillard*
Urban Design: *Dennis Christianson, Alan Bell*

Government Offices
*Junichi Hashimoto, Jim Wright, Randolph*
*Jefferson, Eva Matsuzaki, Yasuo Muramatsu,*
*James K. M. Cheng, Arthur Yesaki, Bob Bida,*
*Tom Robertson, Shanti Ghose*

Law Courts
*Rainer Fassler, Ron Beaton*
*Barry Simpson, Nick Milkovich, Eva Matsuzaki,*
*Rodger Morris, Allen Cheng, Eddie Maifredi,*
*Kirat Anand, Arthur Yesaki, Bob Bida,*
*Tom Robertson, Shanti Ghose*

VANCOUVER ART GALLERY, Vancouver, B.C.,
AEAV, 1979
*Eva Matsuzaki, Noel Best*
*Kon-Hee Ho, Tom Robertson, Barbara Shapiro*
*Arthur Yesaki, Sandra Fraser*
Structural: *Bogue Babicki & Associates*
Mechanical: *Mechanical Consultants Western*
Electrical: *R. J. Wong & Associates*
Lighting: *Incorporated Consultants*

NATIONAL GALLERY OF CANADA (competition),
Ottawa, Ontario, AEAT, 1975
*Bing Thom, Oscar Pereira, Franco Scolozzi,*
*Doris Scolozzi, Richard Stevens*
Joint Venture Architect: *David Boulva Cleve*
Lighting: *Claude Engle*

ROBERT McLAUGHLIN ART GALLERY, Oshawa,
Ontario, AEAT, 1984
*Ralph Bergman, Joan Kilpatrick*
Structural: *Robert Halsall & Associates*
Mechanical & Electrical: *Bayes Yates McMillan*
Landscape: *Paul Ferris & Associates*

KING'S LANDING, Toronto, Ontario, AEAT, 1981
*Ralph Bergman*
*Richard Coombs, Rudy Wallman,*
*Shawn McSweeney, Pui-To Chau*
Structural: *The Maryon Partnership;*
*Rand Engineering*
Mechanical & Electrical: *Rybka Smith & Ginsler*
Landscape: *Paul Ferris & Associates*

EVERGREEN BUILDING, Vancouver, B.C., AEAV,
1978
*Randolph Jefferson, Barry Johns, Paul Berthon*
Structural: *Bogue Babicki & Associates*
Mechanical: *Mechanical Consultants Western*
Electrical: *R. J. Wong & Associates*
Landscape: *Cornelia Hahn Oberlander*

LAUREL POINT INN ADDITION, Victoria, B.C.,
AEAV, 1987
*Rainer Fassler, John Graham*
*Kon-Hee Ho, Sebastian Butler, Thomas Winkler,*
*Brock Cheadle, Gerry Eckford*
Structural: *C. Y. Loh & Associates*
Mechanical: *Yoneda & Associates*
Electrical: *R. J. Wong & Associates*

YORKDALE SUBWAY STATION, Toronto, Ontario,
AEAT, 1974
*James Strasman, Michael Jones*
Structural: *M. S. Yolles & Partners*
Mechanical: *Tamblyn, Mitchell & Partners*
Electrical: *Kalns Associates*

NAPP LABORATORIES, Cambridge, England,
AEAT, 1979
*Alberto Zennaro, Fred Allin*
*Pui-To Chau, Peter Clewes, Richard Coombs,*
*Rudy Wallman*
Interiors: *Francisco Kripacz*
Structural: *Robert Halsall & Associates*
Mechanical: *R. David Mackay Engineering*
Electrical: *Oscar Faber & Partners*
Associated Architect: *Yakeley Associates*

TECK MINING OFFICES, Toronto, Ontario, AEAT,
1980
*Francisco Kripacz, Ralph Bergman*
*Anne Vezina*

ROY THOMSON HALL, Toronto, Ontario, AEAT,
1976
*Keith Loffler*
*Bing Thom, Michael Jones, Margaret Holland,*
*Richard Stevens, Anne Vezina, Alberto Zennaro*
Joint Venture Architect: *Mathers & Haldenby*
Interiors: *Francisco Kripacz*
Acoustical: *Bolt Beranek & Newman*
Structural: *C. D. Carruthers & Wallace*
Mechanical: *Crossey Langlois Firman*
Electrical: *Kalns Associates/Crossey Engineering*
Lighting: *Claude Engle*
Landscape: *EVM*

DOWNTOWN WEST, Toronto, Ontario, AEAT, 1976
*Bing Thom, Richard Stevens, Oscar Pereira*
Joint Venture Architect: *Mathers & Haldenby*

RED DEER ARTS CENTRE, Alberta, AEAV, 1981
*Bruce Trewin*
*James Wright, Rick Clark, Daryl Plater,*
*Sandra Fraser*
Structural: *Halsall-Stanley Associates*
Mechanical: *Hemisphere Engineering*
Electrical: *Morgan Dowhan Engineering*
Theatre: *S. Leonard Auerbach & Associates*
Acoustical: *R. Lawrence Kierkegaard & Associates*
Landscape: *Cornelia Hahn Oberlander;*
*Roman Fodchuk*
Associated Architect: *Robert Merchant Architect*

# P A R T  I V

MINISTRY OF PUBLIC WORKS AND HOUSING
(competition), Riyadh, Saudi Arabia,
AEAT/AEAV, 1977
*Oscar Pereira, James Wright, James K. M. Cheng*

MINISTRY OF FOREIGN AFFAIRS INTERIM
HEADQUARTERS, Jeddah, Saudi Arabia,
AEAV/AEAT, 1978
*James Wright, Wilbert Bruegger*
*Oscar Pereira, Alan Bell*
*Randolph Jefferson, Jon Lightburn*
Joint Venture Architect: *IDEA Center*

AL FALAH SCHOOL (competition), Makkah, Saudi
Arabia, AEAV, 1983
*Alan Bell, Sonya Lukaitis*
*Jonathan Barrett, David Siverson*

KUWAIT INSURANCE COMPANY, Kuwait City,
Kuwait, AEAV, 1983
*Alan Bell, Douglas Muir*
*Rick Clark, Noel Best*
Associated Architect & Engineering: *Al Marzouk &*
*Abi-Hanna*

OFFICE BUILDING (competition), Abu Dhabi,
U.A.E., AEAT, 1975
*James Strasman*

ETISALAT HEADQUARTERS, Abu Dhabi, U.A.E.,
AEAT, 1985
*Richard Stevens, Alberto Zennaro, Bill Colaco,*
*Wyn Bielaska*

ETISALAT BUILDING, Dubai, U.A.E., AEAT, 1986
*Richard Stevens, John Pepper, Colin Hlasny,*
*Christopher Erickson*
Structural: *Robert Halsall & Associates*
Mechanical & Electrical: *MCW Consultants*

PRINCE COURTS CONDOMINIUMS, Kuala Lumpur,
Malaysia, AEAV, 1983
*Kiyoshi Matsuzaki, Rick Clark, Gary Nagamori,*
*Alan Bell*

CHEN HOUSE, Kuala Lumpur, Malaysia, AEAV,
1984
*Nick Milkovich, Susan Stephenson*
Structural: *C. Y. Loh & Associates*

CANADIAN EMBASSY DEVELOPMENT
(competition), Tokyo, Japan, AEAV, 1984
*Kiyoshi Matsuzaki, Wilbert Bruegger*
Associated Firms: *Kenzo Tange & Associates;*
*Takenaka Komuten*

SHANGHAI CULTURE & ARTS CENTRE
(competition), Shanghai, China, AEAV, 1987
*Kiyoshi Matsuzaki, Bruce Trewin, John Graham*
Joint Venture Architects: *P & T Architects;*
*Shanghai Municipal Institute of Civic*
*Architectural Design*

SAWABER HOUSING DEVELOPMENT, Kuwait City,
Kuwait, AEAV, 1976
*Kiyoshi Matsuzaki, Alan Bell, Larry McFarland,*
*Che-Cheung Poon, Wilbert Bruegger*
Structural: *Severud Perrone Sturm Bandel*
Mechanical & Electrical: *Syska & Hennessy*
Landscape: *Schnadelbach Braun Partnership*

MADINAH HOTEL/RESIDENTIAL DEVELOPMENT,
Madinah, Saudi Arabia, AEAT, 1978
*Alberto Zennaro, Oscar Pereira*
Associated Firm & Engineering: *Cansult*

FINTAS TOWN CENTRE, Kuwait City, Kuwait,
AEAV, 1979
*Alan Bell, Kiyoshi Matsuzaki*
*Richard Blagborne, Joachim Halbach,*
*Shahram Moeghbel, Per Palm, Bruce Trewin*
Structural: *Severud-Perrone-Szegezdy-Sturm*
Mechanical: *Kunstadt Associates*
Civil: *Freeman Fox International*
Landscape: *The Schnadelbach Partnership*
Retail Planning: *D. I. Design*

ADMINISTRATIVE HEADQUARTERS, Riyadh,
Saudi Arabia, AEAT, 1978
*Oscar Pereira, Gero Onnma*
Associated Firm & Engineering: *Frank E. Basil*

TECHNICAL UNIVERSITY, Saudi Arabia, AEAT,
1980
*Michael Jones, Richard Stevens*
*Bill Lusk, Ahmad Osman, Chris Knowles,*
*Barbara Vogel, Jamie Goad*
Associated Firm & Engineering: *Frank E. Basil*

ABU NUWAS CONSERVATION/DEVELOPMENT
PROJECT, Baghdad, Iraq, AEAV, 1981
*Alan Bell*
*Jonathan Barrett, Sonya Lukaitis, Douglas Muir,*
*Ted Scott, David Siverson*
Planning Analysis: *Halcrow Fox & Associates*
Civil: *Freeman Fox International*
Landscape: *The Schnadelbach Partnership*
Associated Architect: *Hisham Munir & Associates*

HAMMA GOVERNMENT COMPLEX (competition),
Algiers, Algeria, AEAV/AEAT, 1984
*Alan Bell, Dick Stevens*
*Alberto Zennaro, Noel Best, Wilbert Bruegger,*
*Sonya Lukaitis, Wynn Bielaska, John Pepper*
Associated Firms: *Arcop Associates, Lavalin*

KING ABDULAZIZ UNIVERSITY, Jeddah, Saudi
Arabia, AEAT, 1980
*Keith Loffler, Dick Stevens, Peter Bull,*
*Mustafa Master*
(Campus Consortium Consultants)
Joint Venture Architect: *The Webb Zerafa Menkes*
*Housden Partnership*
Structural: *Quinn Dressel; Nicolet Chartrand Knoll*
Mechanical & Electrical: *MCW Consultants*
Civil: *Cansult*

ISLAMIC UNIVERSITY OF MADINAH,
Saudi Arabia, AEAT, 1983
*Oscar Pereira, Robert Zinser*
*Erik Mustonen, Ahmad Osman, James Wright*
Joint Venture Partners & Engineering: *Frank E.*
*Basil; Dar al Riyadh (Erickson Basil DAR)*

SANCST SCIENCE HALLS, Riyadh, Saudi Arabia,
AEAV, 1982
*Richard Blagborne, Wilbert Bruegger,*
*Douglas Muir, Don Stuart, Gary Nagamori,*
*Joachim Halbach*
Joint Venture Partner, Structural & Civil:
*Dar al Riyadh*
Mechanical & Electrical: *Kunstadt Associates*
Landscape: *The Schnadelbach Partnership*
Exhibit Concept: *Museum Content Builders*

# P A R T   V

KEEVIL HOUSE RENOVATIONS & POOL,
Vancouver, B.C., AEAV, 1983
*Nick Milkovich, Don Stuart, Allen Cheng*
Structural: *C. Y. Loh & Associates*
Mechanical: *J. D. Kern & Company*
Pool: *Shawn Williams, Rockingham Engineering*
Landscape: *Cornelia Hahn Oberlander*

SUKI'S, Vancouver, B.C., AEAV, 1986
*Nick Milkovich, Sonya Lukaitis*
Structural: *C. Y. Loh & Associates*
Mechanical: *Yoneda & Associates*
Electrical: *Schenke-Bawol*

AEA LOS ANGELES OFFICE, California, AEAL,
1981
*Francisco Kripacz, Randolph Jefferson,*
*Marcello Igonda*

PORTLAND MUNICIPAL SERVICES BUILDING
(competition), Portland, Oregon, AEAV, 1979
*Rainer Fassler, Tony Robins, Robert McGilvray*
Joint Venture Architect: *SRG Partnership*
Developer/Contractor: *Dillingham*

HARBOR STEPS, Seattle, Washington, AEAV, 1980
*Rainer Fassler*
*Wilbert Bruegger, Robert McGilvray,*
*Raymond Stern, Roberto Pacheco,*
*Sonya Lukaitis, Rick Clark*
Joint Venture Architect: *Clayton R. Joyce*
*& Associates*
Structural: *Ratti Fossatti Associates*
Mechanical: *John Graham Company*
Electrical: *Sparling & Associates*
Hotel Planning: *Dale Keller & Associates*

THE WINTER GARDEN, Anchorage, Alaska, AEAV,
1985
*Rainer Fassler, Wilbert Bruegger, Sonya Lukaitis*

CROWN PLAZA, Los Angeles, California, AEAL,
1982
*Marcello Igonda, Dennis Cramer, Daynard Tullis*
Structural: *John A. Martin & Associates*
Mechanical & Electrical: *Hayakawa Associates*

MAGUIRE/KNAPP OFFICE BUILDING (competition),
Los Angeles, California, AEAL, 1982
*Yasuo Muramatsu, Randolph Jefferson*

VISUAL ARTS CENTER, OHIO STATE UNIVERSITY
(competition), Columbus, Ohio, AEAV, 1983
*Rainer Fassler, Nick Milkovich, Susan Stephenson*
Joint Venture Architect: *Feinknopf Macioce Schappa*

TRUMP CONDOMINIUMS & HOTEL (competition),
New York, New York, AEAT, 1982
*Oscar Pereira, Peter Clewes*

60 WALL STREET (competition), New York, New
York, AEAT, 1982
*Ralph Bergman*
*Shawn McSweeny, Anne Vezina, Oscar Pereira*

HAROLD WASHINGTON LIBRARY CENTER
(competition), Chicago, Illinois, AEAT, 1988
*Wyn Bielaska*
*John O'Connor, John Ciarmela, Zuhal Ackman*
Joint Venture Architect: *VOA Associates*
Developer: *John Buck Company*
Structural: *Cohen Barreto Marchertas*
Mechanical & Electrical: *ESD*

FAIRFAX COUNTY CENTER, Virginia, AEAT, 1982
*Oscar Pereira, Robert Zinser*
Joint Venture Architect: *Dewberry & Davis*
Structural: *Robert Halsall & Associates*
Mechanical & Electrical: *Syska & Hennessy*

INTELSAT HEADQUARTERS (competition),
Washington, D.C., AEAT, 1980
*Richard Stevens, Rudy Wallman, Peter Clewes*

BEVERLY HILLS CIVIC CENTER (competition),
California, AEAL, 1982
*Alberto Bertoli, Susan Crawford*

MARKHAM MUNICIPAL BUILDING, Ontario, AEAT,
1986
*Oscar Pereira*
*Ahmed Osman, Mustafa Master, Joseph Galea,*
*Erik Mustonen*
Structural: *M. S. Yolles & Partners*
Mechanical & Electrical: *Bayes Yates McMillan*

FRESNO CITY HALL, California, AEAL, 1987
*Alberto Bertoli, Susan Hubbard Oakley*
Associate Architect: *Lew & Patnaude*
Structural: *Structcon*
Mechanical: *W. L. Donley & Associates*
Electrical: *The Engineering Enterprise*
Landscape: *Robert Boro*

THUNDER BAY GOVERNMENT OFFICE BUILDING,
Ontario, AEAT, 1987
*Barbara Vogel, Wyn Bielaska*
Joint Venture Architect: *Reginald Nalezyty*
Structural: *Robert Halsall & Associates*
Mechanical & Electrical: *MCW Consultants*

DISCOVERY PLACE, Prince George, B.C., AEAV,
1986
*Rainer Fassler, Noel Best, John Graham*
Structural: *Bush Bohlman & Partners*
Mechanical & Electrical: *D. W. Thomson*
*Consultants*
Acoustical: *Artec Consultants*
Theatre: *S. Leonard Auerbach & Associates*
Associated Architect: *Tom West Architect*

GRANT HOUSE 1, Woodside, California, AEAV,
1979
*Nick Milkovich, Susan Stephenson*

BRADLEY HOUSE, Carpinteria, California, AEAV,
1979
*Nick Milkovich, Susan Stephenson*

MALIBU HOUSE, California, AEAV, 1981
*Nick Milkovich, Susan Stephenson,*
*Tom Robertson*

KHOSLA HOUSE, Portola Valley, California, AEAL,
1986
*Marcello Igonda, Daynard Tullis, Paul Murdoch*
Structural & Civil: *Rutherford & Chekene*
Mechanical: *Harold T. Kushner & Associates*
Landscape: *Smith & Smith*

LOS ANGELES HOUSE, California, AEAV, 1986
*Nick Milkovich, Inara Kundzins*
*Tom Robertson, Astrid Drikitis, Gerry Eckford*
Structural: *C. Y. Loh & Associates*

PUGET SOUND HOUSE, Washington, AEAV, 1983
*Nick Milkovich, Inara Kundzins*
*Kon-Hee Ho, Tom Robertson*
Structural: *Ray Chalker Engineering*
Mechanical: *Allen V. Creten*
Landscape: *Cornelia Hahn Oberlander*

BIOLOGICAL SCIENCES EXPANSION, STANFORD
UNIVERSITY, Palo Alto, California, AEAL, 1985
*Joseph Collins, Alberto Bertoli, Francisco Kripacz,*
*Elizabeth Widerhorn*
Associated Architect & Lab Planning: *McLellan &*
*Copenhagen*
Structural: *Rutherford & Chekene*
Mechanical & Electrical: *Gluma & Associates*

BIOLOGICAL SCIENCES UNIT 2, UNIVERSITY OF
CALIFORNIA, Irvine, California, AEAL, 1986
*Joseph Collins, James Matson, Francisco Kripacz,*
*Timothy Lambert*
Structural: *Cygna Consulting Engineers*
Mechanical: *Hellman & Lober*
Electrical: *Chen & Kanwar*
Lab Planning: *Earl Walls Associates*

TEXTILE SCHOOL, NORTH CAROLINA STATE
UNIVERSITY, Raleigh, North Carolina, AEAV,
1986
*Rainer Fassler, Wilbert Bruegger, Alan Bell*
Associated Architect: *Hamill-Walter Associates*
Landscape: *LandDesign*

GENERAL MOTORS ADVANCED CONCEPTS
CENTER, Malibu, California, AEAL, 1985
*Susan Hubbard Oakley, James Matson,*
*Timothy Lambert*
Structural: *John A. Martin & Associates*
Mechanical & Electrical: *Jones, Cooper*
*& Associates*
Landscape: *Emmet L. Wemple & Associates*

SAN DIEGO CONVENTION CENTER, San Diego,
California, AEAL, 1984
*Alberto Bertoli, Yasuo Muramatsu,*
*Richard Stevens, Michael Kan, Daynard Tullis*
Joint Venture Architects: *Deems Lewis McKinley;*
*Loschky Marquardt & Nesholm*
Interiors: *Francisco Kripacz*
Structural: *John A. Martin & Associates*
Tent Structure: *Horst Berger Partners*
Mechanical: *Syska & Hennessy*
Civil: *George S. Nolte & Associates*
Lighting: *William Lam Associates*
Audio-Visual: *Con-Tech*
Landscape: *Van Dyke & Associates*

CALIFORNIA PLAZA, Los Angeles, California,
AEAT (competition phase only)/AEAL, 1980
Joint Venture Architects (competition through
Phase 1 Buildings): *Kamnitzer & Cotton;*
*Gruen Associates (California Plaza Architects)*
Structural: *John A. Martin & Associates*
Mechanical: *Syska & Hennessy*
Landscape: *POD*
Lighting: *William Lam Associates*
Interiors: *Francisco Kripacz*

Competition Scheme
*Bing Thom, Tim Vreeland*
*Wilbert Bruegger, Ralph Bergman, Walter Moffatt*

One California Plaza
*Randolph Jefferson, Yasuo Muramatsu,*
*Marcello Igonda, Howard Kurushima,*
*Joseph Collins*

3rd Master Plan, 1986
*Marcello Igonda, Susan Hubbard Oakley*

DANCE GALLERY, AEAL, 1982
*Marcello Igonda, Daynard Tullis, Bob Edwards*
Structural: *Martin & Huang*
Mechanical: *Ayers Ezer & Lau*
Electrical: *Cohen & Kanwar*
Theatre: *John von Szeliski*
Acoustics: *Smith Fause & Associates*
Lighting: *Lightsource*
Associated Architects: *California Plaza Architects*
*(through Schematic Design only); Newell*
*Reynolds*
Special Consultant: *Ove Arup & Partners*
*(California)*

CANADIAN CHANCERY, Washington, D.C., AEAT,
1983
*Keith Loffler, Barbara Vogel*
*Fred Allin, Pui-To Chau, Peter Clewes,*
*Anne Vezina, Douglas Campbell,*
*John Pepper, Wyn Bielaska, David Eckler*
Interiors: *Francisco Kripacz*
Structural: *M. S. Yolles & Partners*
Mechanical: *R. David Mackay Engineering*
Electrical: *BFH/Shawinigan*
Landscape: *Cornelia Hahn Oberlander*

# CHRONOLOGY OF PROJECTS

Dates indicate start of design
**Bold type** = Construction completed or in progress
* = Design and documentation completed; not built
** = Design and documentation completed or in progress
† = Winning competition submission
‡ = Other competition submission
Buildings without notation were not executed, nor were design and documentation completed

1953     **Smith House 1,** West Vancouver, B.C. (with Geoffrey Massey)
1954     **Stegeman House,** Vancouver, B.C.
1955     **Killam-Massey House,** West Vancouver, B.C. (with Geoffrey Massey)
    ‡Civic Auditorium, Vancouver, B.C.
    Donald Erickson Residence, West Vancouver, B.C.
    **McKeen Beach House,** Qualicum Beach, B.C.
1956     **Chilco Street Apartments,** Vancouver, B.C. (with Geoffrey Massey)
    Project 56, Vancouver, B.C.
1957     **Grauer Garden Terrace & Cabana,** Vancouver, B.C.
    **Williamson House Addition,** Vancouver, B.C.
    **Buckerfield Terrace, Loggia & Balcony Additions,** Vancouver, B.C.
1958     **Filberg House,** Comox, B.C.
1959     **Design Forum Shop,** Vancouver, B.C.
    **Children's Gallery, Vancouver Art Gallery,** Vancouver, B.C.
    **Lore Maria Wiener Shop,** Vancouver, B.C.
1960     **Dyde House,** Edmonton, Alberta
    **Boultbee House Remodelling,** Vancouver, B.C.
    Hartree Residence, West Vancouver, B.C.
    ‡Massey College, Toronto, Ontario
    **Pavelich House,** Vancouver, B.C.
    Thomas House, West Vancouver, B.C.
1961     **Danto House,** Vancouver, B.C.
1962     **Harris House Alterations,** Vancouver, B.C.
    **Lloyd House,** Vancouver, B.C.
    ‡Mendel Art Gallery, Saskatoon, Saskatchewan
    **Weston House,** West Vancouver, B.C.
1963     **Bayles House,** West Vancouver, B.C.
    **Perry House,** North Vancouver, B.C.
    **Fuldauer House,** West Vancouver, B.C.

*In partnership with Geoffrey Massey, 1963–1972*
1963     †**Simon Fraser University Master Plan,** Burnaby, B.C.
    **Main Mall and Transportation Centre,** Simon Fraser University, Burnaby, B.C.
    **Library, Simon Fraser University,** Burnaby, B.C., (with Robert Harrison)
    **Gymnasium and Theatre, Simon Fraser University,** Burnaby, B.C. (with McNab, Lee & Logan)
    **Academic Quadrangle, Simon Fraser University,** Burnaby, B.C. (with Zoltan Kiss)
    **Science Complex, Simon Fraser University,** Burnaby, B.C. (with Rhone & Iredale)
    **Point Grey Townhouses,** Vancouver, B.C.
    **Graham House,** West Vancouver, B.C.
    **Baldwin House,** Burnaby, B.C.
1964     **Laxton House,** West Vancouver, B.C.
    **Nalos House Alterations & Additions,** Vancouver B.C.
    **Canadian Pavilion, Tokyo International Trade Fair,** Japan
    **Canadian Pavilion, Expo '67,** Montreal, Quebec (with Evans St. Gelais; Ashworth Robbie Vaughan & Williams; Schoeler & Barkham; Z. M. Stankiewicz)
    **Chess House,** Vancouver, B.C.
    Canadian High Commissioner Residence, Canberra, Australia
    **Smith House 2,** West Vancouver, B.C.
    **Bene House Alterations,** Vancouver, B.C.
    **Women's Residence, Simon Fraser University,** Burnaby, B.C.
1965     **Metal House,** Vancouver, B.C.
    **MacMillan Bloedel Building,** Vancouver, B.C. (with Francis Donaldson)
    **Mitchell House,** Vancouver, B.C.
    **Man in the Community (and Man and His Health) Pavilions, Expo '67,** Montreal, Quebec
    **Erickson/Massey Office Renovations,** Vancouver, B.C.
    ‡Centennial Museum Complex, Vancouver, B.C.
    **Simon Fraser University Landscaping,** Burnaby, B.C. (with John Lantzius)
1966     **Classroom Block, Simon Fraser University,** Burnaby, B.C.
    **Faculty Club Addition & Alterations,** University of British Columbia, Vancouver, B.C.

    **Venezuela Pavilion, Expo '67,** Montreal, Quebec (with Carlos Raul Villanueva)
    Shannon Estates (first scheme), Vancouver, B.C.
    Vancouver Transportation Study, Vancouver, B.C.
    Downtown Core Development Study, Vancouver, B.C.
1967     **Craig House,** Kelowna, B.C.
    †**Canadian Pavilion, Expo '70,** Osaka, Japan (with Nikken Sekkei Komu)
    **Lam Summer House,** Cotuit, Massachusetts
    University of Victoria Campus Development Plan, Victoria, B.C.
    ‡Vancouver Aquarium, Vancouver, B.C.
    **Catton House,** West Vancouver, B.C.
    **Donn Chappellet Winery Offices & Bottling Facility,** Napa Valley, California (with Jeffrey Lindsay)
    **Married Student Housing, Simon Fraser University,** Burnaby, B.C.
    ‡Winnipeg Art Gallery, Winnipeg, Manitoba
1968     University of Lethbridge Master Plan, Lethbridge, Alberta
    Cité des Terrasses, Montreal, Quebec (with David & Boulva)
    **Biological Sciences Building,** University of Victoria, B.C.
    **Project I, University of Lethbridge,** Alberta (with Robins Mitchell Watson)
    **Sikh Temple,** Vancouver, B.C.
    **Erickson/Massey (Arthur Erickson Architects) Office,** Vancouver, B.C.
1969     ‡Institute for the Future, Vancouver, B.C.
    West Seattle Freeway, Seattle, Washington (with Howard Needles Tammen & Bergendorff)
    **Bank of Canada,** Ottawa, Ontario (with Marani Rounthwaite & Dick)
    Fishermen's Quay, Vancouver, B.C.
    Village Lake Louise, Banff National Park, Alberta
    †**Champlain Heights Elementary School,** Vancouver, B.C.
    Buckley House Addition, Stamford, Connecticut (with Norton & Hume)
1970     **Hilborn House,** Cambridge, Ontario
    **Office of the Prime Minister,** Ottawa, Ontario
    Snauq Harbour, Vancouver, B.C.
1971     X-Kalay Mini-Village, Vancouver, B.C.
    ‡Centre du Plateau Beaubourg, Paris, France

Shannon Mews (second scheme),
Vancouver, B.C.
Grouse Mountain Ski Condominiums,
North Vancouver, B.C.
Imperial Oil Office & Shopping
Complex, Don Mills, Ontario
Jawl Offices, Victoria, B.C.
Christ Church Cathedral Development
(Cathedral Place), Vancouver, B.C.

1972　Federal Office Building, Vancouver, B.C.
Museum of Anthropology, University of
British Columbia, Vancouver, B.C.
Vancouver Study, Vancouver, B.C.
University Centre, Queens University,
Kingston, Ontario
Toronto Transit Study, Ontario
Helmut Eppich House, West Vancouver,
B.C.

1973　Robson Square (Provincial Government
Offices and Law Courts Complex)
Vancouver, B.C.
Inner Harbour Development Plan,
Victoria, B.C.
Brookswood-Belmont Area Plan,
Langley, B.C.
British Columbia Medical Centre,
Vancouver, B.C.
Hilborn House, Cambridge, Ontario
East End Lake, Vancouver, B.C.
Arthur Erickson House Remodelling,
Vancouver, B.C.
C.P. Hotel, Vancouver, B.C.

1974　Yorkdale Subway Station,
Toronto, Ontario
Eglinton West Subway Station, Toronto,
Ontario
Kanata Recreation Plan, Ottawa, Ontario

1975　‡Office Building, Abu Dhabi, United Arab
Emirates
Ghajere Ski Condominiums, Iran
‡Midtown Terrace, Toronto, Ontario
Teck Mining Bunkhouse, Kamloops, B.C.
‡National Gallery of Canada (first
scheme), Ottawa, Ontario
Habitat Pavilion, Vancouver, B.C.

1976　Downtown West, Toronto, Ontario (with
Mathers and Haldenby)
Roy Thomson Hall, Toronto, Ontario
(with Mathers and Haldenby)
Sawaber Housing Development, Kuwait
City, Kuwait
Hornby-Smithe Development,
Vancouver, B.C.
Centro Simon Bolivar Expansion,
Caracas, Venezuela
Diego Arria House, Caracas, Venezuela
Anthropology & Sociology Buildings,
University of British Columbia,
Vancouver, B.C.
‡Yarmouk University, Irbid, Jordan
Medical Office Building,
Abbotsford, B.C.

1977　‡Ministry of Public Works and Housing,
Riyadh, Saudi Arabia
Fire Island House, New York
Government of Canada Building,
Vancouver, B.C.

Hotel and Convention Centre, Victoria,
B.C.
‡National Gallery of Canada, Ottawa,
Ontario (with David Boulva Cleve)

1978　Ministry of Foreign Affairs Interim
Headquarters, Jeddah, Saudi Arabia
(with IDEA Center)
Madinah Hotel/Residential
Development, Madinah, Saudi Arabia
‡Abu Dhabi Investment Authority
Headquarters, Abu Dhabi, United
Arab Emirates
‡Arab Monetary Fund Headquarters, Abu
Dhabi, United Arab Emirates
†Administrative Headquarters, Riyadh,
Saudi Arabia (with Frank E. Basil)
Evergreen Building, Vancouver, B.C.
Hollenberg Residence, Bad Homburg,
West Germany
Keevil House, Savary Island, B.C.

1979　Pacific Northwest House, Washington
Fintas Town Centre, Kuwait City, Kuwait
Vancouver Art Gallery (conversion of
F. M. Rattenbury courthouse),
Vancouver, B.C.
Montiverdi Estates,
West Vancouver, B.C.
Reno Condominiums, Reno, Nevada
Hearthstone Condominiums,
Whistler, B.C.
†Napp Laboratories, Cambridge, England
*6 Stamford Forum, Stamford,
Connecticut (with Richard Coates)
Bradley House, Carpinteria, California
Grant House 1, Woodside, California
Beron House, San Mateo, California
Hugo Eppich House,
West Vancouver, B.C.
‡Portland Municipal Services Building,
Portland, Oregon (with SRG)
Laxton and Pidgeon Office Interiors,
Vancouver, B.C.
Martin House Renovation,
Vancouver, B.C.

1980　*Technical University, Saudi Arabia (with
Frank E. Basil)
†California Plaza (Bunker Hill
Redevelopment) Master Plan,
Los Angeles, California (with Gruen
Associates and Kamnitzer & Cotton)
B'nai Shalom Synagogue, Olney,
Maryland (with Komatsu/Brown)
Waterfront Centre, Vancouver, B.C.
**Harbor Steps, Seattle, Washington (with
Clayton R. Joyce)
**King Abdulaziz University, Jeddah,
Saudi Arabia (with WZMH)
*Monte Bre Estates, West Vancouver, B.C.
‡Intelsat Headquarters, Washington, D.C.
‡Sun Life Assurance Complex,
Toronto, Ontario
Main Mall Extension, Simon Fraser
University, Burnaby, B.C.
Teck Mining Offices (interiors), Toronto,
Ontario
Irvine Coastal Development, Orange
County, California (with POD)

*Caledon Housing, Toronto, Ontario
Brentwood College Development Plan,
Mill Bay, B.C.
Grant House 2, Woodside, California
Scaggs House, Cappie's Island, B.C.
Laxton House Additions,
West Vancouver, B.C.
Hwang House, Vancouver, B.C.
Shelter Island Marina, Richmond, B.C.

1981　Songhees Development Theme,
Victoria, B.C.
Songhees Family Townhouses and
Seniors Tower, Victoria, B.C.
*Malibu House, California
Red Deer Arts Centre, Alberta
Abu Nuwas Conservation/Development
Project, Baghdad, Iraq
Marathon Block 80 Development,
Vancouver, B.C.
Simon Fraser University Village,
Burnaby, B.C.
Arthur Erickson Architects Los Angeles
Office, California
†King's Landing, Toronto, Ontario
†Admiralty Place, Dartmouth, Nova
Scotia (with Cowle & Martin)
Georgian Court Hotel, Vancouver, B.C.
One California Plaza, Los Angeles,
California

1982　†320 Taylor Way, West Vancouver, B.C.
†Fairfax County Center, Virginia (with
Dewberry & Davis)
B.C. Place Overall Development
Framework, Vancouver, B.C. (with
Fisher-Freedman and B.C. Place)
Riverbend Estates, Edmonton, Alberta
Keevil House, Hernando Island, B.C.
‡Maguire/Knapp Office Building, Los
Angeles, California
‡Beverly Hills Civic Center, Beverly Hills,
California
‡60 Wall Street, New York, New York
‡Trump Condominiums and Hotel,
New York, New York
Warner Center Marriott Hotel,
Los Angeles, California
*Dance Gallery, California Plaza,
Los Angeles, California
‡Harborplace Square, Baltimore,
Maryland
Crown Plaza, Los Angeles, California
Arrowhead Resort and Hotel,
Vail, Colorado
West Mall Complex, Simon Fraser
University, Burnaby, B.C.
*SANCST Science Halls, Riyadh,
Saudi Arabia (with Dar al Riyadh)
‡National Gallery of Canada (second
scheme), Ottawa, Ontario

1983　East Boston Harborfront Master Plan,
Boston, Massachusetts
Gathering Place, Expo 86, Vancouver,
B.C. (with Phillips Barratt)
‡Visual Arts Center, Ohio State
University, Columbus, Ohio (with
Feinknopf Macioce Schappa)

Islamic University of Madinah, Saudi
Arabia (with Frank E. Basil and Dar al
Riyadh)
**Puget Sound House,** Washington
**Keevil House Renovations & Pool,**
Vancouver, B.C.
*Kuwait Insurance Company, Kuwait
City, Kuwait (with Al Marzouk and
Abi-Hanna)
Al Futtaim Al Esbig Project, Dubai,
United Arab Emirates
†Al Falah School, Makkah, Saudi Arabia
**Canadian Chancery,** Washington, D.C.
*Civic Center Metrorail Station,
Los Angeles, California
*Fifth & Hill Metrorail Station,
Los Angeles, California
Micom Headquarters, Montreal, Quebec
**Ukay Club Villas,** Kuala Lumpur,
Malaysia
*Prince Courts Condominiums, Kuala
Lumpur, Malaysia
Bukit Ceylon Condominiums, Kuala
Lumpur, Malaysia
Ampang Hilir Development, Kuala
Lumpur, Malaysia
Criswell Hotel, Fort Lauderdale, Florida

**1984**
*Saudi Arabian Embassy &
Ambassador's Residence, Ottawa,
Ontario
**Saskatoon City Hospital,** Saskatoon,
Saskatchewan (with Billington Poon
and Folstad & Friggstad)
Chen House, Kuala Lumpur, Malaysia
Lim House, Kuala Lumpur, Malaysia
†**San Diego Convention Center,** California
(with Deems Lewis McKinley and
Loschky Marquardt & Nesholm)
*Nob Hill Plaza Hotel, San Francisco,
California (with Wisler Patri)
‡Market Square, Washington, D.C.
**Robert McLaughlin Art Gallery,**
Oshawa, Ontario
Tanjung Batu Coastal Reserve Master
Plan, Bintulu, Sarawak, Malaysia (with
Hijjas Kasturi Associates)
‡Canada Place, Edmonton, Alberta
**Trudeau Ski Chalet,** Quebec
‡Canadian Embassy Development,
Tokyo, Japan (with Kenzo Tange
Associates)
**†Noel Development Offices &
Residential, Vancouver, B.C.
†Hamma Government Complex
(Assemblée Nationale Populaire and
Palais des Congrès), Algiers, Algeria

**1985**
Watson and Goodstein Houses, Malibu,
California
DeAnza Resort, San Diego, California
‡Museum of History, Science &
Technology, Hong Kong (with Tao Ho)
General Motors Advanced Concepts
Center, Malibu, California
‡Olympic Plaza, Calgary, Alberta (with
Merchant Chomik)
Woodwynn Research Farm,
Saanich, B.C.

**MacMillan Bloedel Building Lobby
Renovations,** Vancouver, B.C.
†**Etisalat Headquarters,** Abu Dhabi,
United Arab Emirates
The Winter Garden, Anchorage, Alaska
*Haggen House, Bellingham, Washington
*Biological Sciences Expansion, Stanford
University, Palo Alto, California (with
McLellan & Copenhagen)
Geffen Office Building, West Hollywood,
California
‡Fine Arts Complex, Arizona State
University, Tempe, Arizona
‡Madrid Fairgrounds, Madrid, Spain

**1986**
Centennial Campus Master Plan, North
Carolina State University, Raleigh,
North Carolina (with LandDesign)
**Textile School, North Carolina State
University,** Raleigh, North Carolina
(with Hamill-Walter)
**Suki's,** Vancouver, B.C.
**Dalhousie University Law Library,**
Halifax, Nova Scotia (with Fowler,
Bauld & Mitchell)
Hillsborough Square Office Building,
Raleigh, North Carolina (with Six
Associates)
*Etisalat Building, Dubai, United Arab
Emirates
†**Markham Municipal Building,** Markham,
Ontario
**Biological Sciences Unit 2, University of
California, Irvine, California
**King Ranch Health Resort and Spa,** King
City, Ontario
**Los Angeles House, California
Kamokogahara Housing, Kobe, Japan
**Khosla House, Portola Valley, California
**1300 West Georgia Street,
Vancouver, B.C.
**Discovery Place, Prince George, B.C.
**Porto Verde Condominiums,** Vancouver,
B.C.
‡Suffolk County Courthouse, Long Island,
New York
Corporate Pavilion, Expo '88, Brisbane,
Australia

**1987**
Aoyama Housing, Tokyo, Japan
**Woodland Park Zoo Aviary, Seattle,
Washington (with Portico Group)
‡Third University, Hong Kong
(with P & T Architects)
†Shanghai Culture & Arts Centre,
Shanghai, China (with P & T
Architects and Shanghai Municipal
Institute of Civic Architectural
Design)
‡Kwantlen College Surrey Campus,
Surrey, B.C.
**New Westminster Quay,
New Westminster, B.C.
*Laurel Point Inn Addition, Victoria, B.C.
**Negishi Housing, Yokohama, Japan
‡University Street Beautification, Seattle,
Washington
**Triad Park Phase II, Winston-Salem,
North Carolina (with Hamill-Walter)

**Sutherland House Additions,**
Georgeville, Quebec
**Two California Plaza, Los Angeles,
California
**Phase 1 Residential Building, California
Plaza, Los Angeles, California
**Fresno City Hall, Fresno, California
**‡Garmisch Resort and Hotel,
Garmisch-Partenkirchen,
West Germany
**Biological Sciences and Chemistry
Building, Western Washington
University, Bellingham, Washington
**Clinical Sciences Building, University of
California, San Diego, California
**Boston Company Interiors, Los Angeles,
California
**Brentwood Branch Library, Los Angeles,
California
‡United Arab Emirates University, Al Ain,
United Arab Emirates
**King's Landing Phase 2, Toronto,
Ontario
‡Napp Research Centre,
Cambridge, England
**Thunder Bay Government Office
Building, Thunder Bay, Ontario (with
Reginald Nalezyty)
Purdue Frederick Pharmaceutical Plant,
Whitby, Ontario
Mundipharma Offices, Limburg/Lahn,
West Germany
‡Metro Toronto Headquarters,
Toronto, Ontario
‡York University Housing,
Toronto, Ontario

**1988**
‡Harold Washington Library Center,
Chicago, Illinois (with VOA)
**Museum of Anthropology Expansion,
Vancouver, B.C.
**Washington State University Downtown
Campus, Spokane, Washington (with
WMFL)
**Karatz House, Newport Beach, California
**Kaiser-Permanente Hospital, Baldwin
Park, California
**Business School, University of Arizona,
Tucson, Arizona (with NBBJ-Gresham
Larson)
**Beit Moshe Centre, Richmond, B.C.

# INDEX